Onward ever
Longwood!!
       taylor

HOW COLLEGE PRESIDENTS SUCCEED

HOW COLLEGE PRESIDENTS SUCCEED

Lessons in Leadership from
Three Generations of Reveleys

Michael Nelson

University of Virginia Press • *Charlottesville and London*

The University of Virginia Press is situated on the traditional lands of the Monacan Nation, and the Commonwealth of Virginia was and is home to many other Indigenous people. We pay our respect to all of them, past and present. We also honor the enslaved African and African American people who built the University of Virginia, and we recognize their descendants. We commit to fostering voices from these communities through our publications and to deepening our collective understanding of their histories and contributions.

University of Virginia Press
© 2025 by the Rector and Visitors of the University of Virginia
All rights reserved
Printed in the United States of America on acid-free paper

First published 2025

1 3 5 7 9 8 6 4 2

LIBRARY OF CONGRESS CATALOGING-IN-PUBLICATION DATA
Names: Nelson, Michael, author.
Title: How college presidents succeed : lessons in leadership from three generations of Reveleys / Michael Nelson.
Description: Charlottesville : University of Virginia Press, 2025. | Includes bibliographical references and index.
Identifiers: LCCN 2024041141 (print) | LCCN 2024041142 (ebook) | ISBN 9780813952871 (hardcover) | ISBN 9780813952888 (ebook)
Subjects: LCSH: Reveley, W. Taylor, II, 1917–1992—Interviews. | Reveley, W. Taylor, III, 1943– —Interviews. | Reveley, W. Taylor, IV, 1974– —Interviews. | Hampden-Sydney College—Presidents—Biography. | College of William & Mary—Presidents—Biography. | Longwood University—Presidents—Biography. | Educational leadership—Virginia. | Educational change—Virginia. | Universities and colleges—Virginia—Administration.
Classification: LCC LD2101.H617 R486 2025 (print) | LCC LD2101.H617 (ebook) | DDC 378.755092/2—dc23/eng/20241211
LC record available at https://lccn.loc.gov/2024041141
LC ebook record available at https://lccn.loc.gov/2024041142

Cover art: The Wren Building, by Thomas Millington. (Thomas Millington Collection, Special Collections Research Center, William & Mary Libraries)
Cover design: Kelley Galbreath

For Linda, again and always

CONTENTS

Foreword by Robert M. Gates — ix
A Note — xiii
Acknowledgments — xix
Chronology — xxi

Prologue: Three Crises — 1

Part I. Paths to the Presidency

1. Taylor Reveley II and Hampden-Sydney College — 11
2. Taylor Reveley III and William & Mary — 29
3. Taylor Reveley IV and Longwood University — 72

Part II. The Reveley Presidencies

4. Fostering Pride and Morale — 99
5. Forging Constructive Governing Relationships — 119
6. Reforming the Curriculum — 141
7. Enhancing the Student Experience — 154
8. Engaging Diversity — 175
9. Advancing Fundraising — 193
10. Leading — 208

Epilogue: Leaving — 225
Afterword by James A. Baker III — 229

Appendix: Insights into Leadership 231

Notes 237

Index 259

Illustration gallery follows page 174

FOREWORD

American history is rich in well-known family dynasties in politics, business, and even entertainment. There is but one dynasty of presidents in mainstream American higher education. It is in Virginia, and it is a story of multigenerational ethical leadership, the successful overcoming of challenges and crises, and the dramatic advancing of the long-term interests of the institutions these presidents led.

This extraordinary book by Michael Nelson is about the lives and leadership of Presidents Taylor Reveley II at Hampden-Sydney College, Taylor Reveley III at William & Mary, and Taylor Reveley IV at Longwood University. Drawing on extensive interviews with the latter two and the papers of the first, Nelson—a widely respected scholar of leadership and U.S. presidents—lets them speak for themselves about how they navigated the perilous rapids of leadership in modern American higher education, their skill self-evident in the long tenure of each. The result is a must-read primer on how to be a successful university president in turbulent times.

What emerges is a significant book about the complexities of leadership in the twenty-first century in all organizations, but especially in what has become the political hothouse—or minefield—of the modern university, where the "power to command" is small (and almost always confined to administrative staff) and the "power to persuade" is nearly all the person in charge can muster. The Reveleys' success in this regard is grounded in patience, tolerance, kindliness, and ethical behavior—plus communicating effectively by speaking and, above all, listening. And each Reveley in turn has exhibited a talent for treating people—even those opposing their initiatives—with respect and dignity, and for "getting things done while bringing people along," a favorite phrase of the Reveleys.

All three presidents took office at a difficult time in the life of their respective institutions that required a restoration of morale among students, faculty, and staff and the fostering of greater pride in their school. All managed to deal with the daily crises of a university while never taking their eye off the long-term interests of the institution—namely, in all three cases, overdue curriculum reform, the creation of effective fundraising programs, enhancing the student experience (including athletics), and engaging issues of diversity and race.

The author's interviews with the Reveleys highlight at least four important lessons. First, they pierce the illusion of the university as ivory tower detached from reality, floating far above worldly matters. In fact, the life of a university president is all about nitty-gritty politics. As Taylor Reveley III says, "You've got students, you've got faculty, you've got staff. You've got alumni. You've got the athletic axis. You've got government at the state, local, and federal levels. You've got the donor complex, actual and potential. . . . You've got all sorts of boards. . . . So it's up to the president to figure out how to hold it all together, how to navigate among the phalanxes and keep pushing the place forward."

Second, their success and longevity owe in no small part to their extensive experience outside the purely academic arena: in the ministry, in athletics, in a large law firm, and on multiple boards and commissions. The book makes clear, at least inferentially, that someone who has spent an entire career in academia is today often ill-equipped to lead a modern university.

Third, the Reveleys never lost sight of the reality that, even as they were respectful of and caring toward the faculty and students, faculty concerns are usually parochial and student concerns are nearly always short term. Only the president (and the governing board, when a university is lucky enough to have a good one) has the role and responsibility always to consider the long-term interest and well-being of the institution, even as he or she must put out the daily fires.

Fourth, a university president must have courage because leadership is all about bringing needed change, challenging entrenched interests, and tackling traditions that have become major obstacles to success or even survival, all the while remaining a calm voice of reason and common sense as waves of social, cultural, and political change wash through the university community.

While this book may seem targeted at readers with a special interest in Virginia history or higher education in the commonwealth, I believe it has many lessons for those in any leadership position or aspiring to such a position, especially those who lead nonprofit organizations and schools of any kind. It should be required reading for any sitting or prospective university president and for all members of governing boards. Indeed, in my view, the only book remotely comparable to *How College Presidents Succeed* in insight, wisdom, and wit for leaders in higher education is *A*

Primer for University Presidents: Managing the Modern University (1990), by Peter Flawn, the longtime president of the University of Texas at Austin.

It was my good fortune to lead four very large, very different institutions: the Central Intelligence Agency and the fifteen other agencies making up the American intelligence community, Texas A&M University, the Department of Defense, and the Boy Scouts of America—theoretically, two with the power to command and two with only the power to persuade. However, even at the CIA and the Defense Department, a leader who wants to be successful in envisioning and implementing enduring change and improvement must bring people along. And even in those organizations, it is imperative that people have confidence that their leader cares about them, about their personal well-being and their professional careers. The lessons in leadership offered by the Reveleys are, I believe, universal.

Texas A&M is many times larger than Hampden-Sydney, William & Mary, and Longwood. Still, the challenges the Reveley presidents faced are those that I and every other university president have faced: curriculum reform, finances and fundraising, enhancing the student experience, uniting a multitude of often discordant constituencies, and contributing to diversity and racial progress, among others. As *How College Presidents Succeed* makes clear, success depends on creating an inclusive and transparent decision-making process; treating faculty, students, and staff with dignity and respect, as well as convincing them that their leader actually cares about them as individuals; dealing successfully with the many stakeholders on- and off-campus (the "politics"); not allowing the daily crises to distract from the long-term agenda; and leading constructive change. Some humility and a robust sense of humor help a lot.

And, as *How College Presidents Succeed* shows us, even as successful presidents lead with the Reveleys' credo of "patience, tolerance, kindliness and ethical behavior," they must have the hide of a rhinoceros and be as tough as woodpecker lips.

Just as three generations of Reveley university presidents learned from one another, now every leader, thanks to Michael Nelson, can learn from them.

ROBERT M. GATES
Chancellor, William & Mary

A NOTE

As a rule, careful scholars avoid superlatives like *best, toughest, only*. Sometimes, however, superlatives are unavoidable. Three such claims follow.

First, the United States has the *best* system of higher education in the world, a claim that is close to beyond dispute. In the 2023 World University Rankings, published in Great Britain by *Times Higher Education*, seventeen of the world's twenty-five highest-ranking universities were in the United States. *US News* placed nineteen American universities in its top twenty-five. Even QS, which included only twelve American institutions in its highest tier, named far more universities in the United States than in any other country.[1]

Among the ranks of public universities in the United States, Virginia's are near or, in the opinion of one recent survey, at the top.[2] Only California has more universities on *US News*'s roster of the nation's twenty-five best than Virginia, home to William & Mary, the University of Virginia, and Virginia Tech.[3] Unlike California's leading institutions, Virginia's have roots extending deep into the country's history, with William & Mary founded in 1693 and the University of Virginia in 1819. And while national public opinion has recently soured on higher education, especially among Republican voters, a March 2023 poll jointly conducted by Public Opinion Strategies and FrederickPolls found that 84 percent of Virginians were proud of higher education in the commonwealth, including large majorities of both Republicans and Democrats.[4]

Second, being a university president in the United States is arguably, to echo former Rear Admiral William McRaven, "the *toughest* job in the nation." McRaven made this statement while ending his term as chancellor of the University of Texas System in 2018.[5] During the three years prior to his chancellorship, McRaven was in charge of the U.S. Special Forces Command.

McRaven's statement was no mere pleasantry uttered on his way out the door. What makes the job so tough, he repeated five years later, are the large and sometimes conflicting demands "of all of the constituents you deal with on a day-to-day basis"—students, faculty, staff, trustees, alumni, donors, journalists, and political leaders, among them—that must be satisfied by presidents whose office lacks sufficient authority and resources to do so. "You're making hundreds if not thousands of small decisions a day," McRaven added. "You hope you get 80 percent of them right, but of course the 20 percent you don't get right" mean that "nobody ever seems satisfied."[6]

In general, former George Washington University president Stephen Trachtenberg argues, a college president "has to play well" with "young and old, near and far, rich and poor, traditional and progressive, entitled and disempowered, supportive and resistant." Presidents "may be called on to meet with students, craft a multimillion-dollar campaign, participate in a faculty meeting, and manage a board meeting—all in a single day."[7] In all, presidents must be, in educational historian John Thelin's apt phrase, "a reconciler of irreconcilables."[8]

A president is also, writes former University of Chicago president Hanna Holborn Gray, "the mayor of a small city" who is called on to "provide a considerable range of services for its residents. These include basic infrastructure, housing, transportation, medical and counseling services, child-care facilities, recreational and meeting facilities, museums and concert halls and theatres, benefits and amenities of many kinds." And "the mayor is held responsible when any of it goes wrong."[9]

Third, Virginia is the *only* state that has spawned a three-generation (so far) family of academic leaders—a unique instance in American higher education. Over a period of six decades, as student enrollment, government funding, and public support for colleges and universities rose dramatically (only to recede somewhat in recent years), W. Taylor Reveley II (referred to subsequently as TR2) was president of Hampden-Sydney College from 1963 to 1977, W. Taylor Reveley III (TR3) was president of William & Mary from 2008 to 2018, and W. Taylor Reveley IV (TR4) has been president of Longwood University since 2013.[10]

The Reveleys are the only trio of grandfather, father, and son to serve as presidents of major colleges and universities. To compound the family's uniqueness, each of them led or is leading a Virginia institution of higher education that is among the one hundred oldest in the country. They are, as a headline in the *Washington Post* overstated it, "Virginia's Academic Dynasty" (overstated because they earned, rather than inherited, the presidencies of three different schools, with no presumption of heirdom).[11] None of the three has led for less than a decade, a remarkable record in an era when the average time in office of college and university presidents has declined to 5.9 years—and falling.[12] Taking note that "the Reveley name is synonymous with higher education in Virginia," the *Richmond Times-Dispatch* only half-facetiously headlined an editorial, "The Commonwealth Needs a University of Reveley."[13]

Why this book—and why me to write it? Second things first: as a longtime scholar of the American presidency, I have sometimes wondered why those of us who spend our careers studying that institution seldom venture into the study of leadership in other important domains: corporations, cultural institutions, or, as in this case, colleges and universities. The last of these omissions is the oddest. Most of us, after all, were trained and have spent our scholarly careers in academic settings led by presidents.

As for the book itself, in an era in which the challenges faced by university presidents—growing public doubts about the value of higher education, severe declines in state governments' financial support, unfavorable demographic shifts that have reduced the number of traditional-age college applicants, ever greater and more conflicting demands from important university stakeholders—increasingly grind presidents down and spit them out, the story of three successful leaders of three very different institutions in three consecutive eras in one state is a story worth telling.[14]

This book tells that story in two parts. Part I chronicles the life experiences that prepared each of the three Reveleys to become president and the processes that led to them securing their positions. Part II describes their presidential careers: how each handled the challenges and opportunities he faced as leader. These challenges and opportunities ranged from the critical but seemingly mundane—fundraising, managing board relations, dealing with government, and so on—to the highly visible, including determining the role of athletics (an aspect of American higher education that is uniquely important by global standards), shaping the curriculum (what is taught and how in an age of rising cultural and political polarization), and negotiating issues of race and diversity during a half century–plus in which the de jure agenda of ending legally mandated segregation evolved into demands for de facto racial justice.

Each chapter in the book glides into the next, propelled by the Reveley presidents' own accounts of how they gained the presidential office and exercised leadership at their institutions. In order that the narrative flow unimpeded, just as events flowed in the lived experience of these leaders and the institutions they led, I eschew one typical approach in books of this kind, namely, tacking on a conclusion at the end of each chapter that tidily wraps things up. Instead, what the Reveley presidents learned and can teach us about effective leadership from their combined experiences is not only a theme of the entire book but the focus of its concluding chapter on leadership and the epilogue, on when leaders leave.

Each Reveley president has been a leader not just of his institution but in other domains of public life as well, including the law, the church, the arts, and higher education more broadly. In addition, their careers intertwined with those of important friends and mentors, especially Peyton Nalle Rhodes, the president after whom Rhodes College was renamed, for TR2;[15] William G. Bowen, the president of Princeton and then the Mellon Foundation, for TR3; and Virginia governor Gerald L. Baliles for TR4. Their paths also crossed in significant ways with those of other prominent leaders, including former secretaries of state James A. Baker III and Warren Christopher, former Virginia supreme court justice John Charles Thomas, former U.S. Supreme Court justices William Brennan, Lewis Powell, and Sandra Day O'Connor, former U.S. senator Bill Spong, and former secretary of defense and Texas A&M president Robert M. Gates, whose foreword graces this book.

How College Presidents Succeed chronicles a long period of time but, as with any book, was written at a particular historical moment. Questions specific to that moment arise that might not have arisen had the book been written some years ago. Twenty-first-century scholars of leadership in higher education—and their readers—appropriately will ask, is this generational family saga a tale of privilege? Of nepotism? The answer to the second question seems clear. Although the examples offered to each other as grandfather, father, and son were clearly beneficial, no improper influence was at work. By the time TR3 even considered taking an academic leadership position (initially as a dean, not as president), TR2's life had ended. Although TR4 joined his father's former law firm, he did so only after turning down a position at a bigger firm in a different part of the country to which his father had no connection. As for TR4 becoming president of Longwood while his father was president of William & Mary, at the start of TR4's presidency the *Times-Dispatch* reported that a Longwood board leader had told him, "No slight to your father, but to the people at Longwood, it just doesn't matter who the president of William & Mary is."[16]

The question of privilege is a harder one, as TR3 and TR4 concede. This is true in specific terms: although TR4 had an excellent high school academic record and was a recruited athlete, for example, it surely did not hurt his application to Princeton that his father was an active alumnus. It is also true in general terms. All three Reveleys were or are well-educated, married white males who, in the case of the son and grandson, had the benefit of their predecessors' example.

In that sense, however, it's reasonable to argue that the flip side of privilege is generational learning of the sort that, for example, John Quincy Adams gained from John Adams, Martin Luther King Jr. gained from Martin Luther King Sr., and countless children have gained from their elders in many areas of life. (Think Ken Griffey Sr. and Jr. in baseball, June Carter Cash and Mother Maybelle in music, Queen Elizabeth II and King Charles III—the list is long.) At the end of the day, the unusual longevity each Reveley enjoyed in his presidential role can only be attributed to his ability to lead effectively. The privilege that may help get one in the door is less likely to enable one to remain inside, as each did for at least a decade.

A book may (like this one) or may not tell a story, but a story lies behind the writing of every book. During my long tenure as a senior fellow at the University of Virginia's Miller Center, I have helped conduct dozens of oral history interviews as part of the center's Presidential Oral History Program. In the course of doing so, I came to know TR4, who was the center's managing director before becoming president of Longwood. As for TR3, although he and I had never met, as an alumnus of William & Mary I followed his decade-long presidency with interest. TR2 died well before my time, but I was familiar with his prepresidential tenure at my own institution, Rhodes College. Indeed, I had written briefly about him as an early contributor to Rhodes's renowned Search course in a book I coauthored about the college's Great Books–style program.[17] Out of that combination of friendship, familiarity, and scholarly interest in leadership came the idea of doing the long series of oral history interviews exploring the three Reveleys' presidencies of important colleges and universities in Virginia that are at the heart of this book, which consists mainly of the Reveleys' own words.

Specifically, from 2021 to 2023 (with brief follow-ups as recently as July 2024), I conducted more than one hundred hours of oral history interviews with TR3 and TR4, drawing on my experience at the Miller Center. The words by and about TR2, who died in 1992, are drawn from a variety of other sources, including his own writings and remarks and an unpublished memoir that his widow, Marie Eason Reveley, wrote about their years at Hampden-Sydney.[18] In as unobtrusive a way as possible, I have inserted contextual material to connect their richly insightful statements, recollections, and reflections, drawing mostly on archival sources, news accounts, and documents relating to their presidencies. This model of oral history–based scholarship has proven its worth in such books as Russell L. Riley's *Inside the Bill Clinton White House: An Oral History* (Oxford University Press) and my own coedited *43: Inside the Presidency of George W. Bush* (University Press of Kansas). It also has caught on in the world of trade publishing, with critically acclaimed oral history–based books about ESPN, *The Wire*, *The Sopranos*, and other subjects.

In terms of coverage, *How College Presidents Succeed* lies at the intersection of leadership studies, higher education studies, and Virginia biography and history. Although it was written with the full cooperation of TR3 and TR4, at no point did either of them attempt to infringe on my editorial independence. The book is these three leaders' stories, crafted by me but told largely in their own words, thereby allowing readers to experience them as leaders teaching leadership of important institutions in an important state during an important era of American history.

Unless otherwise indicated in the text, all of the quoted material from TR3 and TR4, in this book is drawn from the interviews I conducted with them or with their spouses, Helen Reveley and Marlo Reveley, respectively. These interviews were recorded, transcribed, reviewed for accuracy and clarity by the interviewees, and edited by me.

And, by the way, the name is pronounced "Reev'-lee," not "reveille" or "ra-vell'-ee." And the W stands for Walter, which none of them—including the first W. Taylor Reveley, TR2's uncle and a farmer in Rockbridge County—has ever gone by.

ACKNOWLEDGMENTS

Although it's my name on the cover of this book, I am less its author than the vessel through which it has come into the world. I owe debts of gratitude to many for both the words that appear in this book and the process by which the University of Virginia Press has brought them into being.

First and foremost, I owe deep thanks for their words to the three TRs—Taylor Reveley II, who died long before this work began but left a solid legacy of thoughts and memories, and especially his son, Taylor Reveley III, and grandson Taylor Reveley IV, who spent hundreds of hours responding fully and thoughtfully to my questions about their lives, careers, and insights into leadership. I am honored to call them friends and grateful to their spouses, Helen (TR3) and Marlo (TR4), for their hospitality and insights.

The book's origins and development owe much to the great Nadine Zimmerli, the Press's editor-in-chief. She not only nurtured this work from its very beginning, but also provided exceptionally useful guidance at every stage of the writing. If ever Nadine and I disagreed about something, I always knew which one of us was right (it wasn't me).

Other talented members of the University of Virginia Press community also helped to shepherd *How College Presidents Succeed* into being, with consummate professionalism and good grace. I especially thank the managing editor, Ellen Satrom; the project editor, J. Andrew Edwards; the art director, Cecilia Sorochin; the production manager, Joel Coggins; the production coordinator, Rachel Laney; the marketing and sales director, Jason Coleman; marketing associate Clayton Butler; jacket designer, Kelley Galbreath; and compositor, JoAnn Sikkes. Every author needs a good copy editor. I was fortunate that mine was Marjorie Pannell.

Still other individuals and institutions made this book better in various and essential ways. At William & Mary, Brian Whitson. At Longwood, Kay Stokes, Justin Pope, and Matt McWilliams. At Hampden-Sydney and Rhodes College, the staffs of their college archives. At the University of Virginia's Miller Center, Mike Greco. And at the Audio Transcription Center, the many team members who turned the recorded interviews into transcripts.

The joke I told friends as *How College Presidents Succeed* was being designed and produced was that I hoped my name would be detectable on a cover that included two individuals of world historical stature: former secretary of defense Robert M. Gates, whose foreword graces the early pages of the book, and former Secretary of State James A. Baker III, whose afterword brings it to a thoughtful end.

And then there's Linda, to whom this book is dedicated, with endless and ongoing gratitude for her love and support.

CHRONOLOGY

Decade	Year	Taylor Reveley II	Taylor Reveley III	Taylor Reveley IV
1910s	1917	Born in Knoxville, TN; grows up in Canton, NC, with summers in Rockbridge County, VA		
1920s				
1930s	1935	Matriculates at Hampden-Sydney College (BA)		
	1939	Graduates from Hampden-Sydney College (BA); matriculates at Union Theological Seminary (BD)		

xxii CHRONOLOGY

Decade	Year	Taylor Reveley II	Taylor Reveley III	Taylor Reveley IV
1940s	1941	Graduates from Union Theological Seminary (BD); marries Marie Gray Eason; begins pastorate at Loch Willow and Union Presbyterian Churches, Churchville, VA		
	1943		Born in Churchville, VA	
	1944	Leaves pastorate at Loch Willow and Union Presbyterian Churches; enters chaplaincy, U.S. Army		
	1946	Returns from World War II; begins career at Rhodes College; will serve as professor, chaplain, coach, and admissions dean	Moves with family to Memphis	
1950s	1953	Matriculates at Duke University (PhD) on leave from Rhodes College	Moves with family to Durham, NC	
	1956	Graduates from Duke University (PhD) and returns to Rhodes	Returns with family to Memphis	

CHRONOLOGY   xxiii

Decade	Year	Taylor Reveley II	Taylor Reveley III	Taylor Reveley IV
1960s	1961		Matriculates at Princeton University (AB)	
	1963	Leaves Rhodes College; becomes president of Hampden-Sydney College	Moves with parents to Hampden-Sydney	
	1965	Begins twelve-year tenure on board of Patrick Henry Memorial Foundation	Graduates from Princeton University (AB); matriculates at University of Virginia School of Law (JD)	
	1968		Graduates from University of Virginia School of Law (JD); becomes assistant professor, University of Alabama Law School	
	1969	Begins eight-year tenure on Virginia Trust Company board	Becomes clerk for Supreme Court Justice William J. Brennan	
1970s	1970		Concludes clerkship with Justice Brennan; joins law practice at Hunton & Williams	
	1971		Marries Helen Martin Bond	
	1972		Begins research leave at Council on Foreign Relations and Woodrow Wilson International Center for Scholars	
	1973		Research leave ends	
	1974			Born and grows up in Richmond, VA

Decade	Year	Taylor Reveley II	Taylor Reveley III	Taylor Reveley IV
1970s	1975		Joins board, Fan District Association	
	1977	Retires as president of Hampden-Sydney College; becomes fellow at Fitzwilliam College, Cambridge University		
	1979	Returns to Hampden-Sydney College as president emeritus and professor		
1980s	1980		Concludes board tenure, Fan District Association; joins board, Richmond Symphony Orchestra	
	1981		Publishes *War Powers of the President and Congress: Who Holds the Arrow and the Olive Branch?* (University Press of Virginia)	
	1982		Becomes managing partner at Hunton & Williams	
	1986		Joins board, Princeton University	

Decade	Year	Taylor Reveley II	Taylor Reveley III	Taylor Reveley IV
	1990		Concludes board term, Princeton University	
	1991		Rejoins board, Princeton University; joins board, Virginia Historical Society (now Virginia Museum of History and Culture); concludes tenure as managing partner of Hunton &Williams	
	1992	Dies	Concludes board tenure, Richmond Symphony Orchestra; joins board, Union Theological Seminary in Virginia (now Union Presbyterian Seminary)	Matriculates at Princeton University (AB)
1990s	1994		Joins board, Andrew W. Mellon Foundation	
	1995		Joins board, Virginia Museum of Fine Arts; joins board, JSTOR	
	1996		Concludes board tenure, Virginia Historical Society; joins board, St. Christopher's School, Richmond	Graduates from Princeton University (AB); matriculates at Union-PSCE (now Union Presbyterian Seminary) (MDiv)
	1998		Leaves Hunton & Williams to become dean of William & Mary Law School	
	1999			Graduates from Union-PSCE (now Union Presbyterian Seminary) (MDiv); matriculates at University of Virginia School of Law (JD)

Decade	Year	Taylor Reveley II	Taylor Reveley III	Taylor Reveley IV
2000s	2000		Concludes board tenure, Union-PSCE (now Union Presbyterian Seminary)	Holds summer internship at Fulbright & Jaworski
	2001		Concludes second board term, Princeton University	Holds summer internship at Hunton & Williams; marries Margaret Louise (Marlo) Smith; enters practice at Hunton & Williams
	2002		Concludes board tenure, St. Christopher's School, Richmond	Graduates from University of Virginia School of Law (JD)
	2003		Joins board, Virginia Historical Society	
	2004			
	2005		Concludes board tenure, Virginia Museum of Fine Arts; rejoins board, St. Christopher's School, Richmond	
	2006		Begins term as codirector, National War Powers Commission	Becomes Public Service Fellow, Miller Center, University of Virginia; begins as coordinating attorney, National War Powers Commission
	2008		Becomes president of William & Mary; concludes board tenure, JSTOR and codirectorship of National War Powers Commission	Completes fellowship at Miller Center; ends practice at Hunton & Williams; concludes work for National War Powers Commission; becomes managing director, Miller Center, University of Virginia
	2009			Joins New College Institute's Planning Commission

Decade	Year	Taylor Reveley II	Taylor Reveley III	Taylor Reveley IV
2010s	2010			Concludes service on New College Institute's Planning Commission; joins Princeton University's Alumni Council Executive Committee
	2011		Concludes board tenure, St. Christopher's School, Richmond	
	2012		Concludes board tenure, Virginia Historical Society	Concludes tenure on Princeton University's Alumni Council Executive Committee
	2013			Leaves Miller Center, University of Virginia, to become president of Longwood University
	2015		Concludes board tenure, Andrew W. Mellon Foundation	
	2017			Chairs Big South Conference
	2018		Retires from William & Mary presidency	Joins NCAA Division I Board of Directors
2020s	2020			Serves on Governor of Virginia's COVID Response and Recovery Work Group
	2021			Leaves chairmanship of Big South Conference Leaves NCAA Division I Board of Directors
	2023			Chairs Virginia Bar Association's Special Issues Committee

HOW COLLEGE PRESIDENTS SUCCEED

Prologue
THREE CRISES

Late on the night of Tuesday, March 31, 2020, Longwood University president W. Taylor Reveley IV—known to friends, family, and colleagues as TR4—paced around the dining room table in Longwood House, the president's home, with a phone pressed to his ear. On the other end of the call was his father, W. Taylor Reveley III (TR3). Virtually every college and university in Virginia and around the country either had closed its campus and sent students home in response to the rapidly spreading COVID pandemic or, like Longwood, was in the process of doing so. The subject of Reveley's call to his father was how best to persuade his fellow public university presidents in Virginia that they needed to find a way to safely reopen their campuses to students in the fall.

Sons and daughters seeking advice from parents is an age-old story, but in this case the two men had professional as well as personal ties that bound them as colleagues, not just family. TR4 was in his seventh year as president of Longwood, having been named to the position in 2013 at age thirty-eight. His father had been president of William & Mary, also a state university in Virginia, from 2008 to 2018. Both had held previous university posts before becoming president, TR4 as managing director of the University of Virginia's Miller Center, a research institute focused on the American presidency and national affairs, and TR3 as dean of the William & Mary Law School. In those positions they had worked closely together for two years on the Miller Center's National War Powers Commission, cochaired by former secretaries of state James A. Baker III and Warren Christopher. Both TR3 and TR4 were lawyers who, after graduating a generation apart from Princeton University and the University of Virginia School of Law, had practiced with Hunton & Williams, a leading national firm headquartered in Richmond. TR4's experience at the firm included working with the city's hospitals on how best to respond safely (not how to shut down) if, as seemed possible in 2003, SARS (severe acute respiratory syndrome) or some other infectious disease triggered a pandemic.

The urgency of the late-night phone call seemed obvious to both father and son. For Longwood, located in Prince Edward County's Farmville, and Virginia's other campuses to remain closed during the fall 2020 semester would have serious adverse consequences for students, for the faculty and staff who served them, for the communities in which they were embedded, and for the commonwealth as a whole. With Connecticut and a number of other northeastern states indicating that they were leaning toward keeping their campuses closed in the fall, TR4 felt that Virginia's historic stature as a leader in public higher education enabled it to provide an alternative model for safe reopening that would command attention from the rest of the country. This was especially important because the state's K–12 schools were sending the opposite signal.[1]

The key element in TR4's preferred model for the fall semester was an emphasis on how, not whether, to reopen safely. Based on his legal experience dealing with public health concerns, he was convinced that, with proper policies in place—masking, social distancing, diligent contact tracing, and appropriate testing—opening campuses in August 2020 was an achievable as well as an essential goal. The challenge was to persuade his fellow members of the state's Council of Presidents (formally the Council of Presidents of State Colleges and Universities in Virginia) that they should all focus on reopening in the fall, which he saw as an essential step toward persuading the state government to agree.

The immediate occasion for TR4's phone call to his father was a letter he wanted to send to his fellow presidents recommending such a course. The draft letter was formal in tone and admonitory in content. "Dear Council of Presidents," it began. Virginia's public universities "are obligated to do our part . . . to help society responsibly reopen" in the fall and "must also show leadership" in doing so.

Everything you've written makes perfect sense, TR3 told him in an email. But as one who so recently had been a Virginia college president himself and was now a step removed from the pressures of the moment, he knew that the letter's tone would be as important as its contents. "I imagine the COP [Council of Presidents] would be most receptive if your letter were cast as a proposal that should be seriously and quickly engaged than as a concrete plan that must be adopted. . . . Ideally you'd have one or two other prexies on board before sending the letter," and "diplomatically, probably need to let the current COP prexy know what you're planning."[2] For the council's youngest member to tell his colleagues what they needed to do might be a turn-off. Suggesting that they consider devising a common course of action, one sensitive to their own local situations, would be more likely to have the desired effect. You don't want them to feel, as TR3 said during their late-night phone call, "instructed, lectured, told basically that they were wimps and needed to get their act together."[3] And make it an email, he advised, not a more formal-seeming letter.

TR4 revised his letter into an email, infusing it with a "some-thoughts-before-our-call" tone that began "Friends," and offering "some thoughts about sustainable reopening in the future" in the form of "a conversation starter if nothing else." He spoke with the council's president and some other presidents, let the draft email gestate before sending it on April 3, and saw, when the council met via telephone, that, far from alienating his fellow presidents, he had helped motivate them to set the wheels of reopening in motion. The "center of gravity" of the presidents' meeting, he recalls, was as he had hoped: "We see that we need to get in gear in the fall. How do we get there?" His colleagues soon nominated him to work closely with state officials on the commonwealth's official guidance to higher education for reopening.

That his son was dealing with a crisis of university leadership was hardly surprising to TR3. Like nearly all presidents of academic institutions, he had faced crises of varying kinds on multiple occasions. In TR3's case, his first crisis arose instantly, the day he became interim president of William & Mary in February 2008.

The circumstances were these: having lost out to Gene Nichol, himself a former law school dean at the University of North Carolina, in his bid for William & Mary's presidency in 2005, TR3 had renewed his commitment to leading its law school as dean. But Nichol, although enormously popular with most of the college's students and faculty, in part because of promises he made to initiate several expensive new programs, had fallen out of favor with the university's board of visitors (Virginia-speak for trustees). Most board members regarded Nichol's promises as wildly exceeding any reasonable plan to fund them and, more generally, thought he was too inclined to make major decisions without sufficiently consulting the board and key members of the Virginia General Assembly. (Famously, Nichol ignited a national political firestorm by removing the cross from the college's historic Wren Chapel, which is located within its flagship Wren Building.) On February 11, 2008, Nichol was told that his three-year contract would not be renewed when it expired at the end of June. He responded by resigning almost immediately in an angry, widely circulated public letter.[4]

On February 12, the morning of Nichol's resignation, TR3 received a phone call from Michael Powell, who as the college's rector chaired its board, asking him to become interim president. He accepted the invitation, knowing that the challenges he would face in establishing his legitimacy among Nichol's embittered supporters were formidable. He met those challenges by opening his door to any and all who wanted to see him and by seeking out those who did not, starting at noon that day by attending a weekly lunch for Black students at the invitation of Chon Glover, the university's chief diversity officer.

For months, TR3 listened more than spoke and, when he spoke, showed that he not only shared most of Nichol's commitments but also intended to raise the money and build the bridges with the state government needed to fulfill them. Resisting the board's desire to make him president shortly after his interim appointment, TR3 waited until enough stakeholders in the campus community were ready to embrace him in that role. That moment came long before the formal conferring of the title in September—just in time for another crisis, the financial meltdown of 2008–2009 and the Great Recession that ensued.

Unlike his son, TR3 did not have the luxury of consulting his own father when he faced these and other crises of leadership at William & Mary; W. Taylor Reveley II (TR2) had died in 1992. But he was able to draw on his deep familiarity with his father's fourteen-year tenure from 1963 to 1977 as president of Hampden-Sydney College, a private men's college and one of America's oldest institutions of higher learning, founded in 1775.

TR2's path to the presidency was different from his son's and grandson's. A 1939 graduate of Hampden-Sydney, TR2 was ordained as a Presbyterian minister after earning a divinity degree at Union Theological (later Union Presbyterian) Seminary in Richmond. He then briefly pastored a congregation in Churchville, Virginia, and served as an army chaplain during World War II.[5] In 1946, after the war, he accepted a position in Memphis as college pastor and, soon after, as a religion professor at Rhodes College, which, like Hampden-Sydney, was a small private Presbyterian-affiliated liberal arts college. During his seventeen years at Rhodes (including three years away to earn a PhD at Duke University), TR2 did everything from coaching baseball and football to teaching in the college's fabled Great Books program to serving as dean of admissions.

Well into his career at Rhodes and life in Memphis, where his son, TR3, and daughter, Chris, grew up, in 1963 TR2 returned to Hampden-Sydney as president, assuming the helm of a school that, like William & Mary in 2008, was in crisis when he took office. Prince Edward County was the setting for one of the five cases that the U.S. Supreme Court consolidated in *Brown v. Board of Education*.[6] The Southside Virginia locale then became the epicenter of the South's Virginia-led policy of "massive resistance" to the desegregation of public schools that *Brown* mandated. The Prince Edward court case was set in motion in 1951 when Black students led by high school junior Barbara Johns launched a strike to protest the woefully overcrowded and underresourced condition of Farmville's segregated Robert Russa Moton High School.

The awful irony that awaited TR2 when he arrived at Hampden-Sydney in August was that in the nation's first two-college town—Hampden-Sydney, founded in 1775, and Longwood, founded in 1839—Farmville remained the only American municipality whose public schools were still closed lest they be forced to integrate. To no avail, Attorney General Robert F. Kennedy had declared in his May 6, 1961, Law Day address that he did not believe anyone could "support a principle which prevents more than a thousand of our children in one county from attending public school." Kennedy defined the crisis of public education in Prince Edward as one of the three most urgent issues facing the Department of Justice, on the same level as fighting organized crime and corporate price-fixing.[7]

As TR4 understood a half century later while serving as a college president during the COVID pandemic in the same county as his grandfather had served, the costs of closing schools at any level for any reason are profound. When TR2 began his presidency, it was clear that the implications of Prince Edward County's shuttered public schools for Hampden-Sydney were severely troubling. Retaining current faculty and staff with school-age children and attracting new ones at a time when young professors and administrators were in high demand in the rapidly expanding national academic job market of the 1960s was severely challenging unless the college provided an acceptable means for their kids to be educated. Hampden-Sydney's conscience-troubling practice, which TR2 inherited when he began his presidency in 1963, was to pay private school tuition at the new, whites-only Prince Edward Academy. Nor were the college's own hands clean on matters of racial justice. It too was, as it had always been, all white.

As a new president, in ways foreshadowed by his faith-informed writings and actions as a professor and dean at Rhodes, TR2 moved patiently but firmly to phase out Hampden-Sydney's complicity in racial segregation. When the county schools reopened at the start of his second year in office in response to the ruling in *Griffin v. County School Board of Prince Edward County*, a May 25, 1964, Supreme Court decision aimed specifically at the county, TR2 initiated the complicated process of ending the college's private school tuition subsidy.[8] When Congress enacted the Civil Rights Act of 1964 that summer, with its Title VI requirement that colleges and university desegregate in order to continue receiving aid from the federal government, he risked his job by making clear to Hampden-Sydney's less than enthusiastic board of trustees that the college's admissions and hiring policies must be altered to comply. And, in a symbolically important act, when Robert Kennedy decided to visit Prince Edward County that year and was denied the opportunity to speak at Longwood, TR2 invited him to give his speech at Hampden-Sydney. Kennedy's warm reception by a racially integrated audience of students and community members confirmed that TR2's prudential approach to progress at the college had taken root, bearing out the approbation as "a good friend and yokefellow in the gospel" that he received from Reverend L. Francis Griffin, a local Black minister who strongly supported the students' walkout from Moton in 1951.

The six decades (and counting) that, collectively, the Reveleys served as presidents were decades of occasional crises like these, but mostly of more gradual change in higher education. Any account of how they navigated these challenges and led as presidents must begin by describing how they became the people they were by the time they took office. Their paths to the presidency form part I of this account.

PART I
PATHS TO THE PRESIDENCY

What career paths lead to the presidency of a major college or university? Historically, that question has been answered in different ways at different times. In American higher education's early decades, when most institutions were strongly affiliated with one Protestant denomination or another, the path typically went through the ministry. James Blair, the first president of William & Mary, the university that Taylor Reveley III (TR3) later led from 2008 to 2018, was an Anglican clergyman, as were his eight immediate successors. Taken together, they headed the institution from 1693, the year of its founding, to 1814. Hampden-Sydney, the college that Taylor Reveley II (TR2) served as president from 1963 to 1977, was led by Presbyterian ministers at the time of its founding in 1775 and for many years thereafter. Similarly, Methodist clergy filled the ranks of Longwood University presidents during that institution's early decades, starting with its founding as the Farmville Female Seminary Association in 1839.

Princeton University, which Longwood's president since 2013, Taylor Reveley IV (TR4), and his father attended, was Presbyterian in its origins both in 1746 as the College of New Jersey and in 1896 under its current name. Among other things, Princeton provided Hampden-Sydney with its first president, Rev. Samuel Stanhope Smith, who later returned to Princeton as president. According to historian of higher education John Thelin, before the Civil War, 92 percent of college presidents were clergymen.[1]

During the late nineteenth century, as many colleges and universities secularized, longtime faculty members supplanted ministers in the talent pool from which presidents increasingly were chosen, usually from within. "The old-time president," notes Thelin, "taught every member of the senior class and knew most of the students by name."[2] During the twentieth century, institutions of higher education steadily became larger and organizationally more complex. Although the typical career path for presidents still began in the faculty, it rose from the classroom through the ranks of department chair, dean, and provost.[3]

To be sure, minister-presidents did not disappear, especially at church-affiliated colleges. Ordination as a Presbyterian minister was no impediment in 1963—far from it—to TR2's elevation to the presidency of Hampden-Sydney. But, especially with the coming of the twenty-first century, other professions, such as law, and other academic leadership posts, such as vice president of development, broadened the presidential talent pool.[4]

Careers spent mostly in legal practice were no barrier to TR3 becoming president of William & Mary or TR4 becoming Longwood's president. Fueled by the growing legal entanglement between campuses and the federal government that has steadily accelerated since Congress' enactment of the Higher Education Act in 1965,[5] the number of lawyer-presidents rose from forty-four to seventy in the 1990s, 131 in the 2000s, and 251 in the 2010s.[6] In all three cases, however, the Reveleys' presidential appointments were preceded by additional experience in academic posts: admissions dean at Rhodes College for TR2, dean of the William & Mary Law School for TR3, and managing director of the University of Virginia's Miller Center for TR4. Unlike the trend in higher education away from clergy presidents (TR2 was the last of his kind at Hampden-Sydney), in recent decades the law has become a significant avenue to presidential leadership.[7]

The three chapters that follow chronicle the lives and careers of the three Reveley presidents before they took office, including the processes by which each secured his position during a fifty-year period that spanned TR2's hiring at Hampden-Sydney in 1963 and TR4's hiring at Longwood in 2013. In between came TR3's very different experience at William & Mary, where he was the runner-up candidate for president in 2005, a suddenly named interim president in February 2008, and president in every sense of the word seven months later. During that half century, presidential search processes around the country became considerably more elaborate, directly involving multiple stakeholders within the campus community and professional search firms brought in from outside.[8] Turnover among college and university presidents accelerated, with average presidential tenure first falling below ten years and then gradually approaching five.

As these changes were occurring nationally, all three generations of Reveleys became presidents of Virginia institutions, forswore positions in other states and universities in their commitment to remain in the commonwealth, and led their campuses for at least a decade. The chapters that follow describe how each of them became the person he was before he got the job, and then how he went about getting it.

1

Taylor Reveley II and Hampden-Sydney College

Walter Taylor Reveley II—TR2—was born in 1917 and grew up in Canton, North Carolina, and near Lexington, Virginia, the county seat of Rockbridge County. He was the son of a high school principal, Robert Reveley, and his wife, the former Marguerite Grayson, and the namesake of an uncle, Walter Taylor Reveley, a Rockbridge County farmer.

REVELEY III: Reveleys first came to Virginia in the 1700s and his particular strand of Reveleys came to rest on land in Rockbridge County. When he was growing up, two of his uncles managed the farm. One was a retired Presbyterian minister and the other a farmer all his life, for whom Daddy was named. Daddy worked on the farm during summers while playing on a local baseball team. Being one of the hired hands was a great way to stay in shape, he'd say, though you had to be careful when pitching hay onto a truck lest one of the resident snakes fall on you and bite.

Handsome, athletic, smart, and deeply Presbyterian, TR2 was bound for a church-affiliated college in the fall of 1935. While a student he met his future wife, Marie (pronounced Ma'-ree) Eason.

REVELEY III: The Depression was roaring in 1935 when Daddy graduated from high school. So he took what's now called a "gap year," working as a soda jerk in the local drugstore in Canton, North Carolina, to earn some money for college. He wanted to go to a school with ties to the Presbyterian Church and had chosen Davidson, which is in North Carolina, about 140 miles from Canton. Then a cousin, David Reveley, offered to let Daddy live with him and his family on the campus of Hampden-Sydney, another Presbyterian college. It was much farther from Canton than Davidson, but living with his cousin would save money, and money in his family was in short supply. His older sister had just finished college. So that's how Daddy first made common cause with Hampden-Sydney, with its rich ties to things Presbyterian and its deep roots in American history.

MARIE EASON REVELEY: Coach David Reveley was a professor of mathematics, coached the freshman basketball team and the track team, and assisted Coach [Charles "Yank"] Bernier as a football coach. . . . The lingering effects of the Depression made this a gracious and generous offer. When Taylor left home . . . he had never seen Hampden-Sydney.[1]

Hampden-Sydney College, founded in 1775 in Prince Edward County, took its name from John Hampden and Algernon Sydney, influential British Whigs whose commitment to representative government helped inspire two of the college's founding trustees: Patrick Henry and James Madison. In seeking faculty for his favored University of Virginia in 1819, Thomas Jefferson disdained the older college's practice of recruiting professors from "Harvard and Yale. . . . Have we then been laboring merely to get up another Hampden-Sydney?"[2] Presbyterian in identity, the college was also the original home of two other Virginia institutions of higher education that later moved to Richmond. Union Theological Seminary left Prince Edward County in 1822 and the Medical College of Virginia did so in 1838.[3]

At the time of TR2's enrollment in Hampden-Sydney, he was one of about 350 students. The college was on a bit of a roll, having gained national publicity from a widely cited study in the journal *School and Society* showing that a higher percentage of Hampden-Sydney alumni (7.5 percent) were listed in the 1928–1929 edition of *Who's Who in America* than alumni of any other college.[4]

REVELEY III: Along with his studies and other activities, Daddy found real joy and meaning in organized sports, whatever the season. He went from football to basketball to baseball. He excelled at basketball and baseball, not so much at football. He was always in shape, always playing something. He was a significant jock in a small community, with all the attendant acclaim. He was also a significant student, and he was a leader. People liked him. Trusted him. This despite the fact that he was very shy.

When I used to ask him how he managed to garner such respect and affection while being really shy (as I was too when I was young), he would always say that smiling helped a whole lot. When feeling socially uncertain or uncomfortable, he'd smile, and he had a marvelous smile. It parted the waves, along with his athletic prowess and seriously good looks. It mattered, too, that he didn't brag, didn't claim credit, and did his share and more of the work that needed doing. He was a very accomplished, hard-working, genuinely good guy. People were drawn to him.

Another of his comparative advantages was his voice when he was speaking in public. It was deep, melodious, extraordinarily compelling. I rarely, if indeed ever, heard him speak to a group while growing up. On Sundays he was almost always guest-preaching in a different church than the one we belonged to in Memphis, and during the week, of course, he was teaching at Rhodes while I was in school. But then I traveled to Hampden-Sydney when I was in college in New Jersey to attend his inauguration as president. To this day I remember vividly my reaction when his turn came to speak and he stood up, looking great, and started speaking. I thought his voice was absolutely magnificent. Don't remember what he said, just remember being thrilled by his voice.

Small-college sports, ignored by the modern media, were still treated as news in the 1930s.

"Hampden-Sydney Takes Opener with 2 in Ninth," *New York Times*, March 31, 1938: "With Delaware leading 6 to 5, Hampden-Sydney filled the bases and Syd Weed scored on Taylor Reveley's sacrifice fly."

Reveley II: [Football teaches the] willingness to work together, to give of oneself . . . and to make the second effort and even the third.[5]

Marie Eason Reveley: Despite his participation in these many activities, Taylor waited tables and taught a Sunday School class for Black children in a small chapel.

Graves H. Thompson, Blair Professor of Latin and Clerk of the Faculty, Hampden-Sydney College, on TR2: It was almost as if he were the stuff of which legends are made. . . . He had been elected president of his freshman class; of his sophomore class; of his junior class. He had failed to be elected president of his class in his senior year simply because by then he was president of the student body.... At the 1939 graduation he was triply honored with the Tiger Trophy; the Gammon Cup for character, scholarship, and athletic ability; and the Algernon Sydney Sullivan Medallion for "excellence of character and generous service to his fellows."

In the youth you see the man, in the student body president the college president. Here was an individual of wide abilities, destined for leadership, imbued with the ideals of compassion and service.[6]

While a sophomore at the all-male Hampden-Sydney in 1936, TR2 met Marie, a high school senior in Richmond bound for Longwood University, then known as Farmville State Teachers College. Like TR2 at Hampden-Sydney, Marie was elected student body president at Longwood.

REVELEY II: Marie was a senior in high school, and her brother and I played baseball in Richmond one time and stayed the night at their house.... I was pretty slow. But we did get together and dated the next year.[7]

REVELEY III: Daddy said it was love at first sight when he walked into Mother's home and saw her sitting at the piano in the front hall, playing. He thought she was exquisite, and was instantly smitten. He also thought—erroneously—that she was her younger sister, Caroline, who would have been too young for him to pursue. Once that misapprehension was corrected, his innate shyness kicked in, plus he was always incredibly busy. He didn't have a car at Hampden-Sydney, and Longwood was six miles away. Romance moved slowly. Mother used to say she was about to give up on him when he finally got in gear. Their love for one another was a thing of beauty. It was the bedrock on which our family stood.

MARIE EASON REVELEY: A host of marriages took place between Hampden-Sydney men and Longwood girls.... Taylor and I went together all four years at Longwood.

REVELEY IV: The two institutions were very much brother and sister until Longwood, by force of federal action more than choice at the time, became fully coed in 1976.... But Farmville is a true college town, and there's always been back and forth between the two campuses.

Marie Eason Reveley, on Hampden-Sydney students: They looked down on us academically. They said it was Miss Mary's Finishing School.[8]

Marie's family ties to Longwood were strong. Her father, Thomas D. Eason, headed its biology department in the 1910s before joining the Virginia Department of Education and, in 1931, rising to becoming the department's director of higher education. (The year before, when it appeared that Longwood's longtime president, J. L. Jarman, might leave, the *Richmond Times-Dispatch* headlined: "Eason Regarded Probable Choice to Succeed President of Institution," referring to Longwood.)[9] Eason's death in 1939 at age fifty-two, the *Times-Dispatch* editorialized, was "nothing less than a tragedy for Virginia" because it deprived the commonwealth of a public servant who was not just "competent and efficient" but "courteous and considerate, no matter how intense the pressure" and whose "advice and counsel would have been especially valuable in the difficult period which lies ahead" in light of "the confidence reposed in him by educational leaders of both races."[10] Eason's official portrait, recovered from a fire, hangs in TR4's presidential office.

Reveley III: Thomas Eason was an august being by the time my father met him in 1936, in the spring of Daddy's freshman year in college. He died before he and TR2 could have gotten to really know each other, but Daddy would have heard his commencement address at Hampden-Sydney in 1937, about a year after he and Mother started dating. Our family has preserved the text of the address because its theme—the fear that "constitutional government in American is threatened" and the duty of citizens is "to use as much intelligence, fortitude and foresight in preserving constitutional government as your predecessors exerted in securing it"—has had resonance for us through the generations.

Marie's mother, Carrie Eason, herself a Longwood alumna, became a leader in the state Parents-Teachers Association. After seeing her daughter married to TR2 as the culmination of a five-year courtship in August 1941, as well as seeing her grandson TR3 grow to age sixteen, Carrie died in 1959. In the marriage ceremony at Richmond's Overbrook Presbyterian, the Eason family's church, Marie was given away by Tom Eason, the brother who had introduced her to his baseball teammate. TR2 was by then in his final year at Union Seminary.

REVELEY III: After Daddy died, Mother told me he had wanted to be a lawyer, but was urged by many to become a minister. He eventually felt a call to the ministry, which he answered. It was obvious to me that he did have a powerful faith and a deep commitment to the ministry. He was always accepting invitations to preach at churches around town or even out of town. And it was important to him that he teach in a college with church ties. So he ended up practicing two ministerial professions simultaneously, one foot in the church and one in the academy. He worked seven days a week. I've known only one other person with a comparable work ethic, coupled with the capacity to work like a dog, without complaint, while remaining cheerful.[11]

While pastoring Union and Loch Willow Presbyterian Churches in Churchville, Virginia, where TR3 was born in 1943, TR2 felt duty-bound to enlist as a chaplain in the wartime army.

REVELEY III: Though he was a minister exempt from the draft, he volunteered to serve in the Second World War and successfully resisted his superiors' efforts to hang on to him for service in stateside training camps. He ended up in the force that was to have invaded Japan.

Daddy later joked that he'd fought "the Battle of Mississippi" because he was stationed for a time at Camp Dorn. In truth, he had a very strong sense of obligation, since other guys his age who had young families were getting killed and maimed and needed some spiritual comfort. In 1945 he was in the Philippines waiting to be part of the invasion of Japan when Harry Truman used atomic bombs to end the war. I have always been profoundly grateful that Japan surrendered when it did, because otherwise millions of Americans and Japanese would have surely died during the invasion of the home islands. The likelihood that anyone as devoted to serving other people as my father would have survived the carnage was not great.

DAN CALDWELL AND B. L. BOWMAN, ON TR2'S POSTWAR OCCUPATION SERVICE AT THE ARMY'S 27TH GENERAL HOSPITAL: Christmas Eve in Tokyo. There were plenty of sick boys present. They were sick not so much from physical disease as from the thought of Christmas, another Christmas, away from home. . . . After Chaplain Elliott and Chaplain Reveley had been around the wards holding Communion for the patients that were bedridden, a group gathered to sing carols in the halls. . . . There was no race line, for Negro and white had sung together.[12]

REVELEY III: Daddy returned from Japan on an emergency leave because my mother's appendix ruptured just before she gave birth to my sister. The earliest childhood memory I have is watching Mother, in desperate straits, carried on a stretcher out of my grandmother's home in Richmond on the way to the hospital. Her physicians mistook acute appendicitis for the rigors of pregnancy. Infection was raging throughout her body. She was not expected to live. My infant sister and I stayed with our grandmother. Mother slowly recovered, thanks to the new wonder drug, penicillin, and an enormous amount of family care. Thanks also to her indomitable will to live so she could help Daddy take care of the children. In 1946 Daddy began serving as pastor of Fairmount-Hoge Memorial, a small Presbyterian church in Richmond. He thought about returning to Union Seminary to get an advanced degree. His preference, though, was to join the faculty of a liberal arts college related to the Presbyterian Church.

In 1946, after being highly recommended by the president of Union Seminary, as well as by Professors John Osman and Lawrence Kinney, two of his future colleagues at Rhodes College, TR2 received an invitation from Rhodes president Charles E. Diehl. The invitation was to become the institution's first college pastor for a one-year period of "mutual trial" at a salary of $3,900. The need for pastoral care at the time was great, especially for the dozens of World War II veterans and their families whose enrollment at Rhodes was enabled by the new GI Bill. TR2's experience as an army chaplain weighed heavily in his hiring. The college had actually bought thirty-six trailers for married veterans with children.[13]

CHARLES E. DIEHL, LETTER TO UNION SEMINARY PRESIDENT HENRY BRIM, NOVEMBER 26, 1946: You helped us get the Reverend W. Taylor Reveley as College Pastor. He is one of the very few men I have ever engaged as a member of our staff whom I did not know personally or with whom I had not had an interview. However . . . we are very happy over having Mr. Reveley. He is a fine, friendly spirit, is making a place for himself, and is highly regarded both by his colleagues, and by the students.[14]

Although his agreement with Rhodes College was guaranteed for just one year, TR2 bought a small house on Tutwiler Avenue in midtown Memphis, close to campus. It was the family home in which TR3 grew up until he left for college, along with Chris, his younger sister.

REVELEY III: Mother, my sister, and I were still in Richmond when Daddy got the job at Rhodes. She was appalled when he bought the house in Memphis. Houses were scarce right after the war ended, and it cost a lot more than she could imagine paying. More important, there was no assurance Daddy would have a job for more than a year if the college's finances failed to improve. What then? Would they be able to sell the house for what he'd paid?

I never asked Daddy why he bought the house so precipitously and sight unseen by Mother. His basic optimism surely played a part. He was confident that he could do the job he'd been hired to do in a way that would please the college. I doubt he really dwelt on the possibility that Rhodes might not be able to sustain the position financially. He was not very worldly.

Mother, as always, was a trooper. She quickly made the house a home and immediately began helping fund it by renting two of its bedrooms to single women who were working in Memphis and needed a safe, congenial place to live. Arrangements like that were common in that era.

TR2 soon established himself at Rhodes, not only as college pastor but also as an occasional instructor in the Department of Religious Studies (then called Bible), as an assistant football coach, as baseball coach when Rhodes revived the sport in 1949, and as intramural basketball star on the faculty team. His contract was renewed.

The Sou'wester, MARCH 21, 1947: The Faculty basketball team is led by Reveley, a triple threat in looks, legs, and shoulders.

The Sou'wester, JUNE 1949: The baseball team, first in over two decades at Southwestern, was coached by Professor W. Taylor Reveley. It was surprisingly successful for a first-year venture, winning five games in eight starts, several by convincing margins.

TR2 was by now committed to an academic more than a pastoral career. Advised by Professor Kinney that he needed a PhD, he, Marie, TR3, and Chris left for Duke University in the fall of 1950, with no assurance that there would be a place for him at Rhodes when he finished his doctorate. The postwar surge of GI Bill-funded students, which had lifted the college's enrollment above seven hundred in 1946, had run its course. Even so, the Reveleys kept their house in Memphis, renting it out while they were in Durham.

PEYTON NALLE RHODES (DIEHL'S SUCCESSOR AS PRESIDENT), LETTER TO TR2, NOVEMBER 19, 1951: We have four hundred and thirty-two students . . . and are pretty well loaded up [in Bible and philosophy] for that number. . . . Most of your work has been in Bible, but I would like to know what other fields of interest you feel competent to teach in. Would you be willing to do the work necessary to catch up on the Man course? . . . You and Marie belong here and if there is any way which shapes up later to let us invite you to come back, I would go to great lengths to work it out.

REVELEY II, LETTER TO PRESIDENT RHODES, DECEMBER 10, 1951: My work has been in the field of Christian thought (major in ethics and minor in political theory) rather than in Bible so that I could handle some areas in the Man course.

In truth, TR2's dissertation—titled "A Christian Critique of Modern Liberal Democratic Theory as Reflected in the Writings of Jacques Maritain, A. D. Lindsay, and Reinhold Niebuhr"—was ideal preparation for teaching Man in the Light of History and Religion (the Man course), which Rhodes College launched in 1945 as a twelve-credit Great Books–style course that enrolled most students.[15] Man, which then and for years to come was the term men commonly used as a proxy for all of humanity, later inspired similar courses at a number of other southern colleges, including Davidson, Sewanee, Millsaps, and, eventually, Hampden-Sydney, where TR2 brought a version of the course as president.[16] Man later became Search, its current name at Rhodes.

Like the Man course, TR2's dissertation was broadly grounded in the humanities, relating Christian theology to democratic political theory. Especially influenced by the seventeenth-century political philosopher John Locke and the twentieth-century Christian theologian Reinhold Niebuhr, TR2 concluded that "the Christian interpretation of man reveals not only the depths to which sin can bring man but also the heights to which man can rise as a child of God. If the one makes democracy necessary, the other makes it possible."[17] Even with his dissertation unlikely to be finished until 1953, President Rhodes wanted him back, convinced that TR2 could add genuine value to the college. But now TR2 wasn't so sure. He had another possibility at Duke.

PEYTON NALLE RHODES, LETTER TO TR2, JANUARY 14, 1952: We want you back here at Southwestern next session.... As for a title, I suppose that we would have to call you Assistant Professor of Ethics and Humanities.... We could pay you $3,900.

REVELEY II, LETTER TO PRESIDENT RHODES, JANUARY 29, 1952: [Duke has offered me] a promising opportunity—and so near to our parents also. While my initial impulse was to return to Southwestern, I determined to consider both places as carefully and objectively as possible.... The salary is quite adequate.

REVELEY III: Duke was a very appealing prospect, especially for Mother, even though the family had had a wonderful three years in Memphis and still owned a house there. My eight-year-old self assumed we'd go back to 1732 Tutwiler, which was home as far as I was concerned. But at Duke decision time, I was in the third grade and not included in the councils of the mighty.

Family considerations weighed on Mother and Daddy. Duke was in North Carolina, much closer to Virginia than Memphis. Mother's mother, sisters, and brother lived in Virginia. Daddy's parents had retired to the family farm in Rockbridge County, outside Lexington. Memphis was a long way away from them and felt even longer in the era before interstate highways and air-conditioned cars. We'd been in Durham for three years and my parents liked it. Duke was also a much better funded operation than Rhodes.

So, the state of play was: Daddy had left Rhodes to get a PhD so he could be a full-fledged, card-carrying faculty member, got the degree in three years (rather than four, five, or six years—there's that work ethic), and was offered the same salary to return to Rhodes that he had when he left, which was barely enough to keep body and soul together. The offer from Duke did look awfully appealing.

TR2 nonetheless accepted the college's invitation to return, at which point President Rhodes complicated matters by asking him to resume his "old post as College Chaplain." Reluctantly, TR2 agreed to accept the position, but in a limited way, mostly confined to ceremonial occasions, so as not to divert him from his preferred role as professor. Although the promised limits on the chaplain's duties eroded in practice, TR2 was now clearly a member of the faculty and, to his delight, was able to draw on his multidisciplinary breadth of training by teaching the Man course.

REVELEY III: Daddy didn't negotiate much, if at all, when the issue was something he viewed as a personal gain—because he simply wouldn't ask for it. Deep in his bones he believed that his mission in life was to serve others, whether they were individuals or institutions, not himself. He could be very effective, very persuasive when negotiating for institutional or community interests. But that was because he wasn't inhibited by concern he was being selfish.

In 1954, just a year after his return, TR2 was promoted to associate professor of Bible and humanities, with a bump in salary to $5,000—the equivalent of about $60,000 in 2025, less than a new instructor's starting salary at many institutions. He also became cochair of the admissions and student aid committee, later rising to the newly created post of admissions and records dean when Rhodes, like other enterprising liberal arts college in the 1950s, professionalized its admissions process instead of leaving it entirely in the hands of a faculty committee.[18] While serving this administrative role, however, TR2 maintained his scholarly bona fides and a heavy course load and was promoted in rapid succession to full professor. In 1957 he became the first incumbent of the W. J. Millard Chair of Bible and Humanities.

REVELEY II: I was a professor at Southwestern—[19]

MARIE EASON REVELEY:—and an administrator, chaplain, coach—he ran the whole gamut.[20]

In various ways, TR2 focused on issues of racial justice on a campus and in a city where segregation was still the norm and, in many cases, the law. In 1949 he led a group of Rhodes faculty that included physicist and president-elect Peyton Nalle Rhodes in seeking to raise $320,000 for Memphis's church-affiliated HBCU, Lemoyne-Owen College (then called Lemoyne College).[21]

During the summer of 1958, TR2 used a Lilly Foundation Research Grant to write a lengthy paper titled "The Southern Church, the State, and the Negro: An Appraisal." Citing avowedly pro-slavery sermons and speeches by antebellum Presbyterian ministers in the South such as Benjamin Palmer (after whom the main building at Rhodes College was named—until the college changed it in 2019), TR2 considered the situation in Prince Edward County, as well as at his alma mater. He lamented:

REVELEY II: The old tragic pattern repeats itself. In 1958, as in 1860, the region finds itself standing alone in naked defiance of the nation's declared policy.... [To be sure, when] finally in 1954 the Supreme Court decision came declaring "separate but equal" educational facilities unconstitutional, the Church woke both to its danger and to its mission.... Despite the forthright stand of the [Presbyterian Church U.S.'s 1954] General Assembly, however, one must not assume a similar response on the part of the constituency. Church colleges remain segregated.[22]

TR2 never held a pastorate after leaving Virginia for Memphis, but he preached regularly at pulpits throughout the Mid-South. On February 12, 1961, one of his sermons, delivered at Greenwood Presbyterian Church in Greenwood, Mississippi, on the Sunday the Presbyterian Church U.S. had designated "Race Relations Sunday," stirred a hornet's nest. His text was from Luke's account of the parable of the Good Samaritan: "Who is my neighbor?"

REVELEY II, SERMON NOTES: Needs of a minority group: 1. Equality of rights in terms of the structures of society.... 2. Acceptance as person—this [is] the Christian extra mile.

REVELEY III: Daddy and Mother believed deeply in what was then called the "brotherhood of man," which among many other things urged an end to racial segregation. He preached that message from the pulpit and also urged it at Rhodes College, which was still segregated. The "brotherhood of man" was not a welcome message in Mississippi in 1961, and it was often met with violence. An elder who had been instrumental in getting Daddy to come preach in Greenwood quickly took him out of the church to his home and then out of Mississippi. He was afraid there might be physical ramifications to what Daddy had preached. And then Daddy wrote a letter.

REVELEY II, LETTER TO THE GREENWOOD PRESBYTERIAN CHURCH SESSION, FEBRUARY 20, 1961: I cannot apologize for, nor take back anything said during, the sermon. . . . When the Church calls upon its people to consider so pressing an issue as the one which has been thrust upon us here in the South, I believe my first responsibility lies there. . . . For whenever a congregation is willing to hear only pleasing words from its pulpit, it has forsaken its quest for the truth of God's word. . . . "If anyone says, 'I love God,' and hates his brother, he is a liar" [1 John 4:20].

REVELEY III: That was uncharacteristically harsh of Daddy, but he was not about to simply turn the other cheek when basic questions of Christian commitment and fundamental fairness were at issue.

In the fall of 1962, TR2 and fifty-one other members of the faculty—a strong majority—sent a letter to President Rhodes and the college's board of trustees urging that the school begin the long overdue process of admitting Black students, an act that in TR2's case was especially bold because, as admissions dean, he was also part of the administration. But, as TR3 points out, "Even though sending a letter to the board, without consulting the president, is not something you ordinarily should do, it was utterly pursuant to his beliefs about racial justice." By this time, the "strong president" model of leadership in higher education had already begun to move, at Rhodes College and elsewhere, in the direction of shared governance with faculty. At a subsequent meeting of the board in March 1963 the trustees adopted the faculty's recommendation.

Also in 1962, TR2 was invited to become director of the division of higher education of the Presbyterian Church U.S.'s Board of Christian Education.[23] The board was based in Richmond, close to most of his and Marie's extended families. The position interested him. In the fall of 1956 he had taken a semester-long leave from Rhodes College to visit sixty mostly southern campuses as a consultant to the education board's Christian Faculty Fellowship program. TR2's decision to accept the full-time position with the board created a momentary rift in his relationship with President Rhodes, who for more than a decade had been—and soon would once again become—an important friend and mentor.

REVELEY II, LETTER TO PEYTON NALLE RHODES, DECEMBER 15, 1962: I have long recognized your method of putting "bad mouth" on any new project or proposed move and had hoped that this time would be different.

PRESIDENT RHODES TO TR2, DECEMBER 19, 1962: I do not quite follow the "bad mouth" reference. . . . It is just hard for me to think that any job anywhere can be more productive personally or for the Church than the high level administrative post at Southwestern. . . . If anybody can make anything of the Richmond job I think that you can, though I still think you are accepting a considerable "demotion."

REVELEY IV: It's possible Peyton Rhodes was flummoxed because he thought the position wasn't too promising, and also because he was already actively thinking about retiring—which he did just two years later—and wanted TR2 as his successor but wasn't ready yet to actually talk about that possibility, even privately. Discussing retirement from a presidency is complicated, with lots of lame duck risks as soon as the idea is even somewhat in the air.

REVELEY III: My first reaction to the offer when I first heard about the Board of Christian Education job early in the spring term of my sophomore year at Princeton was, "Why on earth would you do that?" (Being a sophomore, I was certain in my views.) The position sounded more important than it was because as a denomination, Presbyterians were not supporting their church colleges very meaningfully anymore, and the colleges were pulling away from their old ties to the church.

My next reaction was: "Why do you think the job is going to stay in Richmond and not move to Atlanta?" Which it soon did. I was not happy at the prospect of my parents leaving Memphis and our house. I was deeply attached to the city, to our neighborhood, our church, my old schools, my friends—and to Rhodes, where I'd had free range of the campus, a job during high school, and lots of friends on the faculty and staff.

I didn't see the frisky exchange of correspondence between Daddy and Peyton Rhodes about the job change until recently. Now that I've been a president, I can understand where President Rhodes was coming from—he wanted to keep Daddy. But it was refreshing to see Daddy push back.

That TR2 was invited to lead a prominent church institution—the first of two invitations that soon would come—was hardly unexpected.

REVELEY III: Daddy got a steady stream of unsolicited job offers. He was always leading. I never knew, or thought to ask, whether this was because he enjoyed leading or felt it was his obligation. Probably some of both. At Hampden-Sydney he was president of his class three times and then president of the student body. At Union Seminary he was president of the student body. When you're a parish minister, you're leading. When he went to Rhodes, he was put in positions to lead again, whether religious or athletic. Then he started being put on countless college committees. When it came to admissions work, where he'd been leading as a committee chair, my guess is he finally decided that if he was going to be sustaining the effort, he might as well do it as a dean rather than a faculty member. He simultaneously carried a teaching load that would be considered cruel and inhuman these days for a tenured professor.

Becoming President

The rift with President Rhodes was soon healed and their warm relationship enduringly restored. At the end of the 1962–1963 academic year, the Reveleys made ready to move to Richmond.

MARIE EASON REVELEY: Our home in Memphis had been sold and I had been to Richmond and bought a home. . . . Our son, Taylor III, was a rising junior at Princeton and had a job at Dupont in Memphis for the summer of 1963. Our daughter, Chris, had finished high school a year early and was already taking a college course at Rhodes.

REVELEY III: While all of us were still in Memphis, Mother, Daddy, my sister, and I were having lunch together one day in early June.

MARIE EASON REVELEY: Dr. James A. Jones, chairman of the search committee, called Taylor long distance and asked him to come and talk about being president of Hampden-Sydney College. . . . Taylor declined. Within fifteen minutes Dr. Jones called again asking both Taylor and me to visit him in his office in Richmond. He was president of the Union Theological Seminary at the time.

REVELEY III: Jones was calling Daddy not to say, "Would you be a candidate?" He was calling Daddy to say, "We want you to be president." After Daddy hung the phone up and told the rest of us what had just happened, there was stunned silence around the table for a moment and then expressions of *joy*. He'd long said the only college presidency he wanted was of Hampden-Sydney. Mother and I knew that, and we also knew Daddy would be deeply troubled about pulling out of the church job. Certainly from his perspective, you don't commit yourself to one thing and then when something more flashy comes along that you'd rather do, throw the first one over the side. But we urged him, really beat on him, to get the church to release him and take the Hampden-Sydney presidency.

TR2 and Marie Reveley met with Jones (known to friends as "Jas A") in Richmond.

MARIE EASON REVELEY: Jas A informed us that the search committee had 200 names submitted or volunteered for president of Hampden-Sydney. Both Taylor and I had already been investigated and Taylor was the unanimous choice. . . . Jas A insisted that the college needed Taylor more than the Church needed him. . . . There was no doubt that Taylor wanted to accept but his sense of integrity would not let him renege on his prior commitment. Within a matter of weeks before Taylor was to assume that commitment, Dr. Jones secured his release from the position.

REVELEY IV: It has occurred to me that if the Hampden-Sydney presidency had been in question when the internet existed, and all the tendrils and trails of what we say and do were as readily available in 1963 as they are now, TR2's very progressive views on race would have been both known and anathema to some of the powers that be at Hampden-Sydney.

PEYTON NALLE RHODES, LETTER TO TR2, JULY 31, 1963: [I saw] that the Board of Directors of Hampden-Sydney had acted and that you now have officially had the noose put around your neck. . . . Of course, if there is anything that I can do at any time to help out just let me know. I am sure that you can handle the situation admirably and maybe I am just a little tired of the job myself.

Peyton Rhodes may have been hoping that TR2 would be available to succeed him at Rhodes College when he retired as president soon afterward. In any case, Hampden-Sydney's need for a successful president was especially urgent in 1963. In the thirty-six years prior to 1955 it had just two presidents, the same number it burned through in the turbulent eight years that followed, which immediately preceded TR2's selection. In contrast to nearly all of their twentieth-century predecessors, neither of the two recent short-lived presidents had been Presbyterian ministers. In that sense, TR2 represented a reversion to the college's historical mean.

No transition period of any consequence attended TR2's appointment as president (with an annual salary of $16,000—about $190,000 in 2025 dollars—plus $2,400 for entertainment and upkeep at Middlecourt, the president's on-campus home). Yet certain challenges were obvious and urgent. The college's most recent president had come and gone in the aftermath of what Marie Reveley described as "an ugly riot in the spring before our arrival" that was "an internal combustion" born of mutual distrust among students, faculty, and administrators. It culminated in a demand that the board fire the dean of men, signed by almost all the faculty.

REVELEY III: A real disturbance of some kind had occurred on campus that really upset the president at the time, Thomas Gilmer, and the board of trustees, and that led to Gilmer's view that he had to get out of the kitchen and the board's view that he really did need to get out of the kitchen. His immediate predecessor as president, Joseph Robert, hadn't lasted long either. Robert was the first president since before the Civil War who didn't emerge from the Hampden-Sydney community, and he was basically driven out.

MARIE EASON REVELEY: Taylor was Hampden-Sydney's third president in eight years. . . . At the time Taylor was hired, the internal unrest at the college was of great concern to the board. Taylor was urged to run the college, to keep things on a steady course.

Merely to "keep things on a steady course," however, was as unlikely a possibility as it was the preferred one. Alone among all the public school systems in the country, the schools in Prince Edward County, Virginia, remained closed in defiance of the Supreme Court's ruling in *Brown vs. Board of Education* nine years before, with damaging consequences for Hampden-Sydney and the surrounding community that its new president would have to address carefully but immediately. On the front page of the *Farmville Herald*, alongside the story on TR2 being named Hampden-Sydney's president, was this headline: "33 Demonstrators Arrested in Week End of Racial Unrest Here." If any reminder of the situation's urgency was needed, it came soon after the Reveleys arrived at their new home, less than one month after TR2 accepted the job.

MARIE EASON REVELEY: The almost tomb-like quietness of the campus, seeming to slumber in the heat of a July afternoon, was in sharp contrast to the scene on Main Street in Farmville. As we sat waiting for a red traffic light to change at the corner of High and Main Streets, we were rammed from behind. The driver of the car was gawking out the window at a line of demonstrators . . . [that] included both black and white members of the Prince Edward community protesting segregation and specifically the closing of the public schools. . . . Both Hampden-Sydney and Longwood colleges were represented in the line.[24]

These issues of segregation and public school closing were to cloud almost every facet of our lives at Hampden-Sydney and to dominate our early years. . . . Like an old but still splendid tiger, Hampden-Sydney lay, *en couchant*, one eye tightly closed and the other open and wary of the slightest movement. Any change in the surrounding savanna would bring both eyes open and a twitching tail gave warning. . . .

We both knew other faculties, programs, and geographic locations. At the same time we looked upon the college with affection and pride, we could honestly assess its situation in a way that was almost certain to elude long-term faculty and local residents. . . . [And because] for generations both of our families had been involved in the life of the college, we could not be easily dismissed as newcomers or troublemakers trying to change "everything."

2

Taylor Reveley III and William & Mary

Unlike his father and, later, his son, Taylor Reveley III spent most of his prepresidential career outside higher education. His father, TR2, who was forty-six when he became president of Hampden-Sydney College, spent seventeen of his first twenty-five working years (68 percent of them) at Rhodes College, including a three-year period in which he left to earn his doctorate at Duke University.[1] His son, TR4, who was thirty-eight when named president of Longwood University, spent seven of his first eleven working years (64 percent) at the University of Virginia's Miller Center. In contrast, TR3 was not only much older—sixty-five—when he became president of William & Mary but had spent only eleven of his prepresidential working years (28 percent) in higher education, including a one-year stint teaching law at the University of Alabama right after completing his own legal education and, starting more than a quarter century later, ten years as dean of William & Mary Law School. His three decades of employment prior to becoming dean involved practicing law at Hunton & Williams, a national firm headquartered in Richmond where TR3 lived while working mostly in New York and Washington, DC.[2]

Growing Up

TR3 was born in January 1943 near Staunton, Virginia, in Churchville, where TR2 was a Presbyterian pastor. When he was an infant, his father joined the wartime army as a chaplain, stationed at various stateside camps in Alabama, Texas, and Mississippi until, at his repeated request, he was deployed in 1945 to the Pacific Theater as part of the force assembled for the anticipated invasion of Japan and, when that proved unnecessary, for its occupation. Until then TR3's existence and that of his mother, Marie Eason Reveley, was peripatetic as they followed TR2 from one army base to another. When TR2 left for the Pacific, mother and son returned to the Eason family home in Richmond. That changed in the fall of 1946, when TR2 became college pastor at Rhodes and the family moved to Memphis.

REVELEY III: It was constant moving around, along with the anxiety Mother felt while we were going from military post to military post, as she drove along unfamiliar roads with a baby, on bald tires and rationed gasoline. But she had an indomitable will and a lot of courage. She loved to sing, loved to dance, loved flowers and made every place we lived more beautiful. She was less willing than Daddy to suffer fools or put up with inconsiderate or incompetent people. Daddy was more empathetic and more willing to clean up messes made by others, without complaint.

And then when I was three we finally were all glued together in the house at 1732 Tutwiler in Memphis. And I looked at them and asked, "Is this our home?" Meaning, are we going to keep moving from pillar to post, or is this our home? And they said yes. I had been having trouble sleeping. And I immediately went to sleep. And didn't have any trouble sleeping thereafter. I'm sure all the moving around under hard circumstances and feeling really safe only at my Grandmother Eason's home in Richmond had a lasting impact on me. For one thing, I've always been attached to home. Big time.

We lived a pretty circumscribed geographical life in Memphis because everything was right there in our neighborhood. I thought people who lived well-regulated lives filled up their car with Esso gasoline, bought groceries at the A&P, shopped at Sears, and went to public schools.[3] Private schools were for delinquent kids, who were shipped off to military academies. In a sense, we lived a small-town life in a big city.

Brown v. Board of Education came down when I was still in the fifth grade. And I can remember standing outside the boys' entrance to Snowden Elementary School waiting for the bell to ring and listening to all the boys around me talking standard racist patter. And thinking, that's not what my parents say, it's not what they think, it's not what my family believes.

Finishing eleventh grade at Central High School, I got nominated to run for senior class treasurer. We had really serious campaigns; they brought in voting machines. I expected to lose—I'd lost other school elections. But I won! And I remember how thrilling that was.

I also remember that growing up I spent a lot of time reading about leaders, thinking about leadership, talking about leadership to other people. The bottom line, I still think, is: if you don't want to lead, the odds that you're going to do a good job at it or even last long in the job are very small. So don't get seduced by the gold braid if you don't want to do the job, even if it's student body treasurer—in other words, if you've got no idea what's entailed and aren't game for the downsides as well as the upsides of leading.

Already, in junior high, I had gotten totally caught up in the Suez crisis and the Hungarian uprising in 1956, and that interest in world affairs never stopped. I decided I wanted to get a PhD in international relations and join the diplomatic corps, become an ambassador someday.

Although still all-male, essentially all-white, and inclined in their admissions practices toward northeastern prep schools, by the early 1960s Princeton University and the nation's other elite institutions were broadening their approach to undergraduate recruitment to encompass high-achieving public school students from other parts of the country.[4]

REVELEY III: I was going to apply for college only to Rhodes, because I wanted to go to Rhodes. And then one day, someone at Central pulled me out of class and said an admissions representative from Princeton is here and no one has signed up to see him—would you? I was urged to "go see him and sound interested, even if you aren't." And I did, just to avoid embarrassing the school. The fellow from Princeton told me about its Woodrow Wilson School of Public and International Affairs. It sounded perfect, exactly what I wanted to study, a mix of history, politics, and economics. So I applied and, when I got in, everybody said, "Oh, little boy, you have to go."[5]

Right before classes started at Princeton, the family put me on an airplane to Washington, after which came a train ride to New Jersey. I'd never set foot on the campus. Finally got there at 7:00 a.m., with no idea where my dorm was. No member of the family had ever gone to Princeton, it was terra incognita.

I went out for the lightweight crew team. My father had played everything and been a serious athlete, and so I wanted to do something. Against all odds, I made the team. And just like winning that election for treasurer, when my boat won races against other schools, after endless hours practicing in all sorts of weather for months and months, it was absolutely exhilarating.

I also worked. If you had a need-based scholarship in those days, which I did, you had to work. My job was to wait on tables in Commons after crew practice. Lake Carnegie, where we rowed, was way down at the other end of campus from Commons. Long walk down to the lake. We would run before we rowed. Then we'd row and row and row. Intense exercise. Come back, take a shower, and go back up the hill, where the Commons was, to serve the freshman football team after their practice. They were exhausted, ravenous, full of themselves. I was equally exhausted, equally ravenous, equally full of myself. Not having my father's sweet disposition, I was really hot at having to do that. I'd like to sit down too and have somebody serve me. Instead, I'm serving these jackasses.

One time, coming in for a landing with a tray loaded with pork chops, I slipped. Pork chops ended up largely on the floor. Picked them up, put them back on the tray, put them on the table. Unlike crew, waiting tables didn't build my character. It probably took a bite out of it.

To avoid working in Commons again, I borrowed money. I also gave up crew after my sophomore year. I'm glad I did it for as long as I did, but I wanted to do other things and I wasn't getting better at pulling my oar through the water.

There was certainly no conversation at Princeton back then about, "If you're feeling anxious or depressed, we're here to help at Centers A, B, C, and D and they're full of nurturing wizards." If you had a problem in the early 1960s, you dealt with it or you went home. I was seriously miserable every day of my first term. And it would have helped if there had been somebody to whom I felt I could say, "Hey, I am really sad, crew's hard, waiting tables is appalling, I'm making bad grades in French and I haven't ever made bad grades. Is this likely to end?" Of course, it did. Second term was much better. By junior year, I was totally awash in orange and black.

And then, on November 22, 1963, fall of my junior year, John F. Kennedy was assassinated. I was deeply distressed. I'd been greatly enamored of him, and when that happened, I decided I ought to go into elective politics. I asked some professors, "What do you do if you want to go into politics?" They said, "Oh, you go to law school." Both because you learn something about government and how it works and because as a lawyer, you have more flexibility in what you do to earn a living. Of course, I never did go into politics or the diplomatic corps. But I did practice law for a long time.

The class of 1965, my class, was really the last gasp of the old order at Princeton, a break point between past and future. We might as well have gone in the 1930s. President [Robert] Goheen told our class that all-male education had worked for centuries and there were no plans to change. Within two years he was leading the move into coeducation.[6]

Bill Bowen

REVELEY III: At the end of my senior year I saw an ad on the bulletin board of the Woodrow Wilson School that Bill Bowen was looking for a summer research assistant. He was the very young director of the school—only ten years my senior—and a young economics professor specializing in labor economics. He didn't know me from Adam, and I was not unduly drawn to economics. But he not only hired me, early in my work for him he said, "Why don't you come live with us? We've got a bed in the basement you can have." And that began an absolutely wonderful summer with Bill and his wife, Mary Ellen, and their two small children, David, who was six, and his infant sister, Karen. They treated me as family from day one.[7]

The book Bill was writing with Will Baumol was *Economics of the Performing Arts,* which became enormously influential for showing that in the arts and other human-centric enterprises, you couldn't reduce labor costs by achieving greater efficiencies the way you could in other organizations because, for example, it will always take four musicians to perform a string quartet.[8] You can't increase productivity by playing it twice as fast or with only half the strings. That insight has obvious implications for education, which is also labor-intensive by its nature.

REVELEY IV: "Baumol's Curse," it's sometimes called, because it drives up the cost of faculty, of lawyers, of dentists, of nurses, of government employees—anything that is of a personal service nature.

REVELEY III: By the end of the summer Bill and I knew each other extremely well, and it proved to be a lasting friendship of deep warmth.

Was he a mentor as well as a friend? We were only a decade apart in age, a gap that felt shorter and shorter as we both got older. That's different from Daddy's relationship with Peyton Rhodes or the one TR4 later developed with Governor [Gerald] Baliles, both of whom were of an earlier generation. But Bill was certainly a powerful role model for me about how to lead and get things done. He was someone whose judgment I trusted and whose counsel I sought. He was hands down the smartest, wisest, most practical, most energetic mortal I've ever encountered. I have never met anybody of comparable ability, work ethic, and capacity to do momentous deeds.[9]

What I was most drawn to about Bill—and, I hope, learned from him—was that he was an extremely warm, collegial, nonhierarchical human being. No overweening ego. No desire to claim credit, even when credit was surely his. Just focused on getting the job done.

Learning and Teaching the Law

REVELEY III: Part of what I'd been told was that if you wanted to go into politics, you should not only go to law school, but go to law school in that state. For me that was Virginia.

I made law review at UVA midway through my first year, and then spent the overwhelming bulk of my time for the next two-and-a-half years working on it. Indeed—and this was counterproductive to learning as much legal lore as I should have—I stopped going to most of my classes and just relied on intense cramming at the end of the term, because the only grade in the course was the final exam.

I did do a couple things along the way that turned out to matter. My last term in law school I took a seminar with A. E. Dick Howard, who was one of the school's bright young stars, on selected constitutional topics. Students each had to come up with a topic and lead the discussion. This was the spring of 1968. The Vietnam War was going on, and so the question I posed to the group was: "Suppose President Johnson tells Congress he needs to send another 500,000 troops to Vietnam to ensure adequate support for our troops already on the ground there and to ensure national security in his judgment as commander in chief. Congress responds instead by passing a joint resolution saying stop spending money on the war and get out of Vietnam entirely in eighteen months, which he vetoes. Both houses override his veto. The question is: Who wins constitutionally?" I had gone to the library to look for the answer and discovered almost nothing had been written directly on the subject. Although this made for a very challenging seminar session, I was hooked by the question and decided to keep doing research and then write a law review article about it.

Meanwhile, Dick had been tapped to be executive director of the state's Commission on Constitutional Revision. Virginia's constitution had been adopted in 1902 basically to disenfranchise Blacks and poor whites and to slow down progress toward universal and high-quality public education. In the summer of 1968 Dick recruited some of us who had just graduated from law school to help. He assigned me to work for Tom Currier on the subcommittee dealing with the bill of rights, the franchise, and education. I did some research and wrote a few memos. Nothing of any moment, but it was great to be part of a process that led to a new state constitution that was approved by the voters in 1971, ending Jim Crow in Virginia and also ending the old pay-as-you-go rule, which kept the state from issuing bonds for capital investments in roads, bridges, universities—all sorts of necessary things.[10]

That same summer, another real star professor at the law school, Dan Meador, recruited me to come teach law at the University of Alabama, where he had become dean in 1966. I was bovinely ignorant about the reality that for each hour you spend in class, particularly if you don't yet know what you're doing, you've got to spend many more hours trying to get ready. I survived, and I hope my students did. Years later, it gave me a real appreciation for what fledgling faculty had to do at William & Mary.

Dan had gone to Alabama with a mission to try and create a genuinely great law school in the Deep South, which had none. And in his first three years there he had strong support from the president, Frank Rose, and made absolutely amazing progress. But then Rose ceased to be president in 1969 and his very young successor, David Mathews, opposed what Dan was trying to do with the law school, including wanting to move it to Birmingham. So when UVA asked Dan to come back to Charlottesville as the James Monroe Professor of Law, he left.[11]

REVELEY IV: You got an early taste of the *Sturm und Drang* of the academy, or at least a foreshadow of it.

REVELEY III: I did indeed. But the law school at Alabama gave me a grant for the summer of 1969 that allowed me to do most of the work on my law review article about the war powers of the president and Congress.

TR3's article, "Presidential War-Making: Constitutional Prerogative or Usurpation?," appeared in 1969 in the *Virginia Law Review*.[12] It argued that the constitutional language concerning the war powers was intrinsically unclear and the Supreme Court was unlikely to resolve the ambiguity.

REVELEY III: The court just doesn't like to get involved in anything it views as basically the two elected branches butting into one another like male bull mooses in heat. Because (a) the court doesn't think it's appropriate and (b) it's afraid it'll get trampled.

With the Constitution unclear and the Supreme Court disinclined to provide clarity, TR3 endeavored to offer a politically realistic proposal to foster cooperation and consultation between Congress and the president. In 1972–1973, while on leave from Hunton & Williams for a fellowship year, which he divided between the Council on Foreign Relations in New York and the Woodrow Wilson International Center for Scholars in Washington, he began the lengthy process of completing his research and turning it into a book. This took a lot longer than expected, especially since he had little time to work on it after returning to practice law in the late summer of 1973. In 1981 *The War Powers of the President and Congress: Who Holds the Arrows and the Olive Branch?* was published by the University Press of Virginia.

The book established TR3 as an authority on the subject who fell between what he described as the then prevailing "schools of thought of really theological intensity: the presidential school and the congressional school." His work led to testimony before the House Foreign Affairs Committee and Senate Foreign Relations Committee, as well as a number of articles, lectures, conferences, and other occasions to engage the war powers.[13] As discussed in chapter 3, in 2007 the book also helped lay the groundwork for the National War Powers Commission, which he helped lead, along with TR4, among others.

Supreme Court Clerk

In 1968, before starting at Alabama law school, TR3 applied for a Supreme Court clerkship with Justice William J. Brennan, one of the leading figures on the liberal Warren Court. At that time each associate justice could annually hire two clerks. They were recent law school graduates who served for a year and helped the justice deal with the complex legal matters that came before the court. TR3 was twenty-six, about the age of his fellow clerks, many of whom had already clerked for a lower court federal judge.[14]

REVELEY III: A Supreme Court clerkship was and is, if you're a lawyer, a distinction worth having and an experience worth having. But they're extremely hard to get. Many are called but few are chosen. I thought I would be a credible candidate but it would take some divine providence to get the nod. But why not try? As for why Brennan, I heard that he actually might be amenable to hiring a clerk from somewhere other than Harvard or Yale, his customary sources.

Each justice had his own selection process, and Brennan's was to let one of his former clerks do the screening. All you could do was work hard on a letter to the justice, do the best you could with your résumé, and send them in. One day in the fall term at Alabama I went down to the faculty mailroom, and there was a small envelope from Justice Brennan's chambers at the court. And I thought, "Great. Envelope's too small. A flush-o-gram." But I opened it and it was a very nice letter from Brennan inviting me to be his clerk for the court's 1969 term.

The Supreme Court heard cases starting on the first Monday in October, following a pattern of two weeks in the courtroom, then two weeks working on opinions. On Fridays the justices would gather to discuss and vote on the cases heard that week. After their conference, Brennan would return to his chambers and meet with TR3 and his fellow clerk, Richard Cooper, a Rhodes Scholar who had served as editor-in-chief of the *Harvard Law Review*.

REVELEY III: He would talk to us about what the conference had done, the decisions that had been made, and in particular about any opinions he was to write, whether for the majority or in dissent, and what needed to be stressed and what needed to be avoided, and how to, in his judgment, hang on to the majority, which was not always easy. He would tell us a lot. He would say, "Here's the vote, here's who was on each side, here's who's picky about this or that." He would tell us where the potential problems were and whose support we had to hold in particular. He would then leave it to Richard and me to decide who would be responsible for working on the opinion, usually based on which of us had time to take on something new. He then set us loose to write a first draft, leaving much, at least initially, to our discretion.

On Monday, October 13, the court heard arguments in *Goldberg v. Kelly*, a welfare rights case grounded in the Fourteenth Amendment's due process clause. In the judges' conference that Friday, Brennan and four other justices voted that before a welfare recipient's benefits could be cut off, their due process rights included a full administrative hearing at which they could present evidence on their own behalf. But the votes of Justices Byron White and John Marshall Harlan II were tentative, subject to change if Brennan's majority opinion went further than the two were willing to go by, for example, stacking the procedural deck too much in the recipient's favor.

REVELEY III: Brennan comes back from conference and says, "We got it. We got five votes. It's going to be hard to hold them. You've got to explain in the opinion why the Fourteenth Amendment applies here, why this is due process, so we've got to work at it, guys." So we did, starting with me.

When we'd take a draft to Brennan, the justice would then tell us what he wanted added, cut, strengthened, restated—whatever. We would rewrite as necessary and keep bringing the draft back until it passed muster. We'd write, he'd edit, we'd edit, and so on.

The justice would then send the draft opinion around to all the other justices, and the negotiating would begin. "I don't agree with this or that," or "If you want to hold my vote you need to say this or not say that." The justice handled all this, letting us know when changes were essential, and we'd do our best to make them in a way satisfactory to all. Hanging on to Harlan's vote was hard. He in particular, and White, were concerned about certain things. And while Brennan preferred the language in his draft, he would make whatever changes were necessary to hang on to Harlan and White. He made clear that he was more interested in holding the result than in his prose or in doctrinal purity. And if that detracted from the elegance of the written draft? Well, life isn't perfect but you get the result if you can.

Brennan preserved his five-vote majority, and *Goldberg v. Kelly* was announced on March 23, 1970. TR3 worked on multiple other cases before his clerkship ended in the summer of 1970, but none that was more challenging or important. In a term that TR3 described as "pretty barren ground for significant constitutional law," *Goldberg* "revolutionized administrative law," according to Justice Stephen Breyer. It was, in Brennan's own assessment, "probably the most important thing that came out of these chambers" during his thirty-four years on the court, a remarkable statement considering that the 461 majority opinions he wrote included landmark cases such as *Baker v. Carr, New York Times v. Sullivan,* and *Texas v. Johnson.*[15]

REVELEY III, IN A FAMILY LETTER: Clerking for Brennan is all that could be desired. The atmosphere is very relaxed and, of course, very stimulating. The justice is clearly one of the world's nicest men—very friendly, accessible, interested in his clerks ... and very willing to have us become involved in the substantive aspects of decision writing.[16]

Clerking for Brennan gave TR3 a sense that the importance of particular words and phrases in Supreme Court opinions can often be overestimated by the legal community.

REVELEY III: Your job was to do what the justice wants to do. But the more you are set free to actually draft the opinion, especially its rationale, the more you are, in reality, expressing your own views. And that's to some extent problematic, when you get this group of hotdog young lawyers writing rationales that legions of judges, lawyers, and law professors then parse closely as if revealed from on high.

Overall, clerking was a great use of twelve months. In professional terms, being a clerk gave you prestige and credibility you wouldn't otherwise have had—a plaque hanging around your neck which, if you were a lawyer, was a big deal. Plus, you got exposed to a whole lot, and you had to do a lot of quick, rigorous thinking and very sophisticated writing. That's great training for just about anything.

Personally, it gave you a measure of confidence and breadth of experience you otherwise wouldn't have had. You had to climb mountains of work. You couldn't begin and then say, "This is too hard. I quit." You had to motor on.

REVELEY IV: And, at an early age, it put you in the presence of people at the apex of American life. You got to see their capabilities and their foibles, realize that they're—

REVELEY III: That they're human. One other thing: the relentlessness of the pattern of the court's work. Hearing cases for two weeks, then two weeks writing constantly—and you can't talk to anybody about the court's work. You have to turn yourself into a vestal virgin for everyone outside the court. This led me to conclude that I didn't want to be a judge. Much more freedom and much less relentless routine in being a practicing lawyer, a dean, a college president.

Although the Vietnam War was still raging during TR3's year as a clerk, no war powers cases were heard by the court. On his own, he spent some time across the street from the court with Senator William Spong of Virginia, a friend and classmate of TR2 at Hampden-Sydney and, at TR2's initiative, a board member at the college. Although he was defeated for reelection to the Senate in 1972, Spong was "a driving force behind what later become the War Powers Resolution of 1973, and a friend. I thought the resolution was fatally flawed in certain respects and told Spong that, but we remained close."

Knowing that his clerkship was only for a year, TR3 had to consider what to do next.

REVELEY III: When I got through with my clerkship, there were two things I thought about doing. One was, the University of Virginia invited me to come join the faculty at the law school. And the other was to go to Hunton & Williams, which was the only law firm I was interested in. I had spent six weeks there during the summer after my second year of law school and really liked it. [Future Supreme Court justice] Lewis Powell, who at the time was one of the prime divinities at the firm, urged me to come when my year with Brennan ended. This meant a lot to me. And George Freeman, for whom I wanted to work if I came to Hunton & Williams, made a trip to the court to recruit me.

I decided that even if I eventually was going to teach law students, most of whom were going into practice, I at least ought to know what lawyers actually do. No one in the family had been a lawyer for a hundred years, and I really didn't have a clue.

No half-million-dollar signing bonus, which later became customary for Supreme Court clerks hired by big firms, accompanied Hunton & Williams's offer, "just one year of gestation credit on the partner track." TR3 and the former Helen Martin Bond married in 1971, with children following in 1974 (TR4), 1978 (Everett), 1983 (Nelson), and 1989 (Helen Lanier). Helen's parents were Everett and Lurline Bond, a prominent couple in Lynchburg, Virginia. In fact, the four parents got to know each other before TR3 and Helen did. Everett Bond was a longtime officer and then president of ChapStick. His brother-in-law was the noted architect Stanhope Johnson. Lurline Bond's Cherokee grandfather, Almon Martin, was born during or soon after the Trail of Tears, the forced removal of Native American tribes from their lands east of the Mississippi River. He became a significant figure in Oklahoma. The wedding of TR3 and Helen was covered in five different newspapers, including the *New York Times*.

Practicing Law: The Shoreham Nuclear Power Plant

REVELEY III: I joined the firm in 1970 thinking I'd be doing antitrust law, which really interested me.[17] I wrote one long memo on an antitrust matter, and that was the end of my antitrust career. In 1972 I took that sabbatical year (unheard of at the firm, but I somehow got away with it) to work on the war powers book at the Wilson Center and the Council on Foreign Relations. When I got back in October 1973 the firm was still pretty small—sixty-nine or seventy lawyers—and desperately needed help with a large client, the Long Island Lighting Company (LILCO), which was trying to get two nuclear power plants built on eastern Long Island in New York State. I had worked for this client before my book-researching year.

Because I was just back and totally unencumbered with other business, and because I enjoyed and respected the people at LILCO, this was an appealing prospect. I liked the challenge of the nuclear power wars on Long Island. And I liked the fact that when I was up there, the firm could charge national rates for my services, not Richmond rates, which were about half as much. So I hurled myself into it body and soul. When I'd first gotten involved with LILCO, my friends at the firm thought it was hilarious that I was dealing with a nuclear power plant, since they knew I knew nothing about nuclear power. Or engineering. Or physics. I took three weeks of physics in the twelfth grade and then quit—that was it.

LILCO had two plants in various stages of development. Shoreham had received its construction permit from the federal government's Atomic Energy Commission, which later after restructuring became the

Nuclear Regulatory Commission (NRC). Construction was underway, and so "there was a legal interlude" until such time as Shoreham was ready to seek an operating license. A second, even larger plant was planned for a different part of the island, Jamesport.[18]

Reveley III: When I got to Long Island, Jamesport was ramping up to get started in the licensing process. It was going to be both a federal process under the Atomic Energy Act and the NRC's regulations, and a state proceeding under the New York State Siting Law, which was rapacious in its demands. I needed help, so even though I was a relatively junior associate at the firm, I began to get associates of my own, which was a man-bites-dog situation. But we got the construction permit for Jamesport, and we finally won a New York State siting permit.

Unfortunately, by then it was clear that the need for power on Long Island—which had been perceived to be enormous—wasn't enormous. So LILCO dropped Jamesport. It just decided, largely for financial and political reasons, not to pursue it any longer. Then all the attention went to getting an operating license for Shoreham.

The NRC has a process for involving the public in the licensing of nuclear power plants. In the past, the usual way these things would proceed was, okay, somebody wants to complain. They come and say what they want to say, and then the decision-making body thanks them and rolls on. As opposed to really organized, dogged, well-funded opposition that comes to litigate. Which is exactly what happened with Shoreham to a degree not approached anywhere else in the country: elaborate, interminable adjudicatory hearings where the parties presented massive amounts of evidence, cross-examined witnesses, filed pleadings and briefs. From a public confidence standpoint, events like Three Mile Island in 1979 and Chernobyl in 1986 were apocalyptic. They gave the opposition new life.

LILCO didn't anticipate any of these challenges when it got started on its nuclear odyssey. So it needed a huge amount of help from our firm. From 1973 on, I was the lawyer leading the band. As the moment of truth for Shoreham's operating license drew near, nine years into the mission, I had thirty lawyers from four different Hunton & Williams offices working on Shoreham relentlessly. LILCO was the firm's leading client for three or four years in the late 1980s. I became a partner in 1976 and was chosen as managing partner in 1982.

We won every legal battle. Shoreham eventually got its operating license from the NRC. Then [Governor Mario] Cuomo killed it. He said, okay, LILCO, you can operate the plant because the feds have said so and they have jurisdiction. But if you do that, I will see to it that the state's Public Service Commission gives you no rate relief—no utility bill increases—for the five billion you've sunk into building the plant. LILCO couldn't financially sustain that. So the deal the company struck with Cuomo was, we won't operate the plant and in return you give us rate relief. This was very sad, bitterly disappointing for me, and extremely bad public policy.

That was the end of my work for LILCO, which lasted until 1992. It made me a seasoned lawyer, battle-tested and experienced at organizing and leading large, complex efforts. I was willing to work brutally hard. I cared desperately about the client and the result. Even though it involved science and engineering, I learned the law and the regulations. I spent a lot of time talking to the media and developed good relations with the reporters who were covering us.

I didn't have any trouble making decisions. And I was a frisky child—pretty shy but very self-confident, very ambitious—and didn't mind herding everybody together and moving the army forward without regard to seniority. On the other hand, I was often quite concerned about other peoples' feelings. I enjoyed being with people, and I think people enjoyed being with me. The one thing that really distinguished me was I was willing to step out and lead, and I wanted to lead.

Practicing Law: Managing Partner

During TR3's decade as managing partner, starting in 1982, Hunton & Williams grew from fewer than two hundred lawyers to nearly five hundred and opened new offices in, among other places, New York, Atlanta, Belgium, and, for pro bono purposes, the Church Hill neighborhood in Richmond. He modernized the firm's administrative and support structures and led an effort to crystallize its core values. None of these moves came without debate, often controversy.

REVELEY III, REMARKS TO THE FIRM, SEPTEMBER 18, 1988: It is impossible to be right about everything all of the time. This cruel fact bores quickly into any decision maker. Paralysis can ensue. If we try to be right in all of our initial decisions, we will take too few risks. More important than initial omniscience is the willingness to acknowledge error and correct our mistakes. We must act, not dither, and then alter course as necessary. A quote on the desk of the seventeenth president of Princeton, now head of the Mellon Foundation [Bill Bowen], is perfect: "If you board the wrong plane and arrive in Moscow when you were on your way to Marrakesh, the magnitude of your error will give it style."

REVELEY III: Lawyers are a risk-averse species, and the challenge is trying to persuade them it's okay to take a leap forward even though it comes with some risk because if things don't go as planned, you can always make a midcourse correction.

The partnership as a whole was not wildly committed to the notion of becoming a national and international law firm. They liked it the way it was. But there were a number of younger lawyers who wanted to drive the firm forward. We wanted it to be more than local, more than regional.

The other big firm in Richmond, McGuireWoods, had brought in John Dalton after his term as governor of Virginia ended in 1982, and that had really worked out well for them. So when Chuck Robb ended his term as governor in 1986, we recruited him, knowing that he would probably run for the Senate, which he did two years later. He brought in a whole flotilla of staff. Everybody enjoyed him, and he enjoyed the firm. And when Jerry Baliles came along next in 1990, we were eager to recruit him. He was harder to land, but along with his flotilla he came and stayed a long time, sixteen years. He was good for raising the firm's horizons, our sense of the importance of having high ambitions and just going for it. He also generated some business and was a very productive member of the firm.

When Justice Powell retired from the court in 1987, he came right back to Richmond. He didn't rejoin the firm, but he was always interested in what was going on there, and he freely expressed his views. As managing partner, I was the prime recipient of these views and saw him often. He stressed the importance of integrity, the importance of unity and harmony within the firm, the importance of service in the community— the centrality of the legal profession's pro bono obligations. And always his concern was that the firm be great and on the move to even greater prominence.

Just as important as these folks, we brought in John Charles Thomas as an associate, the firm's first Black lawyer. John Charles and I have known each other for close to half a century. I saw him as a young Black lawyer gallantly swimming upstream in a white sea. It was critically important to me and others that he succeed in climbing the same intensely demanding and competitive ladder to partnership that other associates had to climb. He did, working under Tim Ellis, one of the firm's stars and, later, an acclaimed federal judge. In 1982 John Charles became partner, making him the first Black lawyer to rise through the ranks to partner in any historically white major firm in the South. A year later Governor Robb put him on the state supreme court at age thirty-two. For health reasons he had to step down in 1989, and we brought him back into the firm. He always has been a magisterial force, doing great good.[19]

As the firm grew, it needed to develop a lot of excellent nonlawyer expertise. The challenges were persuading the partners to pay for it, and dealing with the caste aspects of life, because if you really want to bring in excellent people as chief administrator, chief financial officer, chief HR person, chief technology person, and people skilled at things like communications and advertising, they can't be treated as lesser forms of life by the lawyers. Sure, they don't have JDs. Sure, they don't log billable hours. But they're vital to keeping the firm going and crucial to freeing the lawyers to practice law. So give them full faith and credit.

I also felt like we had to institutionalize the firm's commitment to public service lest it be done by only a small subset of our lawyers, amid the crush of billable work. That meant creating a pro bono committee for each office and one for the firm as a whole. It meant having a partner who was willing and able to oversee the whole effort, devoting himself to pro bono work. That was George Hettrick.

Creating the Church Hill office was a catalyst, a means of putting some real body and flavor and substance into our pro bono commitment. We opened this neighborhood office, and there was a good bit of concern at the firm on two scores. One, what if it's a flop? And two, would we alienate the local Black bar—the Black lawyers in Church Hill—by looking like we were trying to steal their business, which we emphatically weren't, or looking like the great white fathers who were coming from their fancy offices downtown to do missionary work among the downtrodden? But because we took these concerns seriously, things went well in Church Hill from the beginning.

As managing partner, I placed a lot of emphasis on the firm's sense of community and its understanding of where it had come from, its past, and its traditional core values of personal integrity, legal quality, and public service, an emphasis made manifest in helping support and push forth Anne Freeman's excellent book about Hunton & Williams, *The Style of a Law Firm*.[20] But also, especially, on its core value of superior service to paying clients. If you're managing partner, an iron law of survival and success is to ensure the firm's profitability. Feed the partners. Especially if you're trying to do new and ambitious things like opening a New York office or an office abroad. The firm was a marvel of talent and esprit de corps. Randy Totten, my law school classmate, and Dean Pope, whom I'd known since junior high in Memphis, were particular sources of cohesive leadership for the firm in this regard, as well as superb lawyers.

What counts the most in big law firms are clients and revenue. Nothing else gets as much love. If the firm's lawyers can't generate business and hold it and provide service the clients are willing to pay for, the model doesn't work. There's no endowment to help pay the bills, no alumni making annual gifts to alma mater. Although Lewis Powell's appointment to the Supreme Court in 1971 took him from the firm, his legacy was strong. As a lawyer, he rarely missed the business development potential in a lunch. He habitually found a client or potential client to break bread with. He had a preternatural ability to amass clients and retain them. And he would urge younger members of the firm to form relationships with their peers in the client's corporate structure so they could grow together as lawyer and client.

Partners who are highly productive can be very prickly. But they usually understand the importance of the firm's health to their own capacity to be productive. And they also understand that if they aren't at least minimally willing to be good citizens of the firm, there will be adverse consequences for them.

As for deciding on new partners, those issues were, in my experience, the most intractable, painful, difficult issues we dealt with. You could not afford, as a firm, the kind of drain on the body politic that tenure sometimes imposes on universities. Once some people get tenure, they go to sleep at the switch—they stop being nearly as productive as they were. That can't be allowed to happen in a law firm.

REVELEY IV: In the tenure process at many schools, perhaps most, there is almost a sense that if each box is checked, then by right, tenure follows. Whereas in the partnership process at big law firms, there's emphatically not a sense that if each box is checked, you become a partner by right. This creates rampant anxiety among the associates.

REVELEY III: One way I tried to deal with the intrinsic stress and anxiety in a high-powered operation and the differences of opinion, was an open-access policy. Whenever I was in the office, anyone who wanted to see me could, quickly. I also responded to email, quickly. This took time I could have saved if I'd used a gatekeeper. But it was more effective for me to operate that way than if I was hermetically sealed. People needed to be heard and I needed to hear them. Most people who came to see me had a pretty good reason for coming. You can help them, even if it's just by listening and making clear that you understand what they're saying.

But that's not the norm, I think, for leaders. I think most leaders, the longer they're in office, the more isolated they become. The guards at the gate will say, he's very busy. If you really want to see him, here's a slot four weeks from now, and it will probably be fifteen minutes.

Practicing Law: Legal Education

After stepping down in 1991 as LILCO's principal outside counsel and as Hunton & Williams's managing partner, TR3 remained with the firm, initially as head of its energy and public utilities team, but with considerably more discretionary time. As described below, he had already joined and led multiple nonprofit boards at the local, state, and national level. And he had begun working to enhance the relationship among the Commonwealth of Virginia's judges, law schools, and practicing lawyers as a leader of several statewide conclaves that brought together the three legal communities to talk about lifelong legal education. Out of these conclaves came the Virginia State Bar Section on the Education of Lawyers. TR3 was a founding member and the section's first chair.

REVELEY III: The deans of the law schools were hesitant about the conclaves because they thought it might be a means by which the bar would seek to impose certain curricular ideas on the academic community, which was jealously guarding its freedom. And the bench is always diffident about mixing too much with the bar. The three groups weren't really talking much across species lines.

I was eager to get them all to stop circling each other like antagonistic dogs and start communing to see if we could put something together that would make legal learning a lifetime experience and law schools more attentive to what practicing lawyers and judges believe law students need to learn. So we had these conclaves and were able to get them meaningfully talking with each other.

I was always interested in the academy. I'd been on the St. Christopher's School board in Richmond, the Princeton board, the Union Seminary board, and the Mellon Foundation board—and Daddy had been president of Hampden-Sydney. I had produced a serious scholarly book. I liked the academy and knew a lot about it.

I'd also taught a little since joining the firm. After Bill Spong went to William & Mary in 1976 to become dean of the law school, he recruited me to teach an energy law seminar. I in turn recruited my great friend, college roommate, and comrade in arms in the Shoreham wars, Don Irwin, to teach it with me. The class met once a week for a couple of hours. We did it for two or three years. Don would drive, really fast, to Williamsburg while I took a last look at the materials for that day's class. Pedagogically speaking, we did not distinguish ourselves. But, as mortals who were actually doing what many of the students someday hoped to do, we were very interesting. We had a lot of gripping war stories.

Board Leadership

During his long tenure at Hunton & Williams (and for many years after, at William & Mary and in retirement), TR3 served as member and often chair of several significant nonprofit boards. Geographically, these ran the gamut from neighborhood to city to state to nation. Substantively, they encompassed the arts, culture, education, and more.[21]

TR3's first board, which he joined in 1975 and chaired in 1979–1980, was the Fan District Association Board in Richmond.

Neighborhood

Reveley III: The Fan District is an area shaped like an oriental fan because of the way the streets run. It includes Monument Avenue, where Helen and I moved when we came back to Richmond after my sabbatical year working on the war powers. At the time, almost half the nineteen houses on the block where we lived were in commercial use. It was in really bad shape when we moved in and our parents were—

HELEN REVELEY: Horrified.

REVELEY III: Not enthusiastic. One of the association's early objectives was to get the zoning on Monument and throughout much of the Fan changed back to its original purpose of single-family homes. This was complicated by Virginia Commonwealth University's desire to keep expanding west along Monument Avenue and south into a really lovely and historic working-class area. Our view was that VCU's expansion was critically important to Richmond's welfare but that the university should expand north. VCU finally came to adopt this view.

Being a lawyer was really helpful because I was not intimidated by the legal and regulatory aspects of getting things done, which often seem forbidding to nonlawyers. As a practicing lawyer you learn how to identify the key issues in any complicated matter and sort them out. You understand how important factual evidence is in advancing a particular position, and you learn to deal with conflict. You get experience bringing people together to reach a settlement, an agreement on how to go forward. And because you're a lawyer, you're perceived to be more dangerous than the average bear.

HELEN REVELEY: Seeing the Fan turn around was a really great feeling, and it's one of the largest intact turn-of-the century neighborhoods in the country today.

CITY AND COMMONWEALTH

REVELEY III: Around 1980 the Richmond Symphony came to Hunton & Williams and said, "Have you got a young partner who might be good for our board?" And so the firm asked me and I said I would. I stayed on that board for twelve years and chaired it from 1988 to 1990.

I assumed that things were going well, particularly in the life and work of the orchestra's full-time executive director. I was unaware that he was in the midst of a really difficult divorce and was materially distracted and distressed by that. I learned never to assume that all is well just because all was well in the past. You need to keep a close eye on how people are doing, particularly your chief lieutenants.

It was and remains a tough time for symphony orchestras. It was clear from the beginning that crucial to any success was getting the players and the management and board together in a cooperative, not an adversarial frame of mind. But even then there were the underlying realities of an aging audience, expensive ticket prices, players who needed to be paid a living wage, and great symphonic music that was available to people without their having to hear it in person.

That was my first "big board" experience. What I mean by that is the size of the institution, the complexity of the institution, the visibility of the institution, and its significance beyond a small area. It was also where my run of leading the three principal cultural organizations in the city began: the symphony, the Virginia Historical Society, and the Virginia Museum of Fine Arts (VMFA). I served on and at some point chaired all their boards into the 2000s.

The VMFA board was a different kind of experience from the other institutions because the orchestra and historical society are privately owned but the museum is public. State-owned entities are very different from private entities in the way they handle money, the way they get money, the way their boards are chosen, the rules and regs by which they do almost everything. By statute the governor appoints the VMFA board from a slate of names that the museum board gives him. Now—real world—you go in with your slate and the governor or his minions come back and say, "You can have X, but I want Y, who's not on your list." So you get X if he gets Y.

You have much less freedom on that kind of board, and in return you get biscuits from the state, biscuits to operate and biscuits to renovate, build, and maintain. When the state is not providing big biscuits but is imposing its political and regulatory constraints, life becomes fraught. I learned a lot about how the state government works, how complicated and frustrating state regulation can be, and how you need to work the system, including walking the halls of the Virginia General Assembly to talk and talk and talk with people who can help you or hurt you. Of course, public universities like William & Mary and Longwood operate in roughly the same circumstances.

The Sons of the Confederacy always chafed at the fact that all the land and buildings where Confederate veterans and their widows were cared for in their declining years had been reassigned to the art museum. We had it but we didn't completely control the Confederate Memorial Chapel, located on the museum grounds. So the Confederate battle flag often flew there. Life with the Sons of the Confederacy was complicated and at times fraught, but the tide kept running out for the Lost Cause.

Higher Education

REVELEY III: Union Presbyterian Seminary (its name starting in 2009) started on the campus of Hampden-Sydney. The home where my parents lived when Daddy was president, Middlecourt, was built by the seminary. And when the seminary moved from Farmville to Richmond, Hampden-Sydney's feelings were deeply wounded, although it made sense for the seminary to make that move. One of my great-uncles, William Alexander Reveley, was the first member of our family to go to the seminary, and then Daddy did and my sons TR4 and Nelson did. I care deeply about the place.

The selection of a new president shortly after I came on the seminary board in 1992 was a long and at times contentious process, though the person selected, Louis Weeks, ultimately had a successful presidency. But at the outset the going was rough. I was heavily involved in Louis's selection, and was also heavily involved, along with the chair of the board, in helping him navigate the culture wars afflicting Union at the time, which were tied in with some genuine theological differences among the faculty. Some conservative professors felt the seminary was no longer adequately faithful to the Reformed tradition and no longer as academically rigorous as it had been. Culture wars can seriously damage an institution.

I think I was able to do some good there, partly because by the time I joined Union's board I had been on Princeton's board for six of the fourteen years I ultimately served on it. I'd already gotten a close look at the inner workings of an academic institution. Bill Bowen was president through most of my first two years on the Princeton board, followed by his very smooth handoff to Harold Shapiro, who was president of the University of Michigan before he came to Princeton. The university was in very good hands with both of them.

Most of the running of Princeton was left to the president, senior administrators, and the faculty, and the board properly kept its snout out of that. But whenever there was an issue with significant financial, political, or media implications, the board would get involved—and there was no shortage of those. There were some trustees who had very distinguished public careers—James Baker, for example, and Donald Rumsfeld, both of them alums. There were some who had huge financial resources. And there were some like me, neither rich nor famous. What made the board work so collegially and effectively was that nobody waved around their position in life or their money to try to give added weight to their views.

Calls for university boards to divest from investments in companies that did business in South Africa were widespread during the 1980s, as they later would be regarding investments linked to Israel in 2024.[22]

REVELEY III: Early in my Princeton board service, while Bill was still president, he called me late one night, as was his wont, and said, "I want you to chair the Finance Committee's subcommittee dealing with divestiture. And the first things you need to do is codify the principles under which the board has been making decisions about whether to sell our investments in companies that have operations in South Africa," with its awful system of apartheid.[23] Princeton was under considerable pressure on campus to sell everything—to just get out of South Africa. Bowen and most people on the board felt it was better for a company to stay in South Africa if it was doing some good on behalf of the Black population.[24] My subcommittee's first job was to write down the principles guiding the board's decisions about whether to divest or not.

Trying to figure out whether a corporation was doing some good in the midst of apartheid was not easy. The subcommittee had to do it corporation by corporation. And when we came up with one we thought Princeton ought to drop, which was rare, we'd bring it to the full board for a vote. The first time I did that, the subcommittee's recommendation was voted down. This was disconcerting, to put it mildly.[25]

Still, shortly after getting on the board, I had been handed a major task, a delicate task, to do something difficult and important. So by the end of my initial four years, when my time as what Princeton called a "term trustee" ended, I was a proven commodity. And when, after a year's hiatus, I came back on the board as a charter trustee with a ten-year term, Harold—now the president—asked if I'd chair the Student Life, Health and Athletics Committee. This proved to be an extraordinary opportunity to learn and lead and work with other trustees and administrators of compelling ability and commitment. We dealt with a host of issues of real importance

I chaired Student Life, Health and Athletics for seven years, far longer than was typical for a committee chair. It was a great experience. The committee met with lots of people over the seven years, including countless students, for all sorts of reasons. And I found that if you talk to students—or faculty members, coaches, administrators, staff—and actually listen to them carefully, in a friendly, approachable way, you build confidence and legitimacy and amass some political capital you can draw on when you've got difficult issues to resolve. You also have a much better shot at actually understanding what the issues are, what the crucial facts are, what the opportunities to make a difference for the better are.

Take the so-called Nude Olympics, Princeton's variation on the streaking phenomenon of the seventies but a variation that Princeton undergrads, whose sense of college life went back four years at most, tended to think John Witherspoon had blessed when he became president in 1768. The deal was that on the night of the first real snowfall, hundreds of members of the sophomore class would run naked around Holder Courtyard behind a torch bearer. The torch, along with the nudity, was the only connection with the ancient Olympics.

If the kids hadn't been drinking, and some of them howlingly soused, and if a few hundred townies, some from as far as twenty or thirty miles away, hadn't crowded in to see the naked boys and girls running around—but that's how it was. And then one year ten kids were hospitalized with alcohol poisoning, and of course the media were all over it, which elevated it from simply a student affairs issue to a board issue.

So we banned the Nude Olympics and took some heat as killjoys, but I think that, because we had spent so much time listening to students over the years, we had enough credibility that they honored the ban. It helped that, when some students objected that it'd be unfair if only a few of the many streakers got caught by campus cops, the response was that just like with speeding tickets, not all malefactors get caught. The response to the other prime objection—how could male cops lay hands on naked females?—was that they'd use blankets, pursuant to a chaste protocol.

We dealt with a lot of other issues, but let me mention a couple that were much tougher than the rest, starting with race.

The main focus of the racial conversations when I was chair of the committee was, "We know there are racial tensions on campus. How do we begin to more effectively address them?" In particular, how do we get Black kids and white kids to talk to each other about their respective interests and concerns, aggravations and frustrations, happiness and unhappiness? If a Black kid is suffering microaggressions, how to get the white kid to hear why they understandably bother the Black kid so much.

The white kid whose initial reaction is, "Come on, what's the big deal?," needs to hear and grasp the explanation. And the Black kid needs to know that sometimes, maybe often, no malice or ill will from the white kid is involved. I don't think we significantly advanced that effort.

Then there was the issue that caused all hell to break loose, as could have been predicted: Wrestling! This ultimately resulted in an intensive review of all aspects of athletics at Princeton.

The brouhaha started when university administrators, including the president, decided to throw wrestling over the side as a varsity sport. Issues involving the Athletic Department's budget were involved, as well as the fact that wrestling didn't draw many spectators, took up scarce space in the gym, and needed a good bit of medical attention because wrestlers, in combat, are all over each other. What the administration didn't adequately take into account was the long and storied history of wrestling at Princeton and the absolute burning passion of our wrestlers for their sport. Or that Princeton's wrestlers included Don Rumsfeld, who was a trustee at the time.[26]

The board was blindsided by all this. The athletic director had met at length with our committee literally a month before the university announced wrestling would be dropped. He said nothing to us about wrestling being in peril. The president, who was usually extremely sensitive to the need to keep the board in the loop about matters likely to cause controversy, said nothing.

Enraged wrestlers from on campus and off, especially enraged alumni, started coming at the trustees and saying, "Why did you do this? What's going on? You gotta fix this." The media began feeding. You never want board members to first hear about something difficult from alumni, much less the media.

The board was confronted with a major mess it hadn't created and knew nothing about. For my committee, this meant a year of hearings—ten at least, mainly on campus but also in New York. We heard from hundreds of people—faculty, staff, students, alumni, Don Rumsfeld. What we came up with regarding wrestling was to preserve it but as a club sport rather than a varsity sport. That lasted for a while. Wrestling later came back in full NCAA Division I splendor.

With wrestling as the catalyst, our committee embarked on a yearlong study of athletics at Princeton. We learned a whole lot, in particular that there was a growing gap between the coaches and the faculty and, more important, between the recruited athletes and the rest of the student body. Athletes had to be in the weight room, at practice, in meetings, in intercollegiate competition, especially away games—and then do their academic work. Unlike Daddy, who in the thirties had time to be a genuine student-athlete and a genuine student leader at Hampden-Sydney, they didn't have time to do much of anything else, and they were really becoming a caste apart on campus. An extensive written report resulted from the study. I kept the full board informed about our progress along the way. It turned out to be a much larger, more complicated set of interlocking issues than we'd expected. We ended up strongly affirming the importance of athletics at Princeton while urging the new dean of students and the new athletic director to work closely together to help bridge some of the gaps. And they did.

Another campus issue the committee tackled in serious detail was drinking, especially at Princeton's clubs. There was a serious shortage of social activities for kids who didn't want to drink. It was clear that if the university itself tried to provide such activities, they would be DOA. It was also clear that to get such activities going would require funds the students didn't have. We ultimately launched an initiative to have the university provide meaningful funds to groups that then organized and produced dry social events themselves. The idea was good in concept but never really took root. The lasting impact of this initiative was to make blindingly clear on campus that binge drinking is inescapably dangerous, that many students don't want to drink, and that the campus must be a comfortable place for them too.

Back to Bill Bowen. When he left Princeton in 1988 after sixteen years as president, it was to become president of the Andrew W. Mellon Foundation. Mellon was one of the only foundations in the world focused on the liberal arts in leading universities and colleges, and it had vast sums of money for grants.

Bill brought me in as a board member in 1994. The board was small and full of eminences—the president of the University of Chicago, the president of Cornell, the head of the Frick Museum, Bill himself, and so on. I was recruited for my relative youth and as a lawyer to succeed the Sullivan & Cromwell partner who had been the lawyer on the board for many years. Bill trusted my judgment, knew I worked hard, and expected that I would contribute meaningfully to the life of the foundation. Eventually I went from being the child on the board to chairing it, serving until I reached the mandatory retirement age of seventy-two. Along the way I enjoyed marvelous colleagues, learned a huge amount, and, I believe, did a lot of good.

Among Bill's major accomplishments at Mellon was JSTOR. I was there at the creation of the concept, when Bill came back from a board meeting at Denison University, his undergraduate alma mater, where building a library expansion was being contemplated. It occurred to him that building library expansions had become a never-ending process. More and more journals were going to keep appearing, with more and more bound issues needing shelf space. There had to be a better way of dealing with them than just building more and more cubic feet to house them on campus after campus. It was obvious to him that technology needed to provide a solution, and, with some further reflection, that journals needed to be digitized, at least the leading journals in each field, and made available via the internet.

JSTOR started out with precious few people outside Mellon having any idea what it was, and yet it soon became a research tool almost universally known and valued—look it up on JSTOR, go find it on JSTOR. But even though the idea now seems ridiculously obvious, it was enormously hard and complicated to get it off the ground. How on earth could you persuade journals to go this route, persuade libraries to go this route?

The solution was first to identify the most influential and trusted journals in a limited number of crucial fields and recruit them. That worked. And then to have librarians in a limited number of the most influential universities leaned on by their provosts to cooperate, and provosts leaned on by their presidents after Bill leaned on the presidents. It took Bill's prestige and silver tongue plus the Mellon Foundation's willingness to keep pumping in millions of dollars during JSTOR's early years to do the deed. It also took great resilience, dogged persistence, and some real smarts to master the technical and logistical complexities.

Reflections on Board Leadership

Reveley III: In terms of what being on these boards (and many more) has taught me, the first and probably most important lesson is that nothing out of the ordinary, nothing of real significance gets done without leadership. Without leaders, it's very hard for people to do anything but keep repeating what they're used to doing.

When the board chair and the president or director of an organization work together, grounded in a lot of communication and mutual respect, you've got a really powerful engine. The chair needs to encourage and help the president to spend enough time with the board, and explain enough to the board, and be patient enough with the board to get it to engage and understand his priorities and support what he thinks needs to be accomplished, as modified and improved by the board's good counsel. The board chair also really needs to be dealing with the board and saying, "This is what the president is trying to do and needs our help in the following fashion."

One of my strong feelings about boards is that if all members do is show up for meetings, they aren't going to feel like their being on the board makes any difference or is meaningful to them. You need to give them opportunities to serve. You say, here are some areas where you might be especially interested and effective. Which one appeals to you? Boards become meaningful for people when they feel like they're doing something that matters for the institution.

Why did I serve on and lead so many boards? I'm the son of one seminary graduate and the father of two others, and although going into the ministry was never my inclination, my faith has strengthened my view that institutions exist to serve in a way that improves individual lives and improves society overall. So you try to push and pull institutions in that direction.

God expects a lot of human beings, or so I believe. And what God expects is good for human beings individually and collectively. Doing good, particularly when you do it well, is good for the soul. If your only goal while being a lawyer or CEO is to amass an amazing amount of money, you can do that. But it becomes a pretty sterile way to live and doesn't provide much meaning for your life.

Plus, there is a great deal of comfort to be taken from the Christian proposition that while God does expect a lot, it's not up to human beings to save the world or vindicate goodness and justice. You do your bit along the way, but God takes care of things in the final analysis. And if you foul it up, that doesn't mean the enterprise fails, because ultimately you're not the principal driving force.

William & Mary Law School

In August 1997 TR3, still at Hunton & Williams and working on non-nuclear matters, received a phone call from Bill Spong, who after leaving the Senate was an extremely effective dean of William & Mary's

Marshall-Wythe School of Law from 1976 to 1985.[27] After Spong retired, the law school was led for seven years by Timothy Sullivan, who became president of William & Mary in 1992. Since then the school had experienced several years of instability, including three interim deanships and a failed permanent deanship.[28]

REVELEY III: Bill Spong called and said, "Believe it or not, the law school is looking for a dean again." He wanted to know whether I'd be interested—no promises, but would I think about it? They really needed a dean who would stay a while and be able to do the job. And that's why he and Tim Sullivan were interested in me even though if things had been going well at the school, I would have been totally unacceptable to some of the faculty, coming from a big law firm instead of from the academy.

The plot ripened slowly over the next nine months. A whole new life began. I'd enjoyed being managing partner, and what I'd learned from that and from my time with LILCO was that I preferred running the show to playing in the band.

I called Bill back a couple days later and said, "Yes, I will think about it in complete good faith, but the odds of my leaving Hunton & Williams are very small." Bill put me in touch with a wonderful professor at the law school named Dave Douglas, who was heading the search committee.[29] And Dave said words to the effect of, we've got these papers you need to sign saying you revere various pieties in order to become a candidate. I said, "I'm not a candidate. I've got a great job. I'm not looking for a job." Sometime later we agreed the law school would go forward with its normal search process, looking at candidates who signed the papers, and if it landed a dean it wanted, that'd be good for the school and I wouldn't have to think about it any more.

Apparently that didn't work out for them, and so the following April Dave came back to me and said, "Okay. No papers to sign. How about coming and seeing us?" I drove to Williamsburg and had a wonderful day of conversations with different professors. The normal next act, though I didn't then understand the nature of the ritual, was to come back for what I later learned was supposed to be my "job talk."

I showed up for lunch with the faculty. The professors were sitting around a very large table, with their sandwiches and drinks. So I sat down with a sandwich and drink. As Dave had asked, I said a few words about my war powers book. Nothing much more than, "Here's the book. I'll pass it around." And I start eating my lunch and then I start asking them questions. I'm trying to decide if coming to this school was something I should seriously consider doing.

Well, I got very little response even when I asked why a prospective law student should choose to attend William & Mary rather than, say, Washington & Lee. Not a good conversation. Of course, they're thinking, this jerk has come here. He's eating his lunch (not customary). He hasn't given a job talk. And now he's asking *us* questions? I had no idea how many sacred cows I was goring. And the fact that I came from a family of teachers and had been on Princeton's board, the Mellon Foundation board, and Union Seminary's board, learning a whole lot about higher education along the way, and had actually taught law at the University of Alabama, admittedly briefly—none of that cut any ice against the fact that I did not spring directly from the womb of the academy. Instead I had sprung from the womb of a big law firm where I'd been the managing partner for a long time. Would I have all sorts of rules and regs if I was dean about billable hours and productivity and so on? Would I understand and appreciate the rhythms and nuances of the academy? That's what had them worried.

So I drove back to Richmond thinking, this isn't going anywhere.

That night I got a phone call from Tim Sullivan, who wanted me to be dean because he believed I could move the school forward. Tim said, "Don't give up on it yet." I doubt he would have pushed me to come and pushed the school to take me if he hadn't gone through the three interim deanships and one failed permanent deanship. When all was said and done, as president, the deanship was his to offer.

I called Bill Bowen. He thought my going back to school even at age fifty-five would be quite meaningful and I'd be an effective dean. But, he said, "Don't do it if you can't afford it." I ran a bunch of numbers on a yellow pad and decided it would be tight but affordable. Wrong! I grossly underestimated what it would cost to keep the family home in Richmond, acquire a pad in Williamsburg, keep paying tuition for three of our four children who were still in school, and on and on. In the early W&M years, we had to sell some stock and borrow money, a whole lot of it.

Bill also said, "If you do take the job, protect your agenda for what most needs to be accomplished for the school's good. People are going to be coming to you every day wanting you do to this, that, or the other. The agenda of what you believe most needs doing can easily get hijacked. One day you'll realize it's been replaced by everyone else's agendas."

What nobody told me and what I failed to discover myself before coming to William & Mary was that the law school had barely one nostril above the financial waves. The larder was bare—a mouse had made off with the last bit of bread. Fortunately, I'd been told it was SOP to negotiate with the provost for the few modest gifts she could and would give the law school if I came in as dean. I knew enough to get that written down. When I showed up, students seemed thrilled I was there. I was a live lawyer fresh from practice, which is what they wanted to be, practicing lawyers.

The faculty, most of them, were pleased when they saw me take steps to improve their lives, starting by increasing the number and size of their summer research grants, then increasing the number of chaired professorships, and, over time, delivering meaningful salary increases.

I understood about summer research grants because the one I'd had at the University of Alabama was crucial to my work on the war powers article I wrote. I'd watched Daddy deal with chairs at Hampden-Sydney. The desire for them is intense, so thick you could cut it with a knife. What a faculty member wanted was to be able to tell their colleagues, "I am the Goldilocks and Three Bears Professor of Law." I did not say, "Sorry, we don't have any more chairs to award until we find people who will give us big bucks to endow them." Instead I broke bad and took some modest, unrestricted endowments we did have and used them to create chairs. And I worked hard to get salaries up, though that was a much more difficult effort.

TR3 sought to win over the faculty not just with financial support and enhanced status but also by showing them how the law school culture was not entirely different from the law firm culture from which he came. He pointed out that both as managing partner and dean, his job was to understand the organization he was leading ("its people, programs, finances, facilities, and decision-making processes"), identify its "unrealized potential," and find ways to fulfill this potential. Dealing with tenure in the academy and partnership in a big law firm posed similar challenges and opportunities, he argued, and "teaching, research, and writing" were intrinsic to both settings. As for students, "like clients, they want to get what they pay for."

Outside his firm work, TR3 further pointed out, his experience raising funds for various nonprofits was directly relevant to his responsibility as a fundraiser for the law school. In particular, leading the intrinsically public-private VMFA gave him a feel for the situation he faced at William & Mary, which received public funds but could not depend on them for anything approaching what was needed. Still, he noted, "firms' willingness to contemplate institutional change, think like entrepreneurs, act quickly when circumstances so dictate, and avoid unproductive entanglement in 'process' are virtues less fully developed in schools."[30]

REVELEY III: I quickly learned that if I as dean did things that made good sense for the law school, it did not matter much, if at all, that I had not consulted with the university's central powers before doing them.

I made a big thing out of the fact that William & Mary was the first American university with a law school, that Thomas Jefferson created the first professorship of "law and police (policy)" in 1779, that George Wythe was the first professor to hold that chair, and that Wythe taught John Marshall. There's a general presumption about old institutions that age reflects quality because it suggests staying power, the capacity to survive adversity and thrive by seizing opportunity. The law school needed to lay claim to that presumption.

Our Jefferson-Wythe-Marshall connection led directly to the idea of the "citizen lawyer," a concept I celebrated.[31] It was the inaugural idea of the law school, which Jefferson and Wythe in particular pushed very hard. They wanted to train lawyers to serve the larger good, especially in politics. In our day being a citizen lawyer focuses less on public office and more on pro bono work for people and institutions, but it's more than that. Within your workplace, do you mentor those coming along behind you? Do you see to it that there is an ethic of integrity and service? Are you willing to contemplate changing jobs every now and then, maybe go from being a fat cat partner in a corner office to being a judge, at dramatic cost to your compensation? Are you willing to become the general counsel of an arts organization or of a municipality? The emphasis falls on making a difference for the better in your workplace and your community.

At the same time I was stressing the ethos of the law school's founding generation, I became convinced that continuing to call ourselves the Marshall-Wythe School of Law was holding back our efforts to recruit across the country. Once you got out of Virginia, it was hard to market Marshall-Wythe. Which Marshall are you talking about? John?

Thurgood? A benefactor named Marshall? And Wythe, which is invariably pronounced Wy-eth outside Virginia? People had no concept of who he was and why he mattered. None, zero.

The most distinguished law schools, with few exceptions, call themselves by their universities' names: Harvard Law School, Yale Law School, Stanford Law School. We needed to be William & Mary Law School so we could recruit more easily outside the commonwealth and so our students and alumni, when they were asked where they went to law school, could say something that would resonate. Kind of like my mother, who was thrilled when her alma mater, Farmville State Teachers College, changed its name to Longwood College and then Longwood University. Longwood rolls sweetly off the tongue. Farmville State Teachers College didn't.

So I changed the name we used for external purposes. Didn't ask anyone's permission. Just did it. Within the law school family, especially with older alums, Marshall-Wythe is still used at times, though with decreasing frequency. And the school's official name remains the Marshall-Wythe School of Law of the College of William and Mary in Virginia. But otherwise it's now known simply as William & Mary Law School.

Almost immediately, I began pushing for us to grow the student body, especially out-of-state students, since tuition was our main source of desperately needed revenue. Simultaneously, I pushed for us to drive up the academic credentials of the entering class, their median LSAT scores and undergraduate GPAs. Law school applications were booming everywhere during the ten years I was dean, and with the new name and more active recruiting we were able to seize the opportunity. Faculty liked teaching students with stronger academic credentials, and the increased tuition revenue enabled us to recruit new professors more effectively. They had compelling credentials. There are all sorts of splendidly educated and accomplished young people who want to get a job teaching law, and the demand for spots on law school faculties far exceeds the supply. We did well building the faculty.

Progress in hiring women and minorities became a priority, with strong emphasis from me. And even though the most comfortable thing in days past was to bring in qualified, collegial white males, the most difficult professors I dealt with at the law school were older white men who felt like the world had moved beyond them and they were not receiving the due they expected as senior members of the faculty. They became bitter.

Post-tenure review was not working well. It needed to work to ensure that everyone on the faculty was contributing to the best of their ability because we needed all the help we could get. It was also important to the integrity of tenure. We got the process in gear. Most of the faculty was pleased and reassured, though not eager to participate in reviewing their colleagues.

Even if what you're doing as a tenured professor isn't adequately delivering the goods either as a teacher or a scholar, you still can't be forced to retire under federal law. What I could do was say, "If you're really not interested in doing research and writing any longer, you've got to teach more. And you've got to do a really good job of it. And if you don't want to do that, we must find something else for you to do to help move the school forward. In any event, there will be a written performance plan to which you will faithfully adhere."

Coming from years practicing law, when I got to William & Mary I was unusually willing to challenge people who said, "Can't do that at W&M," or "This is how it must be done." If that didn't make sense to me, I would say, "Why?" They would say, "State law or regs, or university policy, or because that's the way we've always done it." Well, I would say, "Show me the text if it's a law or reg or policy." And often it turned out the law, reg or policy wasn't dispositive if in fact it existed at all. So we motored on.

Growing the student body and improving its academic quality, which we did, and adding great young faculty, which we did, and making annual giving by alumni a priority, which I knew from Princeton was the key to so many good things—all of this mattered. So did bringing the school's technology up to speed, renovating and adding to our physical plant. The *US News* law school rankings are an abomination, but getting us up to the low 30s and high 20s carried a lot of weight in all sorts of places. It certainly helped us attract stronger students and faculty. Alumni liked seeing the prestige of their degree appreciate as the reputation of the school grew.

Our accrediting agency told us that the school's faculty and administrative offices were too small and, though our library staff and collections were strong, the library's square footage didn't cut the mustard. All true, given our growth in enrollment and faculty, the breadth of the curriculum, and the range of student activities. Raising the funds necessary to remedy these ills and designing and constructing the new facilities took tremendous effort by a small staff. Deans have to be able to raise money.

In 2006, eight years into his deanship, TR3 was able to announce that construction had begun on the Wolf Law Library, named in honor of Henry (Hank) Wolf's mother. Wolf was a law school alumnus and the vice chairman and chief financial officer of the Norfolk Southern Corporation. He later became rector of William & Mary (the chair of its board of visitors), for two years during TR3's presidency.

Becoming President

TR3 had been dean of the law school for seven years when Timothy Sullivan, the college's president, announced that he would retire in June 2005. Starting in 1971, William & Mary had been in the vanguard of colleges and universities that turned to lawyers for presidential leadership rather than traditional candidates, whose career path ran from professor to dean to provost. Not just Sullivan (president since 1992) but also his immediate predecessor, Paul Verkuil (president from 1985 to 1992) were lawyers. So were both of the leading candidates in 2005, TR3 and Gene Nichol, who at the time was dean of the University of North Carolina School of Law.

REVELEY III: I began to seek the position for two reasons. One, I was urged to do it by a lot of people, including Tim Sullivan as he began to look to retirement. And I felt that if Tim wasn't going to be president, I might as well do it because my general view has been, if I'm going to be involved in something, it's more fun to be the leader. Not always, but often. I also felt like I had punched all the necessary tickets, had all the necessary experience, and knew what needed to happen at William & Mary to make it likely that I would have a really successful presidency. So I threw my hat in the ring.

It was a big search committee that had faculty, administrators, students, alumni, and, of course, members of the board of visitors.

REVELEY IV: Modern-day presidential searches are very much like political elections. They require some campaigning, and I think it's fair to say that in 2005 there wasn't a Reveley campaign in a full-throated way.

One way these searches are like elections is that the electorate, in this case the widely different constituencies of the campus, doesn't necessarily understand the byzantine ins and outs of what the job really does entail.

And so they're looking for almost political high notes to be struck—as opposed to evidence of experience and a rich and demonstrated sense that the person can actually do what needs to be done.

REVELEY III: I had gone into the initial presidential contest with bovine arrogance, assuming of course they will pick me. Look at what I've got to offer, I'm perfect. But when I went through the list of all my higher education credentials, instead of helping it probably hurt me. The reaction of some was, "We're not Princeton, we're not the Mellon Foundation." And I didn't take Gene's candidacy very seriously until the very end, and by then it was pretty clear that he was the more likely choice than I.

Certainly I didn't do as lovely a job as I should have. I learned that when you are asked for your vision for the school's future, people do not wish to hear a realistic appraisal. If you are dumb enough to point out that amid the college's celestial magnificence there are things that we've really got to work on, they don't want to hear that. And they do want you to be funny and gregarious and charming and have a good life story. Well, I didn't have a good life story, meaning I hadn't gone through any particularly difficult turmoil and trial and I wasn't the first person in my family to go to school and I didn't go as a football player and encounter a philosophy professor and discover that the academic world was wonderful. I'd just trundled along as a good boy through school and, worse, went to Princeton, which—they really did not want to hear anything about Princeton.

On one occasion I talked about athletics, even though Tim had told me, "Whatever else you do, do not talk about athletics. And if you have to say something, simply say what a marvelous program William & Mary has and how eager you are to support it as president." Instead, during one session with alumni, somebody said, "Weren't you chair of the Student Life, Health and Athletics Committee at Princeton for seven years?" To which I simply said, "Yes." And I don't know what I did or said after that, but it led to the belief that I would try to abolish scholarships for athletes. And then the athletics axis, which is very strong at William & Mary, became implacably opposed to my candidacy and did a pretty good job of killing it.

EMAIL TO REVELEY III FROM A SUPPORTER OF HIS CANDIDACY, MARCH 10, 2015: I had a call from a big basketball supporter. He was on the alumni interview team and . . . made it clear to me that the athletic supporters are bound and determined to block your appointment.

Reveley III: I wish I'd been given a real chance to speak to the athletics issue because I could have laid it to rest. It became a huge issue, to the point that, as one person later told me, "they would have taken a trained ape rather than you as president—anybody, *anybody* but Taylor Reveley."

Then there was the "hobby" question. I got enough satisfaction from the work I was doing that I didn't feel the need to be building a sailboat in the back yard or playing golf or anything like that. During my presidential candidacy that was a real problem. What was I going to say when asked, basically, "What do you do for fun?" Meaning, are you a dour workaholic with no sense of humor? I didn't have much I could trot out.

As judged by the notes he prepared for his meetings with various stakeholders in the selection process, TR3 had already identified some of the major themes that, with his later selection in 2008, would animate his presidency. In a February 21, 2005, presentation, for example, he highlighted his intention to preserve William & Mary's status as "a small research university with a magnificent arts and sciences program for undergraduates as its crown jewel," as well as to advance its "potential for even greater beauty, when more resources can be committed to the grounds" and to seek "more national and international recognition of William & Mary's historic primacy in American higher education and the role its graduates have played in our national success." He celebrated the college's "Jeffersonian commitment to leadership in the public interest" while highlighting its need for additional "financial support—growth in taxpayer support, growth in tuition, growth in endowment via . . . major gifts to support capital projects; quick powerful growth in annual giving to immediately fuel the operating budget" and provide "generous financial aid for students—fully adequate need-based aid and meaningful merit-based aid."

Reveley III: I told them what I'd do. And also gave them a really long exegesis on all the experience I'd had at Hunton & Williams, at Princeton, and at the Mellon Foundation. Those weren't the sort of things the search committee wanted to hear.

Now when you're a candidate for a job in the maw of the search-industrial complex, great efforts are made to see to it that you don't physically encounter any of the other candidates. But on the day of my initial interview with the search committee, I was at the appointed place and, as is often my lot, went into the men's room to pee, and there stood Gene Nichol, big friendly guy, played football at Oklahoma State. He and I had been friends before, both of us deans of law schools. We looked at each other and we both knew exactly why we were there. So we laughed and laughed and went back into the conference room and had a really good time together. And I thought, "Poor Gene, this is not going to work out for you because I'm going to get this." I was mistaken. And Gene did, in my judgment, a really superb job of being a candidate.

The rector, Susan Magill, when she very graciously, very kindly came to give me the bad news, basically said, "You're too used to running in exalted circles for William & Mary. You're too much." And I thought, "But haven't I been here at the law school for quite a while now?" Helen and I both felt a real sense of rejection. We had offered our bodies and felt like we were really prepared and then crashed on a pretty profound set of misrepresentations about my views on athletics and misunderstandings about my being too "elite university"—too Princeton.

On the very day of the decision, it was useful that I had my two-and-a-half-hour class at the law school, although I was not wildly enthusiastic about teaching that afternoon. But it was better than sitting in the dean's office and replaying the whole saga.

So, back in the law school, nostril out of university matters, supportive of Gene when he needed my help, but focused totally on the law school.

REVELEY IV: In the aftermath, my dad and my mom showed tremendous grace, which was very true to their natures and also undeserved by many of the people that they were gracious toward. There was a very elegant event for VIPs the weekend after the decision. No one in the William & Mary community expected that they would show up. And of course they came, with magnanimity and grace.

REVELEY III: No whining and complaining. And that actually stood me in remarkably good stead when the wheels came off Gene's regime.

Nichol's presidency lasted less than three years, the shortest tenure in William & Mary's history since the late 1840s. Some of the reasons for his truncated term were grounded in decisions that provoked either statewide controversy, such as allowing a Sex Workers Art Show to take place on campus, or national controversy, notably his unilateral decision to remove an eighteen-inch brass cross from permanent display in the college's historic Wren Chapel. Other reasons were more fundamental: his decision to inaugurate the ambitious "Gateway to William & Mary" need-based scholarship program without the necessary funding and his failure to adequately communicate with the board of visitors and the state General Assembly. In February 2008 Nichol was told that his three-year contract would not be renewed when it expired on June 30.[32]

REVELEY III: With me on one occasion he said, "I feel like the wheels are coming off my presidency," which in fact they were. He was in media trouble, he was in political trouble, he was in trouble with the General Assembly and with much of the alumni body. On campus, he was genuinely loved by students and faculty. And he was, in many respects, a very endearing figure who also made all sorts of wonderful promises to the faculty which he was utterly incapable of keeping. Most important, he was in trouble with the board because he did not consult or communicate with them adequately, and he did things that they then had to bail him out on. For example, removing the cross from the altar in the Wren Chapel without letting the board know about it. All he needed to do was appoint a committee, which would have met for six months and thought and thought and talked and talked and then come up with the exact same sort of result, and it would have been a much smaller deal than it was.

In late 2007, TR3 learned that the board was thinking of making a change when Nichol's contract expired at the end of June 2008. In response to previous board pressure, Nichol had already relinquished some of his ongoing administrative duties.

REVELEY III: I had one telling portent. In November or December of 2007 the rector, Michael Powell, and the vice rector, Hank Wolf, asked me to come meet with them. What they wanted to know was, "If we tell Nichol we're not going to renew his contract and we need an interim president, will you do it?" They wanted to be sure before they had that conversation with Gene that they had an interim president in hand. And what I said was, "If you bounce him right now in the wake of the cross controversy and everything else that's going on, there will be hell to pay on campus and hell to pay in the academic press. This is not a good idea. You should not do it." And they then began to explain at pretty significant length why it was going to happen, that he was beyond salvation, and that all they wanted to know from me was, "Will you, on an interim basis, take over?"

I talked to Helen and went back to them and said yes, but the assumption was that this would happen when his contract ended in June, after the campus had a chance to give him a rousing good-bye.

Instead, at 9:30 a.m. on February 12 I got a call from Michael Powell saying, "Nichol has just quit, immediately, and he's about to put out a statement over the internet. Get on your horse, ride over to the main campus, and do something as interim president."

GENE NICHOL, STATEMENT, FEBRUARY 12, 2008: Mine, to be sure, has not been a perfect presidency. I have sometimes moved too swiftly, and perhaps paid insufficient attention to the processes and practices of a strong and complex university.... [But] a committed, relentless, frequently untruthful and vicious campaign—on the internet and in the press—has been waged against me, my wife, and my daughters. It has been joined, occasionally, by members of the Virginia House of Delegates.[33]

MICHAEL POWELL, STATEMENT, FEBRUARY 12, 2008: President Nichol achieved some outstanding things during his tenure. His energy and passion is legendary. He is a truly inspirational figure who has enjoyed the affection of many. After an exhaustive review, however, the board believed there were a number of problems that were keeping the College from reaching its full potential and concluded that those issues could not be effectively remedied without a change of leadership.[34]

HELEN REVELEY: The first round in 2005 had been pretty grim, but then the next time it came up, we both thought it would be a good thing to do. Taylor knew the college was in chaos and needed help, and he's always liked to make things work.

REVELEY IV: A presidency, especially at a place like William & Mary, so ancient and august and accustomed to the big things it can do—a presidency, on the one hand, is a CEO endeavor of knowing what functional thing needs to happen at what functional moment. But in a deeper way it's also an exercise in having the grace and gravitas to, almost by one's presence, be a force for harmony and good. And that's something that my dad and my mom, just by dint of all the things they had known and seen and done over the years, could step into that maelstrom in February of 2008 and have people of different walks understand that they knew how to actually fill the role.

Reveley III: After I got the call, I thought, "What in the name of heaven am I going to do this morning when I get to the main campus?"—which in fact was going bananas. That night, for example, there was a huge candlelight gathering in the Wren Yard with about two thousand undergraduates rallying for Nichol and denouncing the board.

So I go over to the main campus and—I don't know where or how—I run into Chon Glover, who was the university's chief diversity official. Chon says, "Come to my office because every day at lunchtime a group of Black students gets together with me for lunch to talk about things."

I go in and the large group of Black students—they're very angry, they're very worried, scared about what this means, because they had seen Gene as their champion, and he was their champion. So we talked for a long time, and finally one of them said, "We are extremely angry and distressed. But we'll help you." And at that point, I thought, "Well, maybe this is not mission impossible."

And one thing I did early on with students and faculty was say, "Contrary to what is being alleged, we'll keep our emphasis on aid to kids who need financial help, we will continue to be interested in diversity, and we will certainly not be taken over by politicians in Richmond telling us what to do." In other words, no change on these fronts that Gene was emphasizing. The students missed Gene, but they didn't take it out on me. The faculty, particularly the humanities faculty, were a much harder sell. I had to work hard establishing for them that I could be their president too. Then, with alumni, get on the phone with as many of them as we could to reassure them that William & Mary was alive and well. And with the politicians in Richmond, I was an easy sell because it had gotten so bad with Gene. So, easy to reach the alumni and state officials.

I'd say for probably the first three months, I was living and breathing the job utterly, and would go home from the president's office in the Brafferton at night and climb in bed and say to myself, "What are you doing?

The law school was running smoothly. Things were great. Now here you are, trying to deal with this mess."

HELEN REVELEY: It was a lot of reassuring people that we could actually make it work. And then entertaining at the house and attending events—that first year you felt like you had to show up for everything. It was pretty traumatic, especially for him.

REVELEY III: But it got better, quickly. And early on, the rector said, "Just let us make you the actual president." I didn't want to do that because it might have made me illegitimate with the faculty, given the uproar I was trying to calm. The board needed to say they had consulted every dog and cat, and the dogs and cats needed to know they had been consulted. And that took a while. So I held off on being made legitimate until early in September. And because I was the twenty-seventh president in the college's history, the Wren bell rang twenty-seven times, as is its wont for new presidents, and we had a nice modest ceremony.

I declined to be inaugurated formally, because we had just done it lavishly for Nichol. And the other excitement going on in September 2008 was, it looked like the U.S. economy was collapsing. There really wasn't going to be any money—for anything. I thought spending money on an inauguration was just out of the question.

3
Taylor Reveley IV and Longwood University

TR4 was thirty-eight when he became president of Longwood University, more than a quarter century younger than his father when he became president of William & Mary. Unlike TR2, his paternal grandfather, who grew up in North Carolina, and TR3, who was born in Virginia but raised in Memphis, TR4 is a native Virginian who, aside from four years at Princeton University, has never lived outside the commonwealth. More than that, he has always maintained a townhouse in Richmond, even while working in Charlottesville or Farmville.

Growing up in his parents' home on Monument Avenue as the first of four children helped shape TR4 in important ways. So did the other elements of his formative years: school at Richmond's St. Christopher's, college at Princeton, and participation in varsity football at both. The next stage of his life began when he went to Union Presbyterian Seminary (known during the period he was there as Union-Presbyterian School of Christian Education), where he earned a Master of Divinity degree en route to the University of Virginia School of Law. In the summer of 2001, before starting his final year of law school (and her final year in UVA's MBA program), TR4 married Margaret Louise Smith (Marlo), then and now a successful businesswoman in a variety of technology and corporate enterprises whom he met in 1996 through a close mutual friend, Jeremy Radcliffe. Marlo's parents are prominent Texans and deeply familiar with academics—her mother, Peggy, a longtime faculty member at Baylor College of Medicine and her father, Ashley, a University of Texas vice chancellor for government relations.

Like TR3, TR4 became a lawyer with Hunton & Williams. While at the firm, he formed a close relationship with one of its leading partners, former governor Gerald L. Baliles. He then followed Baliles to UVA's Miller Center. In addition to his regular duties as managing director of the center, TR4 worked intensely on its National War Powers Commission, which was cochaired by two former secretaries of state, James Baker and Warren Christopher. He remained managing director until his selection as president of Longwood in 2013.

Growing Up

REVELEY IV: In the neighborhood, in Richmond and around the state, at the law firm, and in larger circles more generally, it was self-evident even to a kid growing up that people looked to my mom, my dad, and my grandparents for leadership, for lack of a better word. One thing that rubbed off on me from observing that is you can do really important things while being a fundamentally good person. You don't, contrary to the mystique that holds among some, have to be a jerk to be a leader of consequence.

One of the chief regrets of my life was that my grandad, TR2, had begun to decline by the time I was eleven or twelve in the mid-1980s, right about when I would have really wanted to talk with him about his experience as a professor at Rhodes and president of Hampden-Sydney, two great colleges of the liberal arts—at a time when that term was not particularly familiar to me.

Here's a vignette that illustrates the problem people still have with "liberal arts." When I was in the tenth grade I got a flyer in the mail from, I think it was, Franklin & Marshall, that in big, bold letters proclaimed something like, "The place for the liberal arts." My mom said, "Don't you think you really want to go somewhere that emphasizes the liberal arts?" This is me: grandson of TR2, son of TR3. But I told her, "No, I don't want to go learn to make art, and I don't think I want to do it at a liberal school."

St. Christopher's is the place where I developed an appreciation—a really keen, devoted appreciation—of the liberal arts, and eventually got familiar with them by that name, while also just doing the normal things kids do at school and in the rest of life, including a great experience with Boy Scouts, making the run up through Eagle scout. I had so many wonderful teachers like Ron Smith for English, the poet laureate of Virginia in later years. Perhaps the one I spent the most time with was Lee Perkins,

PhD in Classics from Harvard, Hampden-Sydney undergrad. He taught me Latin and also Greek, and when I won the Latin Composition Prize my senior year, I used the prize money to buy books and learn Hebrew from him that summer. I majored in Classics at Princeton and my senior thesis was about James Madison's direct use of arguments and thoughts from classical authors as he was helping to craft the Constitution. I might even go so far as to say that the reason I later found myself caring about education so much is in great measure because, in a Madisonian sense, I see education as being vital to democracy.

By the mid-1990s, Princeton was deluged with many more exceptionally well-qualified applicants than it had places for in the entering class. Diversifying the student body, already coeducational, along racial and ethnic lines was one goal of the admissions office. So was admitting recruited athletes and "legacies" (children of active alumni).[1] TR3, already on the board of trustees, did nothing to try to tip the scale in his son's favor, knowing that "any such effort almost certainly would backfire." But the combination of excellent academic credentials, athletic prowess, and TR3's efforts on Princeton's behalf almost certainly made TR4's case an easy one.

Reveley IV: I played football at St. Christopher's—honorable mention, All-State my senior year—on great teams, and also during my first two years at Princeton, again on great teams. But after an accumulation of nagging injuries, I only did it those two years. Princeton is a Division I school. With DI sports in particular, you get a sense of how your mind and body are connected, and that all sorts of aphorisms from the ages— sound mind, sound body—are a reality. I think another thing I learned is the idea of mental toughness. The ability to get yourself out of bed before dawn to practice, and then keep yourself up till nearly midnight to stay current with your schoolwork. The ability to work under pressure during a game. These are habits that serve people very well subsequently. Still to this day, when I am thinking about something hard that I have to do, I tell myself it's not harder than waking up before dawn to go play spring football.

The spirit of teamwork is another real thing, and actually understanding how to achieve it is one of the things that explains the riddle that occasionally surfaces later in life: the A student who isn't successful in the wider world. Often it's because they're not particularly gifted at working with other people and understanding how to rely on other people and let other people rely on them. In athletics you have to learn to do those things.

Seminary and Law School

REVELEY IV: I was drawn to Union Seminary by the prospect of spending a few years really thinking about matters of faith, the chance to think through in great depth how life actually works—and with the hope after that to do something consequential.

I really did think of those three years of seminary, followed by three more of law school, as a path to something. I wasn't sure exactly what, but I wanted to find the right combination of the more ethereal with the more practical between seminary and law school. Presbyterianism, in its nineteenth- and twentieth-century form, post–World War II form, is not as fixated on doctrinal matters as it is on practical effects in the world. And for both my grandfather and my father as well as for myself, faith and church have been geared much more toward what is the thing to do, as distinct from what is the thing to think.

As it turned out, those seminary years really fed my understanding and sensibilities. One particular habit I developed from those early days is reading Ecclesiastes often, in part because you can get through it in an hour or less if you happen to have an unexpected pocket of time. The idea that it was written by King Solomon seems perfectly plausible to me because it seems to give voice to the real experience of somebody who knew what it was like to be in a position of consequence and feel the weariness that can come from that.

Seminary also provided a couple of practicalities that are hugely helpful to me. That's where, in a homiletics class, I really learned to give speeches. And learning about pastoral care has been profoundly helpful at so many levels. As part of the curriculum at seminary, you do some fieldwork, and the fieldwork I did was at Westminster Canterbury, a retirement home in Richmond. I had to make the rounds, walk into people's rooms, some of whom were hurting and really needed attention. I can do that sort of thing now as a matter of second nature, but my twenty-three-year-old self had to learn how.

While I was in seminary I taught an introductory Latin class to ninth-grade girls at St. Catherine's, which is St. Christopher's sister school. I learned that teaching is hard work, very hard work.

I also spent a summer as a planning consultant for the city government. Mike Evans was the head of Richmond's social services portfolio, kind of a suite of departments at that time. He was frustrated that it had been a long time since the city conducted a full-scale review of all the various things it did, let alone capture them in writing and get some sense of the relative focus and importance of them all. And so that's what I spent the summer doing, making my way around to all of the many different parts of the city government and, with my coat and tie on, sweetly telling them I had been sent to try and capture in writing what they do. It gave me a real sense of how government actually works, which strongly informed what I'd learn in law school. Little did we know that Longwood would reunite Mike and me, with Mike serving on the board of visitors and eventually as rector. In Presbyterian circles, seminary is often preparation for work not just in parish ministry—my classmate Wynter Benda also went on to law school and has had a long career in municipal government. In my UVA law school application essay, I let them know, somewhat counter-culturally in my generation of aspiring lawyers, that I was more interested in a career devoted to civic life than in blinkered attention to private success.

Practicing Law

During his law school years at the University of Virginia, TR4 interned at Hunton & Williams in Richmond and Fulbright & Jaworski in Houston. His father, the Richmond firm's former managing partner, was already dean of the William & Mary Law School when TR4 began his own legal career, after close studies (like TR3's) with A. E. Dick Howard.

Reveley IV: The natural gestation of law firms back then—it's still somewhat the case—is you would initially work as a summer associate. The summer of 2000 was my first real engagement with Hunton as a budding lawyer, the summer after my first year of law school. That summer and again in the summer of 2001 I worked at Hunton half the time and Fulbright & Jaworski the other half.

Fulbright & Jaworski—the Jaworski is Leon Jaworski, a towering figure in the law and, for that matter, in broader American history because of his role as Watergate special prosecutor—was and is a marvelous firm, and working there full-time after graduation would have been wonderful.

But I was reasonably committed to living and working in Virginia, and in the course of growing up in my parents' home had come to admire the deep civic traditions of Hunton & Williams and the lawyers of my father's generation who embodied those traditions, people like former Virginia Supreme Court justice John Charles Thomas and former governor Jerry Baliles.

I was at Hunton full-fledged, full-time, starting in 2002, joined soon after by my law school roommate, Aaron Simpson (now a partner). I was doing all sorts of things, including lots and lots of client-billable work and civic engagement–type work with Baliles.

The life of a young associate at a big firm can be unrelenting. There were days and weeks when you'd wake up, get dressed, get to the office, and work until 2:00 or 3:00 or 4:00 the next morning. There could be two, three weeks of that pace, logging vast billable hours, and you learned how to do it. A different skill you begin to acquire when you're working billable hours is a keener and keener sense of how long it's going to take to get something done—to read something until you've got it distilled in your mind, to write something. That's a very useful thing.

From the outset, I was unusual because the entire trend at Hunton & Williams was to highly specialize with one team. In part because I had a little tension of the soul, I wound up crafting an arrangement where I was working with a few different teams.

I could really sense, even as early as 2002, the growing focus on billable activity and moneymaking to the exclusion of other things that make lawyering a calling. And drawing on relationships with my dad's generation at the firm, I made efforts to be countercultural and give some real emphasis to public service and pro bono activity, to the point that four of us—Gordon Rainey, the chairman of the firm; Jerry Baliles; the managing partner, Thurston Moore; and I—met together several times formally to give thought in an organized way to invigorating the service ethos. For me, this centered on ordinary pro bono work helping individuals and classic legal work for smaller nonprofit entities whose boards I'd gotten to be on, but also broader engagement in public affairs. And in the meantime, I'd found myself more drawn to working with the "Gov"—Governor Baliles.

The major client matter that the Gov and I worked on was the Harvest Foundation and its effort to create a new public college in the southwestern part of Southside Virginia. (Unlike my dad, who was only about ten years younger than Bill Bowen and called him Bill from early on, I never addressed the governor, who was more than thirty years older than me, as Jerry, even though he wouldn't have minded that a bit.)

The Harvest effort gave me a sense of what it was like to deal with the state government. In a nutshell, Martinsville really wanted a college. And it had the Harvest Foundation, which was the product of the sale of a previously freestanding community hospital to a hospital chain that resulted in the creation of a large foundation—$200 million—in the early 2000s. Hunton represented the Harvest Foundation.

The Gov and I were off to the races. But the state was wary of having another piglet at the trough. "What about the other parts of the state that are doing better from a population standpoint?" It was uphill, but we got close. In 2005 we got the state to create a thing called the New College Institute, which is like an airport through which other institutions offer baccalaureate programs. At the institute you can take courses from Longwood or James Madison or Virginia Tech or George Mason, usually in hybrid fashion, and get your degree from that university.

The politicians could say, "Oh, that works out fine." But from a Martinsville standpoint, it's got none of the compounding virtues of having a campus. There's no choir that sings at Christmastime, no dormitory that draws students to the local coffee shop, etc. It became clear to me then that in the Virginia General Assembly, higher education no longer has the same mandate of heaven it had a generation or two before; it's no longer conceived of as a self-evident good.

I also did a lot with hospitals along with Matt Jenkins, one of the country's great health care lawyers. One facet of my hospital work—the SARS (severe acute respiratory syndrome) outbreak of 2003—prompted a hospital client to ask us, "What happens if this becomes a full-blown pandemic?" As a result, when COVID came along in early 2020, I had a wealth of background that not many other college presidents had—a prebaked, pre-assembled understanding of what authority various levels and entities of government had and didn't have. And through that work I acquired a layperson's background in the science of pandemics as well as how the Centers for Disease Control intersected with various other parts of the federal government and state government, what types of things were likely to unfold, what types of things were not likely to unfold.

Hospitals, like universities, are a set of wheels within wheels, and so learning how that animal ticks from a governance standpoint has been very helpful in understanding how universities tick. Just the different layers of decision-making and what they each have the authority to decide. What responsibilities do boards of directors have? How do officers and members of the board interact with one another? How do bylaws work, and how do you change them? I did a lot of work of that nature, and then lots of work regarding finance and mergers and acquisitions, and really came to understand how to read financial statements, including the notes to financial statements, where the pressure points likely are.

I was in kind of the middle innings of the partner track at Hunton when UVA came to the governor in the late fall of 2005 and said, "The Miller Center, the great hub of research on the U.S. presidency, needs a new maximum leader. Would you consider becoming the director?" He did and told me he thought it would be a good idea if I were to come along with him.

This was a genuine point of decision for me, because I was doing really well at the firm. But the prospect of being there without the governor was not one that held as much appeal. I flipped into my occasional creative mode and figured out a way to do both, to still be at the firm while having a "secondment" that embedded me with the client, in this case the Miller Center, for a year or two, say from 2006 to 2008. I'd be there mostly to work on the National War Powers Commission, which Baliles had launched. But by 2008, the commission was moving to its conclusion, and I needed to either go back to the firm or jump to UVA.

REVELEY III: When Taylor started talking about maybe staying at the Miller Center with Jerry Baliles, I said, "Oh, Jerry is wonderful. Working with him, studying presidential regimes, probably fascinating. But you know, you've been doing really well at Hunton & Williams. What is the post-Baliles career path if you go the Miller Center?" And Taylor was very sweet in listening to me but basically took his own counsel and went to the Miller Center.

REVELEY IV: As my dad also told me, if you successfully stay in a law firm, you get to a point where you have very elegant golden handcuffs and you can't easily escape them. As much as becoming a partner at a major firm is a meaningful credential, it's not easy to get away once that happens.

REVELEY III: Yeah, that's very true.

Miller Center

REVELEY IV: At the Miller Center, I became the managing director. The governor, in somewhat law firm style, was like the chairman, and I was like the managing partner. And in those years, I very much acquired the experience of operating a consequential undertaking and overseeing a number of direct reports.

The Miller Center was like a university president's office in that it had a governing board. Also, I was dealing with fundraising on a scale that, at the time, was larger than Longwood's. Wound up having lots of experience with physical plant things—that was helpful. It's good to know what you need to do—or, better put, have others with the know-how do—when the A/C for your headquarters is not working. Lots and lots of IT experience. And lots of what could be categorized as VIP experience, which a president's office is dealing with all the time. The governor was beatifically happy to outsource our hiring, firing, compensating to me. Being inside the bosom of the university was also eye-opening in that it clarified the extent to which the academy has its own deeply grooved set of British constitution–style norms that you can't know from the outside.

While at the Miller Center I was a freedom fighter against the central regime and always eager to maximize the latitude we had with regard to what central UVA wanted or didn't want. That was edifying when, much later, I worked to develop my understanding of the levers of influence at Longwood. I had a sense of what gets on the nerves of freedom fighters.

Had lots of interactions with the media. I was tremendously lucky to learn at the knee of Jerry Baliles and later James Baker the art of dealing with journalists. The most fundamental thing I learned was that the media play a role as essentially another branch of government with its own responsibilities. Something that's useful when you've dealt with the media a great deal is that your skin becomes thicker, and you know that headlines come and go.

There were other lessons. I did not know before getting to the Miller Center that not everybody is a fan of the university's president. Another eye-opener was that when the Gov had some success in making sure that the Miller Center's scholarship got proper recognition in the national media like the *New York Times* and *Washington Post*, it was met with eye-rolling disdain from a small contingent of faculty who thought these outlets weren't sufficiently academic.

But I developed an appreciation for the purity of their scholarly focus too, and the 2013 external review of the center's academic work, by a committee chaired by Stanford's eminent historian David Kennedy, was especially gratifying.

2013 EXTERNAL REVIEW OF THE MILLER CENTER'S ACADEMIC PROGRAMS, REPORT FROM COMMITTEE CHAIR DAVID KENNEDY OF STANFORD: Over the last several decades, the Center has served an especially valuable function as arguably the principal institution that has nurtured the study of politics within the disciplines of History and Political Science. Though the study of political institutions and behavior long constituted the heart of both disciplines, in recent years that kind of inquiry has been pushed somewhat to the academic margins. Our committee noted only partly in jest that, like the legendary Irish monks who kept the lamps of learning kindled through Europe's "Dark Ages," for a long scholarly generation the Center has conspicuously sustained the subdisciplines of political history within History and the historically informed approach known as American Political Development (APD) within Political Science.

National War Powers Commission

The impetus for the Miller Center's creation of the National War Powers Commission lay at the intersection of TR3's longstanding scholarly work on war powers, TR4's deep interest in the subject, and the widely conceded failure of the War Powers Act of 1973 to achieve its goal of fostering genuine collaboration between Congress and the president in the exercise of the constitutional power to enter, conduct, and end a war.

REVELEY III: When Jerry Baliles was still at Hunton & Williams but leaving for the Miller Center, I went into his office one afternoon just to talk, and he asked if I had any thoughts about a major subject the Miller Center could take up. And we kicked around some ideas, and then I said, "How about the war powers, the way the United States goes about deciding questions of war and peace?"

REVELEY IV: The Miller Center had this tradition of assembling blue ribbon bipartisan commissions. My dad's suggestion resonated with Baliles. I found myself quickly, in the way I'd done by that point countless times with the Gov, beginning to think through the substance and mechanics of what to do.

Long after he left Virginia's governorship in 1973, Linwood Holton was still very active at the Miller Center. And that became relevant in two practical ways. One was that Holton is Tim Kaine's father-in-law and Kaine has become the U.S. senator who is most focused on war powers issues. The other way is that Holton was quite close to Jim Baker. My dad and Baker also knew each other from their time on the Princeton board.

The first act in April 2006 was for Baliles and Holton to get in touch with Baker. He was reflexively interested, and one of the things that Baker and Baliles talked about was bringing in Warren Christopher as cochair. That was a fraught question because Baker and Christopher had been the leaders of the opposing phalanxes in Florida in the aftermath of the 2000 election.

REVELEY III: Recruiting two former secretaries of state from different parties who had done bloodcurdling battle with one another in a crucial presidential contest was a masterstroke. It made it much easier to recruit the rest of the commission, evenly drawn from elephants and donkeys.

REVELEY IV: A different masterstroke was recruiting John Jeffries, the dean of the law school at UVA. He is one of the most prominent experts on questions of standing in federal court. And in addressing the tantalizing idea of getting the Supreme Court to figure out the war powers, John was the one who could definitively say to the commission, "No, that issue is not part of the Supreme Court's constitutionally denominated original jurisdiction and, as a political question, the court is profoundly unlikely to choose to take such a case."

The Miller Center's board, the Governing Council, then blessed the commission idea, and with Baker and Christopher signed up, every single person they recommended said yes immediately. From the start, the commission had an air of gravitas; it felt like an important thing that prominent people wanted to be a part of. It also became a mix not just of Republicans and Democrats but also executive branch and legislative branch officials, with the judiciary present, and the military itself. There was an appetite for true ideological breadth, with Ed Meese perhaps at the conservative end and Abner Mikva at the liberal end.

Reveley III: It was pretty clear from the beginning that the commission wasn't going to come up with: "This is the Constitution's answer to whether the president or Congress owns the war powers." Emphatically not to do that but to try to come up with something that brought the two branches together in a way that worked.

Reveley IV: If there was a loose division of labor, TR3 was Dr. Substance and the Gov, staff director Andy Dubill, and I were Dr. Make It All Happen. And Providence smiled on the endeavor because TR3 had the time to pay attention to this, which he would not have had if his William & Mary presidency had begun earlier than 2008.

At the commission's first meeting in April 2007, I don't think anyone started out with preconceived notions. They just wanted to find something that would work and that would be politically viable since if it wasn't politically viable, it definitionally wouldn't work. One of the most interesting aspects for me was watching Baker and Christopher—these two giants of the public process in the United States—very graciously and with good humor lead this commission to produce a result.

The commission's first three meetings were consumed by the iterative work of letting all the assembled brains get into harmony as to the fact that there was no clear-cut answer in the abstract and instead there needed to be a practical framework that allowed for consultation between Congress and the president. There came a point in about the fourth meeting where TR3 and Baker and Christopher and Meese and Mikva and Brent Scowcroft began figuring out what the best thing to do would be, and talking it through in substantive detail. It was a sight to behold, seeing them sitting around a table, at times with sleeves rolled up, just marking through paragraphs and coming up with the language of the War Powers Consultation Act.

Reveley III: If these seasoned politicians didn't think the proposal had a fighting chance to be sold to other seasoned politicians, then we really weren't getting anywhere, we were just producing another report that would languish.

Reveley IV: The fifth meeting in Houston was where the most important substantive steps were taken. From that meeting on, we were no longer hearing from outside experts by and large. Meetings five, six, and seven were all deliberative.

In political circles there's the staff/principal divide. John Williams from Baker's Houston office, Matt Kline from Christopher's office in Los Angeles, and Andrew and I from the Miller Center were on the staff side of that equation, seated away from the table. TR3 and Jeffries and Baliles, of course, were very much among the principals, alongside the commission members. That was especially true of TR3 because by that point he had been serving on boards with some of them for twenty-five years or more. In February of 2008, of course, William & Mary suddenly changed presidents and he became very, very busy. Had that happened even two months earlier it would have been difficult to come up with as strong a draft of the proposed legislation.

Our last full meeting as a commission was in April at the Miller Center in Charlottesville. That was where the last substantive touches were put on the draft statute.

The War Powers Consultation Act that the commission drafted defined "significant armed conflict" with some precision and required the president to consult with a newly created, well-staffed Joint Congressional Consultation Committee before initiating such a conflict. The committee would consist of both political parties' House and Senate leaders, as well as the chairs of the key standing committees in both chambers. The act also charged Congress to vote up or down on any significant armed conflict within thirty days of its initiation.

REVELEY IV: Christopher and Baker very deliberately chose to roll out the report and its proposed statute in Washington on July 8, a moment of natural lull in the 2008 presidential campaign when the news cycle would intrinsically be slow. And then lie low until the election was over before really mounting the case again. The idea was to give both parties and candidates a maximal chance to develop a real familiarity and comfort with the commission's recommendations and not have it appear to be partisan in any regard.

Virtually all the members of the commission were there. Our shuttle bus from the Hay-Adams staggeringly managed to get lost on its way to the Capitol—it got stuck in an alley and had to back out, which was both vexing and amusing to Baker and Christopher. When we got there, Speaker Nancy Pelosi arranged for a quick briefing for Hill staffers, and then the press conference happened right after. We were the lead story on

NPR's newscast that morning and in other outlets. During an interlude, Baker personally took a copy of the report to the White House and spoke with President [George W.] Bush in the Oval Office.

Blue-ribbon bipartisan commissions like this one once were momentous occurrences in American life that could drive real change. The National War Powers Commission has been one of the last of its kind on any subject—heavy hitters working hard and coming to a common accord on a policy of fundamental importance.

Alas, fast-forward a couple months to the financial crash in September 2008, which knocked the well-laid plans of the commission off stride. Still, [President-Elect Barack] Obama did have Baker and Christopher come to his Chicago transition office and brief him. The House Foreign Affairs Committee and the Senate Foreign Relations Committee had them come testify. They'd talked to [Republican presidential nominee John] McCain too, who was interested. It's just that the political climate created by the crash and then the new president's intense focus on health care reform in 2009 simply removed the possibility during those initial Obama years that something definite might happen.

Even without it becoming law, though, the Obama administration did begin to implement the commission's proposed consultative mechanism as a matter of practice. The Afghanistan surge in December 2009 was undertaken after having gone through the process of bringing the leadership of the House and Senate and the chairs and ranking members of the key committees together to talk with the president about it.

Although the political moment had passed—the financial devastation was too real, and the attention to health care had begun to completely dominate the political conversation—over the long term, Senator Kaine became very focused on the issue, as did Senator McCain while he was still alive. In 2014 they introduced the War Powers Consultation Act, based squarely on the draft legislation the commission wrote. Kaine continues to keep it alive in the Senate.

All that said, the commission will always count as one of the formative experiences of my life. My dad and I developed a knack for being able to work together on really important things in a fashion that strikingly does not seem awkward or off-putting to others. And, of course, it was very special to get to see some of these lions of American national life working on something that they cared about and to see how they did it. The manner in which they worked and the spirit with which they went about it, the care, the deliberateness, the wisdom. The issue of how power is balanced between the executive and other bodies is something that for university presidents is a live, practical matter.

Reveley III: Getting smart people of good will to try to work through seemingly intractable problems with you certainly does help. You see that in a university setting when the president is dealing with the board. You want them to help figure things out so that they're clearly on board when the plane takes off. And second, if you've got a really good staff that is working together effectively, that's crucial if you're a university president.

As for the outcome, the one iron law of reality concerning American use of force and armed conflict—of getting into it, conducting it, getting out of it—is that if the president and Congress don't cooperate with one another, don't learn from one another, things go very badly. So what we did in this commission was produce a way of going about it that speaks to this reality.

"GLB Lessons"

In 2019, six years into his presidency at Longwood, TR4 wrote a letter to Governor Baliles, shortly before he died. He theme was "GLB lessons, . . . which were rarely delivered in so many words, more typically by variations on the Socratic method." Some examples, embedded in TR4's subsequent reflection, follow.

Reveley IV: First lesson: "When in a crowd, mingle. Introversion is fine except for accomplishing much of a public nature." That is not my disposition, and so he would put his hand on my arm and say, "Get out there, just start talking to people." And eventually I got the drill.

Reveley III: It is not something that comes naturally to any of the Taylors, including my father. We do not draw energy from working a room. Rather, it sucks energy from us. We are not Bill Clintons. I'd love to have been.

Reveley IV: Next lesson: "Wherever you go, dress with the expectation that others will expect a certain dignity of you." As I often experience now, you never know who is going to cry out, "President Reveley!" and if you are unshaved and in shorts and sandals, it will be notable to the person who's talking to you.

Next lesson: "Suffering fools is necessary and something of an art." To get things done, you often have to deal with fools, and you just have to meet them where they are and occasionally do some ingratiating thing for them. It means indulging some quirky details and long meetings and, even if you sometimes think it's a bad idea, at least entertaining their pet project.[2]

REVELEY III: If they're important for other reasons; otherwise, you're just nice when you're with them.

REVELEY IV: So, the next lesson: "Absolutely everyone deserves a kind word and the warm courtesy of attention, most especially those behind the scenes or far from the focus." I think maybe I am naturally inclined in that direction, but that's something I unfailingly noticed when Baliles was out and about.

Next lesson: "Details matter." He was very gracious when I screwed up, but obsessive about details, almost to the smallest degree.

Related lesson: "Presenting [your board] an elegant and thorough briefing binder conveys that the details are in good order." Another virtue of this is just doing the work of getting the binder ready, as Bill Bowen has written about. It's the fact that the in-laws are coming and so you clean the house.[3]

Becoming President

REVELEY IV: An interesting aspect of the "family business" is that neither my father, my grandfather, nor I particularly set out in life thinking that it was what we would ultimately do. But by 2012, although things at the Miller Center were going quite well, it was becoming more evident that the governor was eager to begin thinking about retiring, and it became clear to me that I needed to think about what might come next. And he said, that summer, "You're still young"—I was thirty-seven—"but I think what you really ought to squarely consider is a college presidency. So cast your eyes out there and see what spots in Virginia might be possibilities." I think the natural draw I had to intellectual matters is part of what prompted him to think that. He also had begun to take a dimmer view of public life and politics, and encouraged me to think about the kinds of good that could be done in academia.

I began to look around, just as Marlo and I were preparing for the twins to be born, May and Quint. It was a particularly hectic stretch. I was an executive producer for *Doomsdays*, the first feature film by my and Marlo's great friend Eddie Mullins, as well as musing in a formal way with our friend Scott Nystrom as he considered building an investment firm. But the time felt right. Although I was young by college president standards, I had been doing a variety of complicated big things from an administrative standpoint with the Miller Center, and so I felt ready in that regard. And something my dad and I had talked about over the years is that around age thirty-five you're basically old enough to be taken seriously by society at large. You're still young but not prohibitively young.

The governor, in his careful way, sent some search firms in my direction and, quite quickly, the Longwood possibility was on the radar.[4] It seemed like it would be a very natural fit for me for several reasons: the long family connection not just to Longwood but to Farmville, which is the nation's oldest two-college town. Both Longwood, which my grandmother and others attended and loved, and Hampden-Sydney, which my grandfather attended and loved and led, have been together, in exactly the same spot, longer than any other institutions of higher learning in America. Then there's the fact that it was a public university and the governor had contacts on the board, including his former secretary of natural resources, John Daniel, and was able to get a sense of the lay of the land. The governor's and my and both TR2's and TR3's longtime friend Charlie Guthridge was also a key adviser.

Although the Longwood that TR4's grandmother and other family members attended was a women's college, it had long been coeducational by the time he became a candidate for president. In 1972 Congress enacted Title IX, which among other things forbade single-sex education in "any education program or activity" receiving federal financial assistance. The act exempted undergraduate colleges like Hampden-Sydney "that traditionally and continually from its establishment had a policy of admitting only students of one sex." Although Longwood claimed to fall into this category despite having enrolled male students during and after World War II, in 1973 the U.S. Department of Health,

Education, and Welfare ordered it and 150 other single-sex colleges to "eliminate sex discrimination in admissions" no later than 1980. Longwood elected to comply in 1976.[5]

REVELEY IV: Right before the Christmas holiday season of 2012, I got a call saying the search committee very much wanted to speak with me. It was a board of visitors committee that also had nonboard members on it: a student, several faculty members, student affairs and advancement staff, athletics, alumni—probably fourteen or fifteen people in all.

My dad's unsuccessful candidacy at William & Mary in 2005 underscored the extent to which the process of selection is intrinsically political, far more like a political campaign than a dry, merit-based selection. It's small-p political in the sense that it's not partisan, but it does involve a large, varied group of people making a decision that relies on all facets of their human understanding and human nature. Certainly the Gov was reinforcing that view to me. And so throughout the selection process I was thinking about it as persuading sequential groups that hiring me was a good idea from their standpoint: students, faculty, staff, alumni, the Longwood Foundation board, and some actual political figures—and each had their own sets of things they were most focused on.

The issue of being young was one that I needed to overcome, but I think I quickly did. I carried myself with enough of a sense of gravitas, I guess would be the word for it, that the issue began to fade away. The issue that was maybe paramount in a lot of people's minds was, "Would this just be a way station? Was I really interested in doing great things for Longwood, or was I simply interested in being here to hop somewhere else?" But I could genuinely say, I'd like to be at Longwood a long time because I see all the ways it can do great good in an era that really needs it. The rector, Marianne Radcliff, at the time—we did not know each other, but through mutual friends I made sure she knew that this was not a way station, and that I really cared for Longwood intrinsically. And from an early phase she became very eager to see it happen.

In general, I don't think that the political nature of the current-day search process is beneficial. It can reward theatrics, and so it depends on having someone at the center of the process who can see through all that and judge substance. Fortunately, that is a spiritual gift of Marianne's.

My platform, so to speak, had a few elements. I could tell quite quickly that Longwood's basic bones were in good order; that it had a lot more financial wherewithal than it understood itself to have; that the campus needed some tender loving care but was basically strong and lent itself to more development and more beauty; that the basic spirit of everybody who made up Longwood was good—warm and engaging as opposed to defeated and prickly—and that Longwood's position as a public university in Virginia gave it real enduring strength in all sorts of ways, financial and otherwise, and also a very meaningful opportunity to make a difference. Higher education in Virginia, in the relatively decentralized way it's set up, allows for public universities to make long entrepreneurial runs in the way that Virginia Commonwealth University, George Mason University, James Madison University, and, more recently, Christopher Newport University have. So I could see that as a possibility too.

The fact that Farmville was also poised for a bit of a renaissance, I felt I could see, and the prospect of continuing the attention my grandparents [Marie and TR2] and my great-grandfather [Thomas Eason] had given to matters of racial reconciliation and civil rights in Farmville was deeply appealing to me. I saw that as a potentially great strength for the school. I wanted to help find a way to make Farmville's painful but also powerful history a source of inspiration, both for itself and for the broader world, Virginia in particular.

And if there's a thing I maybe disagree with Bill Bowen about, it's the great good that Division I sports can actually do, both for an individual institution and also for the way the sports people really want to watch can serve as a powerful point of connection between a mass democracy and an otherwise elitist endeavor.[6] The fact that Longwood is DI and was eager to make headway with that was very attractive to me as one of the few former DI student athletes who is a college president.

Basically, if you distilled all that, Longwood, with some moxie and attention, could make genuinely great strides, really reviving and strengthening the way—and in this effort hopefully becoming a beacon to others, too—in which the liberal arts do active, positive good for civic life.

I got the offer, formally, on my mom's birthday, March 23, 2013. It was a Saturday morning. I had driven to Farmville that morning with Marlo. It was a live interview session with the whole board, though it was known to me that if I did not do something really egregious, things ought to work out. The session went very well. It was very fun to give my parents a call right afterward.

REVELEY III: A great triumph for both Taylor and Longwood. He handled the process with far greater wisdom than I handled my first run at William

& Mary—having, in my case, simply assumed I would be anointed. Why didn't they just get on with it? By the time I figured it out it was too late.

TR4 was the first lawyer president in Longwood's long history (other than his immediate predecessor, Patrick Finnegan, who for health reasons served only briefly in the office after a legal career in the army), but his recent experience in academic administration fit the mold of the university's twentieth- and twenty-first-century presidents. Nor, because none of his predecessors were Longwood alumni, was that an impediment to his hiring in the way that it often had been at Longwood's brother institution in Prince Edward County, Hampden-Sydney College.

Neither TR2 nor TR3 had the benefit of a transition period between becoming president-elect and president, TR2 because he was detaching himself from the Presbyterian board position he had just accepted (and from the house he and Marie had bought in Richmond) and TR3 because of the suddenness of his elevation. TR4 took advantage of the opportunity his own transition period afforded.

REVELEY IV: My start date as president was June 1, 2013, so about a nine-week transition. I began to rely on Lara Smith, who's the provost now—she chaired what we called a transition committee—just to begin to collect information on the queue of decisions that might be forthcoming. I also met three or four times with Marge Connelly, the interim president who had just been rector, and she was very helpful.

I spent an afternoon in April with my dad at William & Mary. By that point, I had accumulated a set of relatively granular questions, and it really helped to have somebody that I need feel no shame with to talk them through. "Do I really need to send this form to Richmond? What are the prosaic inner workings of FOIA (Freedom of Information Act)? How much paperwork do you think that I ought to be affixing my signature to? Here are some varieties of what the troops keep stuffing in front of my face. Does this seem reasonable?" "No," he said, "that's far more than is necessary."

REVELEY III: "Do I have to have all of these meetings? Does each of my direct reports have to come sit at my feet once a week? And how should I be signing my name to messages to the campus? Should it be 'President W. Taylor Reveley IV, JD'?" A lot of presidents make a mistake on that and sign all of their name with PhD after it. I said, "No, just sign it 'Taylor.' They're going to call you president. You don't have to make a big deal of that. Just sign it 'Taylor.'"

Reveley IV: There were also bigger, more important things, like how to make the advancement operation really sing. Then and after, we talked about that plenty because in all honesty, TR3 had just helped William & Mary finish making powerful strides to get its already quite consequential philanthropic operation into true intergalactic form. And Longwood, by contrast, needed to make the jump from Triple A to Major League, which is a different type of challenge but with many of the same types of things in play.

I set my start date as June instead of the more customary July because of my concern about the planning and design for what would become the Upchurch University Center, which had been a contested matter at Longwood for several years that I'd gotten pretty attuned to. And it was also clear to me that those involved were precariously close to pressing go, in a way that might be very costly to unwind, on an architectural design for the building that would've been jarring to the aesthetic of the campus. So I wanted to be on the ground as quickly as I could so that I could have bearing on that, which I did. As it then developed, it's a really very beautiful building that ultimately opened in the fall of 2018.

A broader reason was that, maybe with U.S. presidents in mind, I had a general sense that the early months were going to be fleeting, and so I wanted as much of the summer to be in gear as I could.

PART II

THE REVELEY PRESIDENCIES

As shown in part I of this book, each of the three Reveleys followed his own distinct path to the presidency of a college or university in Virginia.

TR2 grew up in the 1920s and 1930s, matriculated at Hampden-Sydney College, was ordained as a Presbyterian minister, served as an army chaplain during World War II, and earned a PhD at Duke University in the course of spending seventeen postwar years as a professor, coach, chaplain, and administrator at Rhodes College. The invitation to lead his alma mater came unexpectedly in 1963, in a phone call that both solicited his interest in the position and offered it to him.

Dwight Eisenhower often distinguished between the types of challenges leaders face: those that seem urgent and those that are enduringly important. Often, he emphasized, urgent matters are not very important, and leaders needs to learn not to be distracted by them. Yet sometimes the urgent really is important, and therefore the leader must act.[1] TR2 faced two such challenges when he took office at Hampden-Sydney: righting a ship that, after decades of steady leadership, had thrown off two presidents in the previous eight years, and addressing the racial crisis that kept local public schools closed and divided the college over its own and the community's failure to integrate.

Once stability was restored to the campus and both the college and the local schools were integrated, TR2 was able to focus on matters that were important but less urgent. He inherited a weak—indeed, unstaffed—fundraising operation and worked to build it, despite opposition from those who resented the expense of doing so. By the time he left office the college's endowment had doubled and a number of new buildings had been constructed. The faculty grew by about 50 percent, as did the student body, while remaining all-male at a time when the vast majority of single-sex institutions were becoming coeducational. (This was a matter of some ambivalence for TR2, who had attended all-male Hampden-Sydney but happily taught both men and women at Rhodes.) He also inherited a curriculum that was outdated and, with an ancient language requirement for all students that had become unmoored over time from the rest of their studies, was somewhat incoherent. He brought with him from Rhodes College a new general education curriculum that immersed students not in Greek and Latin as languages but in the full sweep of Western philosophy, literature, religion, and history.

As the 1960s unfolded, TR2 faced the same sort of resistance from Hampden-Sydney students to the prevailing practice of colleges acting in loco parentis on matters of sex, alcohol, religious observance, and general deportment that was being expressed on nearly every campus in the nation. These challenges took him and most other presidents whose own experience as students and, later, as leaders was grounded in the old ways by surprise. TR2's approach was to bend in order not to break—for example, to allow near beer to be sold on campus and to permit dorm visitation across gender lines. None of these decisions came easily to him, but he managed to make them without either surrendering to every student demand or provoking the sort of angry protests that marked many other campuses.

Over the course of the fourteen years TR2 served as president of Hampden-Sydney, the job grew harder. As Warren Bennis wrote in 1971, midway through TR2's tenure, "more and more, college presidents have found themselves caught squarely between the zealously defended claims of a self-protective, professionalist faculty, a restive and extraordinarily idealistic student body, and a gusty old-guard troupe of trustees, alumni, and businessmen."[2]

TR2 retired as president in 1977 and, after a sabbatical spent at Cambridge University, returned to the Hampden-Sydney faculty for several additional years of teaching. He died in 1992 after a lengthy struggle with Parkinson's Disease, predeceasing his wife Marie by fourteen years.

TR3's path ran from childhood in Memphis during the 1940s and 1950s through college at Princeton University, followed by a half-century-long legal career that encompassed three years of law school, a year teaching law, a Supreme Court clerkship, a year studying the Constitution's war powers full-time, twenty-eight years of high-level legal practice, and ten years as dean of the William & Mary Law School. Along the way he led important local, state, and national boards, ranging in subject from neighborhood preservation to the performing and visual arts, at major academic institutions and foundations. In 2005 he waged an unsuccessful campaign for the presidency of William & Mary before being elevated to the office literally overnight less than three years later.

During TR3's first year as president, he worked hard to still the waters roiled by his popular predecessor's stormy resignation only to face the sudden challenges that the 2008–2009 global financial crisis posed to funding for higher education. Once calm was restored on campus, TR3's presidency was marked by a transformational fundraising campaign, For the Bold, that ultimately raised $1 billion, a goal previously unrealized by any public university of William & Mary's size. Additional revenue was generated through significant tuition increases for those who could afford them, accompanied by the new "William & Mary Promise" that the price of tuition would remain stable for all four years of a Virginia student's education and that more financial aid would be available for those with family need. A building boom took place in the form of new and renovated structures, newly acquired and repurposed real estate, and carefully landscaped grounds. A new and integrated general education curriculum was developed and implemented that placed a premium on interdisciplinary learning and lasted all four undergraduate years, culminating in a senior research project. TR3 worked hard to reclaim the finer elements of William & Mary's long history, including four alumni who became presidents of the United States, while coming to terms with the university's slaveholding past; the latter efforts extended into a greater emphasis on diversity and inclusion. Having become interim president (and soon president) at age sixty-five, he retired ten years later in 2018, a time of his own choosing.

TR4, the third of the three Reveley presidents, grew up in Richmond during the 1980s and 1990s and, while following his father's path from Princeton into legal practice and his grandfather's path to seminary (but not ordination), he parlayed a managerial position at the University of Virginia's Miller Center into a well-conceived, successful candidacy for president of Longwood University in 2013. Unlike TR2, whose first year was shadowed by racial conflict locally and the assassination of President John F. Kennedy nationally, and TR3, whose first year was marked by the onset of the financial crisis of 2008–2009, TR4, as he gratefully recalled, was "initially spared from anything calamitous happening." By 2020, however, he was dealing with the COVID pandemic.

TR4 was thirty-eight when he became president of Longwood and, ten years later, was still the youngest of the commonwealth's presidents. His first decade in office saw the university's endowment more than double, even as annual tuition increases remained among the lowest in Virginia. He led initiatives that culminated in Longwood hosting the 2016 vice presidential debate and forging a new partnership with Farmville's historic Moton Museum, the only partnership of its kind between a university and a civil rights museum. He oversaw construction of new buildings and the renovation of old ones with a New Urbanist's eye toward beauty, walkability, and openness to the surrounding community. Like his father and grandfather, TR4 initiated a new general education curriculum, Civitae, with a coherent theme: citizenship in a democracy. In dealing with COVID, TR4 led the way among Virginia's public universities toward a safe reopening of their campuses in the fall of 2020, well before most of the rest of American higher education.

Although each of the three Reveley presidents' path to the presidency was distinctly his own, some common threads clearly marked their pre-presidential lives and careers, shaping who they were before and after they took office. These included:

- a love of the liberal arts, especially as pursued in academic settings;
- experience as college athletes;
- the cultivation of important mentors;
- a strong attachment to Virginia, both family and commonwealth;
- a commitment to active public service;
- a love of the law, whether in the form of TR2's intense study of Lockean political theory or TR3's and TR4's full-time professional practice;
- despite the difference in their age on becoming president (TR4 at thirty-eight, TR2 at forty-six, TR3 at sixty-five), a great capacity and stamina for hard work; and
- in TR3's and TR4's cases, frequent opportunities to learn personally from TR2's and each other's experiences as president.

As shown in the chapters that follow, this mix of shared and distinctive qualities helped shape the ways in which the three Reveley presidents led their Virginia institutions in important areas, understanding always that in order to succeed, a college president must both shepherd the campus community and represent it to important outside constituencies.

Foremost among the challenges they faced were, in their view, fostering morale and pride of place among students, faculty, staff, and alumni (discussed in chapter 4) and forging constructive governing relationships with important external constituencies, especially their governing board, and, in TR3's and TR4's cases, with government officials (chapter 5).

These two chapters are followed by others chronicling their efforts at reforming the curriculum (chapter 6); enhancing the student experience, including intercollegiate athletics (chapter 7); engaging issues of diversity (chapter 8); and advancing fundraising (chapter 9). Each chapter details how the three Reveley presidents dealt with these issues, each in his own time and place. The narrative flow continues from chapter to chapter uninterrupted by tidy conclusions, a format consistent with the lived experience of the three presidents, in which every day brought some combination of these challenges.

Intrinsically, however, the neat segmentation of the president's job into relatively discrete topic areas grossly schematizes what doing the job actually entails. The book's concluding chapter and appendix present their hard-won insights into leadership. The epilogue offers their thoughts about leaving their positions as college and university leaders.

4
Fostering Pride and Morale

Apart from their need to establish constructive relationships with important external constituencies, especially the institution's governing board (the focus of chapter 5), presidents must lead a wide range of campus stakeholders, notably faculty, staff, and students, whose interests are varied and not always in obvious harmony. At a minimum, for example, different cohorts' sense of time varies. Students pass from matriculation to graduation in a few years, while many faculty and some staff are there for the long haul. For a new president, fostering pride and morale in the institution as a whole can be an effective way to bind these groups together.

All three Reveley presidents took office at a difficult time in the life of their institution. Nothing indicated this more than the unstable leadership that preceded their arrivals. Historically, Hampden-Sydney, William & Mary, and Longwood had usually benefited from presidents who served long enough to provide steady leadership but not so long as to atrophy in the job. But by 1963, when TR2 took office at Hampden-Sydney, he was the college's fourth president in less than a decade. TR3's immediate predecessor at William & Mary lasted less than three years before resigning stormily in 2008, having served about the same length of time as the president who preceded TR4 at Longwood and who resigned for health reasons in 2012, a year before TR4 took office. All three institutions were rattled by this instability, with obvious consequences for campus morale. To the Reveley presidents, restoring morale among students, faculty, and staff and, over the longer term, fostering greater pride in alma mater formed one of their most urgent and important leadership challenges.

Reveley IV: A public company CEO is expected to materialize on Day 1 and begin barking the strategic directives immediately, and the assumption is that they will then be executed faithfully by the at-will employees up and down the line. A U.S. president has that same bias toward action, but tempered by all sorts of political and constitutional realities. An academic president, in contrast to both, can run onto the shoals by overlistening. I definitely did not want to radiate the sense of "All I will be doing for the first year is listening." I did make the rounds and meet with people over the summer, but pretty quickly—not days, but not months either—began to make a series of decisions about matters like staffing, facilities planning and architecture, and the curriculum reform effort I wanted to launch.

REVELEY III: Given the uproar going full blast on the main campus over my predecessor's sudden resignation, the first thing I did was walk the few blocks there from the law school, wondering what on earth I was supposed to do. So I just began talking with people. At lunchtime that first day I met with a group of Black undergraduates who were very angry and deeply concerned about what was happening. Soon came a meeting with the provost and other senior administrators. As quickly as the calls could be arranged, there were mass gatherings by phone with alumni who wanted to know whether William & Mary had run off the tracks. My main message was W&M had been through a rocky period but we were still breathing and ready to make progress again.

When walking on campus, I spoke to everyone I encountered. Often this jarred them off their smartphone screens. If someone wanted to take a selfie with me, we did it. I learned to leave extra time for pictures when going from place to place.

Whenever I got an idea or complaint from someone on campus, my standard reply, quickly and by email, was, "Come see me." As at the law firm, this took time I could have saved if I'd used a gatekeeper, but it built bridges. If someone wanted to see me, I saw them as soon as feasible.

Typically, I was candid about what I thought. Nonanswers—pablum— from people in charge have usually seemed counterproductive to me. Sometimes candor creates problems. More often, it is disarming.

Prodded by our communications and advancement people, I began appearing in videos, usually for greetings or development purposes.[1] After a while these gigs grew on me, and the troops produced a steady stream of hits, especially with students and alumni. My career in films coexisted surprisingly well with the dignity and elegance the president owes the office. At times it was a close call but well worth the candle.

If you care about people and like them, you hope they will respond in kind. It enhances your effectiveness as president and makes the job more fun.

Morale

REVELEY IV: There's a saying that morale is to the physical as three is to one. You can have all the resources and support and supply lines imaginable, but if morale is low, you're in tough shape. And if, by contrast, the bridges are all burned and food is scarce but morale is high, you can carry the day.

In my grandfather's case morale was pretty low at Hampden-Sydney in 1963 after two consecutive failed presidencies, and some bad will that had arisen between the students and faculty and administration on a range of issues. But, just by virtue of who he was, TR2 was universally seen at the outset as the hero arriving on the scene, the native son come back to save the kingdom. That bought him a lot of good will and willingness to follow right from the outset.

EDITORIAL IN THE *Hampden-Sydney Record* WHEN TR2 WAS APPOINTED: It would be hard to name a Hampden-Sydney graduate of the past fifty years with a more distinguished undergraduate record than Taylor Reveley, '39. . . . He became something of a campus legend. . . . This is the past that is prologue to a future which, *Deo volente*, must be brilliant.[2]

REVELEY III: My ascension at William & Mary did not evoke that sort of response. But I knew in my bones how important it was that institutions be proud of themselves. So I got to work on pride, urging W&M to get its light out from under the bushel, to stop being so understated and reticent about itself.

I talked about the four U.S. presidents with ties to William & Mary, and urged us to get much more serious about George Washington. He got his surveyor's license from W&M when being a surveyor was a big deal, and he didn't get an academic credential at any point from any other school. He was William & Mary's first American chancellor, serving for eleven years. I urged us to recognize the splendid undergraduate education Thomas Jefferson got at W&M and remember how attached he was to his alma mater until the idea of a university he could see from Monticello consumed him. I said we needed to get more excited about James Monroe, another alum whose presidency was unusually successful (and who, unlike Jefferson, did not defect to the University of Virginia). We also needed at least to acknowledge John Tyler, a less successful president but a president nonetheless whose only higher education came at William & Mary. Not everybody was wildly enthusiastic about elevating all these dead white males, but I was a president in good standing. I wanted to get it done, and we did.

I also talked a whole lot about William & Mary's glittering run of modern chancellors: Chief Justice Warren Burger, Prime Minister Margaret Thatcher, Secretary of State Henry Kissinger, Justice Sandra Day O'Connor, and Secretary of Defense Robert Gates. I pointed out the number of senior federal positions held by W&M alumni in recent years—secretary of defense, directors of the CIA and FBI, the head of the National Park Service, chair of the President's Council of Economic Advisers, and majority leader of the House of Representatives.[3]

I pointed out that William & Mary was the largest and best funded of the colonial colleges, with an innovative curriculum; that it became a university in 1779 with the creation of its law school; that the undergraduate education it now provides is among the very best in the country; and that its commitment to train leaders for the larger good burns as brightly now as it has for centuries.

I was always on message, always the troubadour, about why the Alma Mater of the Nation should step out from the shadows.

REVELEY IV: Watching all that unfold at William & Mary, I drew from TR3's experience very significantly. Longwood itself has honest claim to real antiquity. It's one of the hundred oldest existing institutions of American higher education, meaningfully older than Cornell, Johns Hopkins, the University of Chicago, and Stanford. Every other institution on that list is better known than Longwood, which told me that we had unused potential to become much better known as well. But as with my dad at William & Mary, when I came on the scene Longwood did not have an easy pride in itself. I've worked really hard to get Longwood to comprehend its place in the celestial order.

REVELEY III: Like it or not, and I emphatically don't, *US News* rankings have become a fact of life. They affect your capacity to recruit not just students but faculty also. They affect morale on campus and among alumni. The media and politicians notice them. So in years when the rankings go well, you shamelessly trumpet how you did. In years when they don't, you gnash your teeth and note how sorry an approximation of quality they are.[4]

REVELEY IV: Since I've gotten to Longwood, we've started to reliably be in the top ten of regional public universities in the South, which we were not before. And yes, that's given Longwood alumni and the broader Longwood community a real shot in the arm. We've been pretty artful in telling the tale of why we've done well, one reason being our small class sizes, which are a meaningful part of those rankings.

A huge turning point in Longwood's sense of itself came when we hosted the 2016 vice presidential debate. I'd realized that the only two things a university can do to really jump quickly into national focus in a good way are to host a debate or make a basketball run.

REVELEY III: It was a triumph about which his father had been Cassandra-like. I'd been told at William & Mary, whatever else you do, don't get us involved in another presidential debate—we'd hosted a Ford-Carter debate in 1976. It's enormously time-consuming, eats millions of dollars, just not worth it. I also thought, erroneously, it would be virtually impossible to persuade the Commission on Presidential Debates to come to Farmville, outside the bright lights of a big city, and simply making a case to the commission would itself take a whole lot of time and effort.

REVELEY IV: Centre College had already successfully hosted two debates in Danville, Kentucky, so the debate commission wasn't scared off by Farmville not being a metropolis. And I had a story to tell that appealed to them, about Farmville being at the crossroads of the final days of the Civil War and the courageous student protests a century later that ultimately became one of the cases the Supreme Court consolidated into *Brown v. Board of Education*. Our Farmville-related mantra was, "Where the Civil War ended, and Civil Rights began."[5]

The process of seeking to host one of the 2016 general election debates involved an initial application by the university, extensive campus visits by representatives of the debate commission, the publication of a list of finalists in June 2015 (Longwood was one of fifteen institutions that made the cut), and the announcement of four dates and hosts three months later.

REVELEY IV: You had to be willing, when you applied almost twenty months out from the election, to get the vice presidential debate instead of one of the three presidential debates. When we got the vice presidential debate, it was a little bit of a letdown, like we had scored a touchdown but then missed the extra point. It was not yet predictable even by then that the 2016 presidential contest would be between Donald Trump and Hillary Clinton and would be so angrily divisive. In contrast, the vice presidential debate between Mike Pence and Tim Kaine wound up being, in some very real sense, the last normal moment in American politics for years to come—a reasonable, if feisty, debate between two established figures that wouldn't have been out of the ordinary in any previous election. For all the rancor surrounding the presidential candidates, we were free to treat the run-up to our debate in the usual bunting-and-marching-bands way.

But even before it became obvious that this was the case, the effect on campus was electrifying. Here was Longwood in the national spotlight in a way that it had never been and that relatively few colleges were or ever would be, at least for good things. Every major news organization was on our campus, and Justin Pope, who had come to Longwood with me as chief of staff after a career with the Associated Press, wove the top-line melodies for Longwood with enormous panache. The debate itself—Live from Longwood University!—was seen by nearly 40 million people.

Of course, I got requests from all sorts of Longwood VIPs asking for one of the relative handful of tickets we had to distribute, and the solution we ultimately stumbled on was to give virtually all our 150 tickets—including mine—to Longwood students, which among other things solved a lot of campus politics and was also a morale boost for the students who had worked so hard in a number of volunteer capacities and now had a chance to be in the actual debate hall. I watched it outdoors with thousands of others on a big-screen TV.

From September 2015, when we got the go-ahead, until October 4, 2016, the date of the actual debate, it was an operatic undertaking for me and the core team, just working our hearts out while trying to keep the rest of the university going at the same time. Victoria Kindon, one of the key leaders I'd been lucky enough to hire, brought experience and perspective from Obama's 2008 presidential campaign, and Jeff Chidester of the Miller Center brought know-how to the debate effort while holding a joint appointment with us for the year.

The value of the debate to Longwood was enormous. Pride, morale, confidence—full stop. At a prosaic level, the campus got all sorts of improvements in hardened IT, building enhancements, and the like. The debate got us national and international attention on a scale you can't replicate—more than $80 million worth by one credible estimate. It also provided an occasion to pilot new courses that would help our ongoing effort to refocus Longwood's core curriculum, with democracy as its North Star *(see chapter 6).*

And then, a thing that had really lasting value, the debate required important people from all across the campus to work together on a massive and complex undertaking. It produced all sorts of muscle memory that did us great good in dealing with COVID when the pandemic hit in early 2020. For instance, our university spokesperson Matt McWilliams had already become a trusted voice to the campus on weighty matters. We were able to an extent we otherwise would not have been to respond to unforeseen circumstances with seamless teamwork because we could freshly activate the cross-campus neural network that was made strong by our experience hosting the debate. On so many levels, it truly is a shame that the Commission on Presidential Debates looks like it may have reached the end of its three-decade run in 2024, with both major parties turning on it, likely ceding control of future debates to the television networks and the campaigns.

Concern was widespread on college campuses when it became apparent that Trump had won the election. William & Mary was no exception. TR3's ability to restore calm was facilitated by his longstanding practice of refusing comment on political matters that were not directly related to the university. As the *Richmond Times-Dispatch* editorialized in 2017, "Reveley did not consider his office a political platform. His ideological sympathies are unknown outside his inner circle."[6]

REVELEY III: William & Mary's 2016 election story was fairly typical of what happened on college campuses nationally. Most people in Williamsburg thought Trump would lose. But he won. Shock and anguish! Social media went into overdrive. One rumor hit the internet that I'd canceled classes the next day so that everyone could retreat to their rooms to recover. I had not canceled classes. Wild animals could not have gotten me to cancel classes. Another rumor began circulating online that cotton had been planted on one of our playing fields, as if the era of slavery was with us anew. It was fertilizer. The students who'd voted for Trump felt they couldn't celebrate. It was not a great Wednesday for anyone.

But for Longwood, 2016 was the year of the debate, and it turned out to be a great morale-building, confidence-raising, exposure-generating triumph.

Ceremony

The effectiveness of traditional academic ceremonies as binding agents within a campus community was a casualty of the 1960s emphasis on informality and relevance. In large part because of their long connection with the Presbyterian Church and their previous experience at other institutions, all three Reveley presidents strongly believed in the power of ceremony to remind the varied members of the campus community of what united them.

REVELEY III: Schools that are really glued together have moments in their annual cycle that are positively liturgical, a balance of faith in the institution and its meaning and the importance of celebrating it. TR2 would be sad to see how the ties to the church have disappeared at Rhodes and Hampden-Sydney, just as they have from almost every other campus that once had close links to a mainline Protestant denomination. This is certainly the case at William & Mary. But there are other things that compensate for that absence.

Charter Day at William & Mary, for instance, is an annual celebration of the signing by King William and Queen Mary of the royal charter that created W&M. When I became president, the way Charter Day was celebrated had grown tired. For starters, it was held at 10 a.m. on a Saturday morning in February, much too early to draw a crowd of students. And it wasn't all that interesting. So we moved the celebration to Friday afternoon and added elements such as having one of the campus singing groups, a different one each year, deliver a rousing rendition of "Happy Birthday" to William & Mary that had to be creative in some way. The first group sang it as a fugue. We even sent each student an invitation, and they began to show up—several thousand instead of a hundred or so.

REVELEY IV: You know, a preacher's son like my dad has a liturgical flair for how to make a ceremony move and have verve.

REVELEY III: Same thing with the annual Homecoming Parade in October. It had fallen on hard times because it started at 8:30 on Saturday morning, when a lot of students were still in bed. Student interest in building floats had slowly ebbed away. So we moved the parade to Friday afternoon and provided some support for float building. The parade began to draw crowds again. Some alumni mourned, but the salad days of Saturday morning parades, with legions of floats setting the stage for the Homecoming football game, were long gone.

The point is, each year, throughout the year, schools need ceremonies and rituals that bring people together and engender confidence and pride in alma mater. For William & Mary some occasions were there to remind everyone how deeply the university's roots are planted in America's history. Other occasions were opportunities, when they had flair and personality, to just have a good time together. Still others celebrated our teaching, research, and learning and those among us who were unusually good at them.

REVELEY IV: The Yule Log ceremony over the holidays was another real high note, something the Reveleys certainly enjoyed as a family.

REVELEY III: Yule Log took place right before people left for the holiday break. It was in the courtyard of the Wren Building, lit by torchlights, with a great crowd on hand—lots of splendid singing, readings from various faith traditions, an original poem in the manner of *The Night before Christmas* composed and delivered by the student affairs VP, and huge Yule logs carried by a cohort of strong undergrads into the Great Hall of the Wren and thrown on a blazing fire in an enormous fireplace. Celebrants then moved through the hall to throw sprigs of holly on which they'd placed their cares into the fire to be carried away up the chimney. I would materialize, dressed as Santa Claus, with a full beard that invariably got stuck in my mouth, to read *The Grinch Who Stole Christmas*, just like my presidential predecessors had done—don't know if they had to eat their beards too. The students, who knew the story quite well, joined in at crucial moments. They enjoyed seeing the president looking like a moth-eaten—but festive—Santa.

REVELEY IV: I think a very real and important aspect of human nature is that the fullness of our understanding is only partially verbal or written. Every true community, when it's in full flower, has a liturgical dimension to it, even if it doesn't overtly recognize that. There are things like the beauty and elegance of our surroundings and the elemental force of communal liturgical activity—ritual—that contribute deeply to our sense of how the present connects to the past and the future. When it's time for convocations, commencements, other grand occasions, the places that do them well, with genuine verve and meaningful ritual, stand apart from places that give them short shrift.

Faculty

OWEN NORMENT (LONGTIME PROFESSOR AND DEAN OF THE FACULTY, HAMPDEN-SYDNEY COLLEGE): Faculty hiring was largely a presidential matter when Taylor [Reveley II] became president of Hampden-Sydney. When I was hired in 1966, the sequence of events was: an initial exchange of letters with the president, a short visit to the campus, a brief and casual meeting with the academic dean in his garden, lunch with the president and department members, and, within a few days, a letter of appointment from the president.

Ten years into his presidency the process was far more complex, having become externally subject to federal and AAUP (American Association of University Professors) guidelines and professional society recruiting procedures and internally involving departmental initiatives, classroom appearances, faculty committee advice, student opinion, and so on.[7]

REVELEY III: When I was dean of the law school, I saw a lot of the faculty and made it an ironclad practice to be accessible whenever someone wanted to talk. My colleagues knew that. As president, with the university's enormously larger faculty, I didn't engage professors the way I'd seen my father do or that I did as dean. I left most close contact with the faculty to Michael Halleran, our exceptionally able provost, and to the academic deans. If any faculty member wanted to see me, I was still available as soon as possible. But William & Mary needed me to focus elsewhere.

It's vital that a leader create a context in which other people in the organization can relax, hold anxious gossip to a dull roar, and get on with doing their best work. As long as they believe there's a firm hand on the wheel, the ship isn't about to hit the rocks, and it's sailing on a promising course, they're fine.[8]

My first year as president coincided with the 2008–2009 financial crisis. The state went into budgetary arrest. And it wasn't a great time to be raising money from alumni and friends. We were unable to provide raises on campus for several years. It was tough. The board of visitors kept offering me pay increases, which I kept declining until we could provide raises for the faculty and staff as a whole. Until then, I stuck with the salary I'd been paid my last year as dean of the law school. This was good for campus morale, to the limited extent it was known. It made me feel better.[9]

Reveley IV: Unlike my dad and, to a lesser extent, me, the everyday rhythm of the faculty is something that TR2 dealt with a great deal before becoming president. And it was during his presidency that the tenuring process came to Hampden-Sydney in the 1960s, something we think of as engraved in ancient runes but for which widespread adoption is really just two-and-a-half generations old. He advanced that and made it happen.

TR2 persuaded Hampden-Sydney's board of trustees to institute tenure in conformance with what had recently become standard practice in higher education. As the college's enrollment grew from about five hundred to eight hundred during his fourteen years as president, he oversaw a commensurate increase in the size of the faculty.

Reveley III: One thing you've got to assume if you're president is there are going to be some people who have agendas inconsistent with yours or even vehemently opposed to yours who're going to work against you. Tenure protects them, but this doesn't mean you shouldn't try to stay on top of what they're doing and take steps to protect the school and the presidency. Daddy was always reluctant to think ill of anyone. I used to lean on him to guard the ramparts more.

Patience and generosity of spirit toward others were qualities of TR2's that people remarked on at every stage of his life, from fellow students at Hampden-Sydney in the 1930s to colleagues at Rhodes College in the 1940s and 1950s to faculty while he was president of his alma mater during the 1960s and 1970s. When he announced his retirement, nearly every faculty member signed a letter of gratitude, partly for the tangible improvements in the college's enrollment, endowment, compensation, and physical plant that he helped bring about but even more for the decency with which he led:

> We see one of the clues to your success: at all times you have shown yourself a gentleman and a Christian, with a door open to those who wanted to talk and a willingness to hear those who might disagree. There was a patience, a tolerance, a kindliness, a sense of ethical behavior that marked a truly noble character.[10]

REVELEY IV: At the outset of TR2's presidency in 1963, racial integration of Hampden-Sydney was something that a number of old-line potentates on the faculty were stridently opposed to. He listened to them with genuine patience and, with equal patience, explained why he thought it had to happen and should happen.

REVELEY III: Tenure in its modern form is something rich schools can pay for without undue angst. Same for schools that don't make any meaningful effort to have most of their undergraduates taught by full-time professors in secure position. We live in a time when course loads for tenured and tenure-track professors have gotten quite light to make time for their research and writing. So if the school can't pay to have legions of tenured professors, it turns to pedagogues with little or no security of position to do much of the teaching, usually adjuncts who appear on campus briefly to teach a class and then head off to their next part-time gig. Understandably, these itinerant scholars usually aren't around enough to mentor students or write references for them. They barely feel part of the institution's life.

Along with an abiding commitment to tenure, I pushed hard at William & Mary to create a category of full-time, non-tenure-eligible faculty with renewable contracts who were expected to be splendid teachers and mentors of long duration but not expected to produce publishable research.[11] They were to teach meaningfully, more than their tenured colleagues. They were to be treated as card-carrying members of the faculty, not lesser life forms, except when certain matters such as tenure were at issue.

Predictably, this was not an easy sell in some campus precincts. But there was no desire among the tenured to return to the heavy course loads of the past. And funds were not available to expand their number enough so that all students could be taught by tenured or tenure-track people without reducing their time for scholarship. Everyone agreed that exceptional teaching was William & Mary's gold standard. Something had to give.

A member of our board of visitors, Robert Scott, helped push us along. Bob, formerly a very successful dean of UVA's law school, was a master teacher and prolific scholar who had kept his teaching and scholarship going even while moving mountains as dean. He had bullet-proof credentials in the academy. In meetings with our faculty, he said, in essence, "We can't afford to do it the way Harvard and Princeton do it. We've got to come up with an alternative. If we're going to have tenured and tenure-track faculty who teach relatively little compared to the past and do a lot of important scholarship, we also need full-time teaching faculty who don't come and go like adjuncts but get to know the students well enough to mentor them and write effective recommendation letters." Bob was a crucial voice in planning and domesticating this step forward.[12]

Strategic Planning

There's nothing glamorous about strategic planning, but both TR3 and TR4 regarded it as useful in giving all campus stakeholders a way to be heard and the board of visitors a sense of direction. And although the process opened the door wide to voices other than the president's, it also served as a vehicle for building support for his own agenda.

Strategic planning's entry into the academy came indirectly, from its military origins to the corporate world in the 1960s to colleges and universities a decade or two later, often at the initiative of board members from the business community. Although the development of a strategic plan was not part of the academic culture during TR2's tenure at Hampden-Sydney, it had become an expected presidential activity by the time TR3 and TR4 came along.

REVELEY IV: Strategic planning is really a phenomenon of the last generation. If TR2 in 1963 had said, "We're going to start doing a strategic plan," Hampden-Sydney, like any campus then, would not have had a sense of what that meant. It is a vast irony that this military concept—"strategic" comes from the Greek word for general, *strategos*—has been adopted and to some extent fetishized by higher education.

REVELEY III: But it kind of makes sense. Campus denizens like to get together to share ideas, in particular to opine about what the school ought to be doing. People who care about the institution invariably have thoughts about how it can get better. Strategic planning is made for that sort of conversation.

The law school was in the early stages of a strategic planning effort when I left suddenly to become interim president. Once I had a moment to breathe on the main campus, it became clear that a good bit of time had passed since the last strategic plan and there was appetite for another run at one. The ship needed a renewed sense of direction. Equally important, people, faculty especially, needed a chance to be heard and to know they were being heard. For this reason alone, a rigorous planning effort made sense to me, even though it would take a whole lot of time and energy and would probably prove mostly aspirational for lack of funds. The provost and our vice president for strategic initiatives, Jim Golden, led the way. The process produced not just a highly articulated plan but also a way to review it annually and make midcourse corrections. The fact that the university was planning strategically was another boost for confidence and good cheer.

From start to finish, my overriding strategic objective for William & Mary remained as it had been from the first, to build the university's financial foundation. Without a radically greater endowment, only so much more than what was already afoot could come to pass.

Because of the robust search and transition processes that culminated in TR4 becoming president of Longwood in March 2013, in which myriad groups of faculty, staff, students, alumni, and board members were involved, he felt that many of the virtues of an elaborate strategic planning process already had been achieved by the time he took office in June.

At a meeting of the board of visitors at the close of his first semester as president, TR4 won its initial endorsement of a one-page, seven-item strategic plan that, because of the groundwork already laid, had baked-in support from board members and much of the campus community. He did so in an effort to avoid a common failing of strategic plans for academic institutions—namely, that "in the effort to please everyone, . . . strategic plans end up being either general to the point of uselessness or a long, unfiltered wish list that includes everyone's highest priorities."[13]

REVELEY IV: Strategy is most effective when it is concise and nimble. Our first strategic plan focused on what most needed to be done in the next six years. It hit hard on enhancing student retention and graduation, on revitalizing the core curriculum (later named Civitae) to focus on cultivating "citizen leaders," on enhancing our national marketing as one of the nation's fifty oldest NCAA Division I schools, on encouraging increased foot traffic on campus by alumni and townspeople, on fostering prosperity in Farmville and Prince Edward County, on strengthening the university community with increased compensation and greater diversity, and on making the various components of that community fit together better.

Obviously all of these objectives needed fleshing out, but limiting the plan itself to seven items on one page—half a page, really, apart from introductory and concluding text—gave us a clarity of purpose that much longer strategic plans often lack. As we began to implement the plan, the spirit of fresh momentum and new beginnings was almost self-evident, in part because the new rector, Colleen Margiloff, and I were both younger than forty when the new academic year started.

When that six-year plan drew to a close in 2019, we devised a new strategic plan to carry us through to 2025. It renewed the original plan's emphases on diversity and compensation while adding items like further enhancing "the beauty of our residential campus" and making "the culture of philanthropy . . . more robust."

The (Un)changing Role of the First Spouse

In all three cases, the Reveley presidents were aided in their efforts to foster pride and morale on campus by their spouses, albeit in ways that changed as the larger culture changed.

REVELEY IV: The president's wife at Hampden-Sydney and other colleges and universities when my grandfather was president in the 1960s and 1970s was expected to be a full-fledged part of the functioning of the institution, albeit unpaid. Whereas I think the expectation now is that it's relatively likely a married president's spouse will have a range of outside interests that are consequential and not necessarily tied to the university. And yet it's still the case that the university community has expectations of at least seeing the president's family at social events and marquee occasions and probably, in some unstated way, more expectations than that.

REVELEY III: Hampden-Sydney in the sixties and seventies was a village where everybody worked for the same company. It could be a warm and supportive community, and usually was, where people really did know one another and cared about one another. But it was also a community where everybody had opinions about almost everything and gossip flowed freely. Middlecourt, the president's house, was pretty much right in the middle of the village. The president and his wife were the main attraction.

MARIE EASON REVELEY: Everyone had an inalienable right to a viewpoint about what you did, often expressing this viewpoint in no uncertain terms.[14]

REVELEY III: In every regard other than purely academic matters like curriculum, Mother was Daddy's partner. He wanted her thoughts about things and took her judgment heavily into account. They were deeply devoted to each other. But she felt it was hard for him to grasp all that she needed to do at Middlecourt to entertain and even house people. To say, "We need more staff at Middlecourt"—it took wild animals to get him to do that. Or to get the house painted when the paint was peeling or to get done the basics of what the grounds needed. Wholly beyond the pale was to ask to be paid more, even though it was clear to Mother that his reluctance on that score was doing the college no favors and hurting the family. But anything he perceived as asking for something for himself jarred his celestial sense of Christian responsibility. This rattled Mother's cage a lot.

MARIE EASON REVELEY: Women believe in their secret hearts that men regard what women do as unimportant. . . . The problem of inadequate staffing not only placed a heavy burden from the standpoint of cooking, housekeeping, gardening, and hostessing but as butler too. Guests arrived with heavy luggage when I was the only one to receive them.

Beyond the traditional duties associated with first spouses at the time, Marie Reveley was instrumental in creating a kindergarten on campus for Black and white children, working alongside Marlene Miller, the wife of a faculty member. In 1967, at TR2's request, the session (governing board) of the College Church, which is on the Hampden-Sydney campus but somewhat independent of the college, authorized the kindergarten to operate within the church building "without regard to race." A year later, after a number of church members expressed their opposition to the continued operation of the racially integrated kindergarten in the church, it relocated to a college building known as the "Log Cabin."[15]

MARIE EASON REVELEY: An irate [Hampden-Sydney] board member became very abusive when Taylor gave a routine report of what was happening on campus. . . . He alleged that the integrated kindergarten was in violation of the use of college property and had to be removed at once.

Taylor instantly responded. . . . No law was being broken; no college rule was being violated; no damage was being inflicted upon the house. Mrs. Miller very definitely had Taylor's blessing.

Marie Reveley's interactions with the board were always gracious and hospitable. But a few years after the kindergarten issue was resolved, she felt compelled to speak up. Gathered on campus on the eve of a late 1960s commencement, the board's executive committee learned that a few graduating seniors planned to wear a white armband on their robes in protest of the Vietnam War. Although Hampden-Sydney was not a hotbed of antiwar activity, its all-male student body was especially concerned about being drafted into the army and deployed to Vietnam after graduation.

MARIE EASON REVELEY: David Squires, who was then chairman of the board, called a special late-night meeting of the executive committee to address the problem of the arm-banded students. . . . What was being proposed was that a graduation diploma be withheld from any student wearing a white armband.

By midnight Sara Squires had become very concerned for Dave's health as he had a serious heart condition. She enlisted my help in urging the men to retire. With some trepidation I went to the ground floor where the men had sequestered themselves and knocked on the door. . . .

"Gentlemen," I asked, "would any court in the land uphold a decision to withhold a diploma from a student who had met the requirements for graduation on the basis that he was wearing a little white rag around his arm?"

"Besides," I said, "who knows, I might be wearing a little white arm band under my sleeve." Of course, I wasn't wearing a band but my unexpected disclosure . . . brought a smile to their faces. Very shortly they disbanded.

HELEN BOND REVELEY: When Taylor became dean of the William & Mary Law School, we still had two children in school in Richmond. Our son Everett was beginning his sophomore year at Princeton, and young Taylor had graduated from there two years before. I was working full-time in Richmond. So we kept our home on Monument Avenue and I drove back and forth to Williamsburg constantly. There definitely were things at the law school I had to be there for, a lot of meeting and greeting people, getting to know donors, entertaining. Naturally the scale of all this ramped up when he became president.

REVELEY III: Helen had a very large role in all the entertaining that goes on in the President's House (known as the PH) and for certain events on campus, such as presidential tailgates before football games. She was very involved in the care and tending of the PH, everything from its history, dating back to 1732, to what needed to be done when something broke.

William & Mary's "Historic Campus" consists of the PH, the Wren Building, and the Brafferton, which is where the president's and provost's offices are. Helen and Louise Kale, the executive director of the Historic Campus, had an unusually warm and productive friendship. Helen provided wise counsel about certain aspects of the restoration and renovation of the Brafferton, which was nine years older than the PH and was slowly sinking into the primordial ooze when I became president.

Helen was also extremely interested in the campus grounds. Obviously, buildings are important to how a school looks and feels for the people who live and work there, as well as for visitors. But so are the trees, shrubs, and flowers that surround them—the grass too. All of it needed attention. Helen developed a strong relationship with the staff who worked on the grounds. She knew them, cared about them, worked with them. She came across not as, "I am Madame President giving you orders," but as, "Let's work on this together." And she knew what she was talking about. They did wonderful things.

There's been a lot of change in what's expected of presidential spouses from when Mother was at Hampden-Sydney. The spouse no longer needs to be committed to the campus utterly, and so Helen was able to keep working full-time in Richmond during the first half of my presidency and also complete the course of study required to become a master gardener. But much is still expected of spouses, and when they pull their oar, it makes a real difference for the better. Helen pulled her oar.

MARLO REVELEY: Helen's encouragement to me was, "You need to run your own race. Focus on what's important to you and shut off other noise." When Taylor became president of Longwood in 2013, we had just had the twins the July before. I was on the executive track at Allianz, the twentieth largest company in the world. And I was fiercely defensive of "Holy moly, I'm not going to be a first lady who sits there pouring tea and making pleasant conversation, and they'd better understand that because they didn't hire me." Taylor never asked me to stop what I was doing; he supported me without question. And it's true that cultural expectations have changed very significantly, embracing the idea of families with two hard-charging careers in parallel.

But I am involved at Longwood, and when I get involved I get very involved. One big example is the president's house, Longwood House, which is gorgeous and two centuries old. It's about a mile and a half from the main campus and had been an underutilized gem. And when we were getting started, it was really compelling to me that we figure out how to turn the house into a welcoming place for everybody where people truly wanted to come, a place that's light and airy and easy to adapt so the family who comes after us in the fullness of time can make it their own.

Early on when we were starting, Longwood had a board member who was in a wheelchair, and they had to move the ramp every time he came and even at that, there wasn't a bathroom big enough for his wheelchair. That alone was compelling to me, that we fix that. It took the preservation people, the ADA (Americans with Disabilities Act) people, the builders, and three different lawyers to figure out how to do this in a way that was functional and still beautiful. And we did it, which was really important to me, making that sense of inclusion real for everybody.

All of the Reveleys have been very lucky with these historic houses. I know Taylor's grandparents loved Middlecourt at Hampden-Sydney. Taylor and Helen and all of us loved the President's House at William & Mary. And we love Longwood House, and have seen its important role in catalyzing activity and advancing pride and spirit.

5

Forging Constructive Governing Relationships

As with the presidents of the United States whom TR3 and TR4 studied as scholars, presidential leadership in higher education involves interacting successfully not just with internal constituencies—the students, faculty, and staff who live, work, play, and study on campus—but also with the external constituencies with which the president shares governing authority. All three Reveley presidents were hired by and accountable to governing boards entrusted by law and tradition with powers that potentially could be used to facilitate, impede, or end their presidencies. As presidents of public universities in Virginia, TR3 and TR4 also were accountable to the commonwealth's governor and the Virginia General Assembly, even as they relied on "Richmond" for a decreasing but significant share of their universities' funding. Constantly evolving state and federal regulations further impinged on aspects of campus life, as when in 2024 the General Assembly made Virginia one of the first states to forbid legacy admissions—that is, favorable treatment of applications from alumni and donor children—at its public universities. And like all colleges and universities, the Longwood, Hampden-Sydney, and William & Mary campuses are embedded in local jurisdictions, making the fostering of constructive town-gown relationships an important presidential challenge.

Other than in the surrounding neighborhood, most members of a campus community have little interaction with these external constituencies and are at best partially aware of how important they are. Board members—called trustees and headed by a chair at Hampden-Sydney and visitors, headed by a rector at William & Mary and Longwood—typically make only brief and occasional appearances on campus. Most of their time there is spent with the president and other high-level administrators.

Legislators and governors appear even less frequently on campus, if at all. But however much "out of sight, out of mind" may characterize the campus community's awareness of what trustees and public officials do, all three Reveley presidents knew that they must keep the board's and government's concerns and interests—and those of the ever-present news media—constantly in mind in order to lead successfully.

The Board

TR2 had some experience dealing with boards before becoming president of Hampden-Sydney in 1963, both as the pastor of Presbyterian congregations and, increasingly, as he rose up the ranks, as an administrator at Rhodes College. TR4 and, especially, TR3 brought considerable experience as board members and leaders to their presidencies.

REVELEY III: The summer of 1963 was a fraught time for Daddy to begin a presidency. The Prince Edward County public schools were still closed as part of Virginia's "massive resistance" to school integration.

REVELEY IV: Closed in a way that had drawn attention from the Kennedy administration and the national media because by then, Prince Edward stood alone nationally in still having no functioning public schools.

REVELEY III: And what Hampden-Sydney should do about it fretted the faculty and drove their deeply felt opinions, which the trustees heard all about because when the board met, the trustees spent the night in faculty homes. There were no nearby hotels or motels to put them in.

REVELEY IV: One result was that TR2's Hampden-Sydney experience, frequently to his frustration, was witness to a good bit more faculty-board interaction than my dad or I have experienced. Present-day Farmville is amply supplied with hotels.

Of the twenty-five board members TR2 inherited on becoming president, all were white male Virginians and twenty-one were Hampden-Sydney alumni.

Marie Eason Reveley: In upbringing, education, and viewpoint, they were remarkably similar. They tended to be conservative, very conservative. . . . Basically, they were content with the college the way it was.

Reveley III: The trustees, who were almost all alumni from earlier eras, tended to fondly remember their own college days when Hampden-Sydney's students and faculty were all white and the surrounding community was rigidly segregated. It took a lot of diplomacy and persistence for Daddy to persuade the board that the college had to integrate and be a force for integration in the local school system. He had to draw heavily on his fund of political capital as the good son returning home to lead the college forward. It helped that a couple years after he started, the federal government began leaning on higher education to admit Black students.

Reveley IV: Things got better over time. The fact that Bill Spong, an alum and a close friend of TR2's with all the prestige of being a U.S. senator, soon came on the board was also a boon. The board began to see the light on this issue and to help.

Reveley III: In time, the archconservative reaction faded. Some members left and others arrived.

And a related small thing—though based on my own board experience over the years, perhaps not that small: Mother finally persuaded Daddy that when the trustees came to town and gathered at Middlecourt, many of them wanted to have a drink, a real drink, not coffee, tea, or punch, and the fact that he didn't drink and didn't think drinking was a good idea or in accord with Presbyterian practice didn't cut much ice. The trustees were men who enjoyed a drink and were accustomed to having one on social occasions. They didn't have much traffic with teetotaling as a matter of religious conviction or sound body. As Mother knew it would, providing liquid refreshment made a difference because board members became more relaxed and convivial. And who knows regarding those early controversies at Hampden-Sydney? More relaxed and convivial board members perhaps were more agreeable to Daddy's initiatives.

Owen Norment: With respect to the college's relationship with the Presbyterian Church, toward the end of his presidency Taylor influenced the

1975 decision of the board of trustees to rescind the single legal tie to the church, the responsibility of the Synod of the Virginias to elect (or confirm the election of) members of the board. This was an eminently respectable move, necessary to remove any semblance of a sectarian impediment to receiving state or federal financial assistance. The move was followed by a kind of covenant relationship with the church, an informal but conceptually useful vehicle for continuing to affirm . . . what remained always for Taylor of major importance: the essential, historical character and responsibility of Hampden-Sydney as a Christian college, though free and independent of any sectarian controls.[1]

In their relations with their own institutions' boards, TR3 and, through him, TR4 were heavily influenced by the example of Bill Bowen at Princeton and the Mellon Foundation. As historian Nancy Weiss Malkiel has written, Bowen personally welcomed new members to the board, "communicated constantly" with all board members, did an "unusual amount . . . of advance planning" for each meeting, showed "great patience in the way he listened" so that "no one left board meetings feeling angry or disrespected," "fram[ed] issues and discussions so that the members themselves would . . . get to his desired endpoint," and "painstakingly identified . . . the people he wanted to take on specific responsibilities."[2] Like Bowen, both TR3 and TR4 regarded the board as a powerful asset to their leadership rather than an impediment.

REVELEY IV: Even though other countries run their universities without boards, I think they are deeply part of the magic of American higher education. The important function the board plays is that, not unlike civilian control of the military, it ensures a robust and rounded connection between the institution with its particular concerns and the hopes and sensitivities of the larger body politic. When a board is at its best, it cares deeply about the institution but is alive to considerations from beyond the campus. Private college and university boards can sometimes get hived off from the currents that swirl outside the academy, but the boards of public institutions are highly cognizant of them all the time, which can make things hard for a president but ultimately is for the greater good of the institution.

One thing that is true for both my dad and me—obviously my dad much more than me, but me in a meaningful way also—is that we'd had considerable experience as members of boards dealing with their institutions' executives.[3] We could see things through the board's eyes. There are rightful things that board members have natural questions about, natural instincts about. Having a keen understanding of that is enormously helpful for a president, and much more likely if they've been board members themselves.

That kind of experience is relatively unusual for university presidents. So many of them, especially those who've gone through a kind of pure academic progression before becoming president, don't have that perspective. As creatures of the academy they're tempted to think of board governance as an imposition from the corporate world, not knowing that it is corporations that borrowed the model from American higher education once upon a time. And because they don't understand the historical context or have meaningful board experience, they can get over-prickly about their executive prerogatives. "How dare you ask a question about what I'm doing?"—they don't always say that out loud, but they feel it in their bones. They often see a board as a problem to be managed as opposed to what it really is at its best: a fount of practical wisdom that helps to navigate the enterprise, both toward good opportunities and away from trouble. TR2 got similar perspective from his deep experience with Presbyterian polity and, while president, on other boards.

REVELEY III: You learn all sorts of practical things from being on boards. One example: how endowments work and what the investment universe looks like for schools. More broadly, how boards go about dealing with issues, especially tough ones.

By the time I became president of William & Mary, I had been on a whole lot of boards, including those of three schools—Princeton University's for fourteen years, Union Seminary's for nine years, and St. Christopher's School's for twelve years. I was comfortable with boards. In contrast, some presidents view boards as alien infestations of the campus that need to be fenced in and constrained as much as possible. As opposed to working with the board as an ally to get some big stuff done.

REVELEY IV: And I'd say, as a general rule of thumb, those are presidents who have not had a range of experience serving on meaningful boards themselves.

Reveley III: Apart from anything else, it was the board that hired you and the board that at any minute can dispose of you.

TR3 and TR4 both emphasized the importance of the relationship between the president of the university and the rector, or chair, of the board.

Reveley III: You need a rector who'll deal openly, no hidden agendas, with the president, and work in ways that suit both the rector and the president. As I found from my own experience as a board chair, when the chair and the president work together, you've got a powerful engine. It really helps if they like each other. The relationship between the board chair and president greatly affects the president's relationship with the board as a whole. It needs to be healthy.

Next, the rector should know how to organize and lead other people, starting with how to run a meeting on time, cheerfully; how to get decisions made, small ministerial ones and huge, hard-as-hell ones; and how to be sure everyone is heard but no one is heard too much. If there's a disruptive, discordant board member or two, people who actually are vexing the mission, somebody has to keep them from doing serious damage. The rector needs to take the lead in curbing them.[4]

Third, you need a rector who's willing and able to work hard, sometimes like a dog, for the school. Chairing a university board and dealing with all the ceremonial functions of a chair takes countless hours, including many, many visits to the campus. When things get rocky or major initiatives are afoot, the hours put in by the rector can be staggering.

Reveley IV: All of those things are true in my experience, too. I would add an additional virtue—perspective. It really matters if the board chair can readily differentiate things that matter from things that don't matter. There's flak coming in all the time, and if somebody has not had the experience of dealing with flak or of operating at a consequential level, it can be easy for them to think that the latest round of flak is the most important thing that's going on, and that rarely is true.

Part of perspective is the board chair's willingness to talk with the president about challenging things but then, when the president makes a decision that is very much his or hers to make, to stick with them. By contrast, for the board chair to have an obsessive zeal for the details being exactly one way just won't work. It's hard to keep all the balls in the air as president and so you need somebody who is giving you wise counsel but not wanting the paper clips a half inch from the side of the page rather than a quarter inch. I've always been so fortunate that way with Longwood, but have seen it awry in my own board service elsewhere.

Unlike the self-perpetuating boards that govern Princeton, where TR3 was a member, and Hampden-Sydney when TR2 was president, the boards of Virginia's public universities are appointed by the governor. Over the course of the single four-year term that Virginia's constitution allows governors to serve, they can substantially remake a majority of the board in their own political image, a risk that has been mitigated in recent decades by the Virginia electorate's alternation of Republican and Democratic governors.[5]

REVELEY III: Many board members are not reappointed for a second term.

REVELEY IV: Especially when there's a change of party with the election of a new governor, which has occurred fairly often in elections during my and my dad's presidencies.

REVELEY III: New governors know they'll be gone in four years. So they're in a hurry, a white heat, to pay political debts and reward friends with board appointments. Of course, governors also focus on the substantive caliber of those they appoint. What I always hoped for, and most presidents hope for, are appointees of high caliber and good judgment, some standing in the body politic, and a willingness to work hard for the school and dig deeply into their own treasure to help. It's good, too, to get people who come already knowing the school and caring about it. That usually means alums. Every now and then, a non-alum joins the board knowing virtually nothing about the school, and falls in love with it. They have splendid potential. On the negative side of the scale, you do not want people who come with preconceived agendas or gubernatorial axes to grind. Once on the board, their overriding commitment must be to the university and what's best for it.[6]

REVELEY IV: Even apart from political considerations, because of the one-term limit on the governor's tenure, substantial turnover on the board is a fact of life for public universities in Virginia, in contrast to some other states and, especially, to private institutions, where there's some turnover but considerable stability. On top of everything else, almost all of our public institutions besides William & Mary have a term limit of two years at a time for a board member to serve as rector. So what often happens is that people become rector toward the end of their tenure on the board, and then they're term-limited off it after serving their two four-year terms. And so the champion that recruited the new president is gone from the scene even as the board itself is going through its usual significant turnover. The result is that you're hired by a different set of people than you're working with as president. It's a measure of good luck and circumstance that this was not a problem for me or my dad.

Reveley III: I was advised when I became president, "Don't try to influence appointments to the board, too risky, too much sensitivity about this on the board, and too much state politics at play." But I decided early on that appointments were too important not to try. So I began conversations with state decision-makers to make clear what William & Mary needed. Usually I could count on getting one of my asks, but not more. Sometimes two, once nothing. It was a political process. You had to roll cheerfully with what you were dealt. This is an area, I believe, in which private schools, free to choose the most promising people for their boards, have a significant advantage over public institutions.

But I shouldn't whine. On the whole, my boards of visitors were talented, constructive, and willing to pull their oars. The rectors with whom I served were manna from heaven—Michael Powell, William & Mary's first Black rector; Hank Wolf, our first Jewish rector; Jeff Trammell, our first openly gay rector; and then Todd Stottlemyer, a powerful leader during the last five years of my presidency. I was blessed. This was so even though I usually kept my paws off the board's selection of its own officers.

Reveley IV: I've had genuinely superb boards the whole way through. I've just worked at it hard and been incredibly lucky. And even the political nature of gubernatorial appointments can be helpful. An appointed board is likely to be diverse in all important regards—diverse in background and diverse in perspective. That prevents the university from being secluded from the full range of public opinion because by its very nature, the composition of the board keeps us thinking about what is on people's minds. That's especially important in a state like Virginia, where the governorship and one or both houses of the General Assembly are often controlled by different political parties. Longtime Longwood board member, twice rector Marianne Radcliff has given me peerless perspective on how to navigate the university in this regard, to our great good. The navigating is important and, honestly, fun as we've worked together.

As an aside, unlike my dad, I do get pretty involved when the board is electing a new rector. There is some peril in that for sure, but the bond between the president and the rector is so consequential.

All of the Reveley presidents stressed that regular communications between the president and the board chair and, only slightly less important, between the president and the entire board are essential.

Reveley III: I began a custom, an iron discipline, of sending the board of visitors a weekly email, usually on Sunday night, about my sense of things during the prior seven days. This was a real chore some Sundays when writing another message wasn't high on my list of fun things to do, but these weekly emails were a remarkably efficient way for me to speak to every member of the board in one fell swoop. You don't want to surprise the board.

Reveley IV: They really, really don't like surprises. Even good news not delivered correctly can ruffle feathers. Bad news not delivered correctly can create real and appropriate disturbance on the board. They want frequency of communication from you in your own voice that is keeping them in early alert mode on anything of consequence. If you don't understand that—if you outsource communicating with the board to others—trouble awaits.

Reveley III: It's especially damaging for the board to first learn in the media about something bad that's happened at the university, or for a board member to be asked about something significant at the school and know nothing about it. This is disconcerting and embarrassing for the board member. It doesn't build confidence in the president's commitment to keep the board informed. And Taylor is right, the board doesn't want to be caught off guard even by good news.

One thing for certain: whenever something happens that casts the university in an unfortunate light, or has political import for the institution, or gets undergraduates' parents seriously disturbed, the president needs to alert the board ASAP, even if details are scarce.

REVELEY IV: All true. What makes it hard is that in a university there are dozens of things happening on any given day that could register on the scale, most of which the board actively does not want to know about. So having the discretion and wisdom about which of those things to focus their attention on, and at what stage in the progression of a particular thing—that's an art rather than a science. For example, on those rare occasions when a student passes away, which is truly horrific, or goes missing or is arrested on a major charge, I contact the rector immediately and email the board in real time, as best I can. You want the board to hear about it from you. And again, prior service on boards probably helps you make those judgments.

Communicating to the board is one thing, but both TR3 and TR4 emphasize the value the president can derive from listening to it.

REVELEY IV: I'm a big believer in actual deliberation at board meetings, as opposed to show-and-tell. Board members really want to be able to think matters through together. And there are things you can do to create the right atmosphere for that. You want to have a convivial meal together the night before the meeting because that adds to good spirits, as my grandmother finally persuaded my grandfather needed to happen at Hampden-Sydney. Food and libations aside, dinner together is an important chance for them to get in synch with each other, catching up on kids and vacations and things they've just read so that the harmonizing early aspects of a meeting have already occurred by the time the meeting begins in full the next morning. And because there are new members every year, I have them come to Longwood before their first meeting and have a long lunch with me and the rector and then take an extended tour of the campus.

REVELEY III: We did that too. There are a lot of ways to skin the cat, but you have to give new members an opportunity to feel comfortable, to bring them in gracefully. We had each new member come visit the campus to look around and talk with campus leaders, as well as a relaxed lunch with me at the President's House, when I'd have the new member ask me anything on his or her mind. It's important too to find ways early on to involve new members in meaningful work so they feel it matters that they're on the board. If they come to meetings and it doesn't seem to make any difference whether they're there or not, pretty soon they may stop showing up faithfully or come but spend large chunks of time in communion with their iPhones or laptops. You gotta push hard to find something each member of the board can do for the school that he or she finds fulfilling and the school actually needs. This isn't always easy, but it's worth the effort.

REVELEY IV: There is a great Bill Bowen theory that four-fifths of the fruit of a board meeting is the executive-side preparation you do in advance.[7] The work of getting the house in order on a routine basis because the in-laws are coming is itself of fundamental value. And so, if you've laid the groundwork well between meetings, as my father says, in preparation, and on the night before, then the meetings can be enormously fruitful.

One early goal of mine was to connect Longwood in a close and formal way with the Moton Museum in Farmville, which originally was the Robert Russa Moton High School for Black students where Barbara Johns, who was in her junior year there in 1951, organized the strike that began the march to *Brown v. Board of Education*. Both formally and informally, meaningful conversations with the board enabled them to ask the questions and make the suggestions that were on their mind, and then emerge as a body strongly in support of the endeavor.

REVELEY III: An example from my experience at William & Mary involved BHAGs. Well into my presidency, the board got intrigued with how "Big Hairy Audacious Goals" might come to William & Mary. BHAGs were an idea from an influential business book at the time called *Good to Great*.[8] The board wanted me, apart from our normal strategic planning process, to identify some major steps that, if achieved, could do great good for the university. The emphasis was on being bold. "Don't just come up with stuff that is already in the bag or easily nailed. Come up with goals that, if achieved, would move W&M ahead big time and really set it apart from the competition." So, after much conversation with my vice presidents, I came up with something like ten BHAGs and took them in draft to the board. Meaningful debate ensued, with the board ultimately agreeing to an amended and evolving list. It was a group effort, collaborative and fun, and drove momentum.

The BHAGs were aspirational in nature. They included goals such as "William & Mary will provide the best undergraduate education of any college or university in the country," "William & Mary will experiment aggressively with digital technologies," and "the 'William & Mary Way' for varsity athletics will set the standard nationally for how intercollegiate athletics should be done." At a minimum, they gave TR3 and the board an even clearer and more widely shared sense of direction and, in some cases, quantitative benchmarks to measure progress. These included goals such as "at least 60 percent of our undergraduates will have an international experience" and "our endowment will grow to $1.5 billion," thereby doubling in size.

"Richmond"

Although, as discussed in chapter 8, the federal government's civil rights policies helped give TR2 the leverage he wanted to advance racial integration, Hampden-Sydney's status as a private college meant that his interactions with Virginia's state government were few. That was not the case for his son at William & Mary or his grandson at Longwood. TR3 and TR4, as presidents of public institutions owned by the commonwealth, found that dealing with "Richmond" was a crucial aspect of the job. Gubernatorial appointments to their boards, discussed above, were one component. Maintaining good relations with the commonwealth's General Assembly and administration officials was another.

Recent patterns in Virginia politics provided distinctive challenges and opportunities for both TR3 and TR4. Since 1998, when TR3 became dean of the William & Mary Law School, the commonwealth has been led by three Republican governors and four Democratic governors, with similar shifts occurring in the General Assembly. When TR3 was president of William & Mary from 2008 to 2018, the forty-member state Senate was, at various time, narrowly Republican, narrowly Democratic, and evenly divided between the parties. The one-hundred-member House of Delegates remained reliably Republican, but the governorship swung during his tenure from Democrat Tim

Kaine to Republican Robert McDonnell to Democrat Terry McAuliffe. TR4 has experienced similar oscillations in partisan control since becoming Longwood's president in 2013. For instance, as a result of the 2023 state legislative elections, Republican Glenn Youngkin remained governor, but both the House of Delegates and the Senate had narrow Democratic majorities.

Because the governor appoints new members to each public university's board of visitors and the General Assembly reviews those nominations and appropriates funds for the universities' ongoing operations and construction of new buildings, maintaining good relations with both Republicans and Democrats in Richmond has been an especially important part of the presidential job description in Virginia.

This is a task to which TR3 and TR4 have been well-suited. TR3's long legal career before becoming dean and then president of William & Mary kept him out of partisan politics. His firm, Hunton & Williams, produced the Republican-appointed Supreme Court justice Lewis Powell and brought in former Democratic governors Gerald L. Baliles and Charles Robb as partners. TR4's most important prepresidential years were spent at the University of Virginia's nonpartisan Miller Center. While he worked there, Baliles was the center's director and former Republican governor Linwood Holton was the senior member of the center's governing council.

With ties to both political parties but publicly identified with neither, both TR3 and TR4 were able to credibly represent the universities they led to Republican and Democratic governors and legislators. But in order to make the most of this advantage on behalf of William & Mary and Longwood, they needed to walk the halls of government in Richmond, both literally and figuratively, to make their university's case.

Reveley III: At the outset of my forays into the legislative process, I needed an experienced field guide to help me find my way through the byzantine reaches and hidden lairs of the old General Assembly building. I'd had considerable experience walking those halls and talking with the people who could help you or hurt you when I was board chair of the Virginia Museum of Fine Arts. But you need someone to handle the logistics of getting appointments with legislators, and wise counsel about each one's proclivities, as well as the current state of play on matters important to your university. When politics are turbulent, the challenge is to stay in good stead with legislators of all persuasions. A lot of time and energy go into government relations, both offensively and defensively.

Much the same drill goes on with the executive branch of state government, but there are far fewer senior players there and, unlike the General Assembly, where one party might control the House of Delegates and the other party the Senate, only one party rules at a time. The nonpolitical civil servants, however, continue from administration to administration, with knowledge and influence. Presidents must till the vineyards in both branches.

REVELEY IV: Fortunately, Fran Bradford was William & Mary's splendid governmental affairs liaison, splendid for my dad and a great friend to me from prior work we'd done together. She later became the commonwealth's secretary of education.

Virginia, like all states, does things its own way. In the budgeting process, the General Assembly really is the determining factor. The governor and the administration, in the analogy I've sometimes heard and deployed, decide where to place the football, but the game takes place in the General Assembly until the ball gets back into the governor's hands near the end of the game, in what's called the veto session. In other words, the governor proposes a budget, which then gets chewed on very substantially by the General Assembly.

In terms of its public universities, Virginia has arguably been pretty light, relatively speaking, on the amount of money it provides for operations.

REVELEY III: Quite light.

REVELEY IV: On the flip side, Virginia is very generous with regard to capital funding for construction projects and maintenance of buildings. That's been true on both sides of the aisle, Republican and Democratic. Longwood's good fortune is that our own government affairs expert, Emily O'Brion, is able to peer into the state budget as the process rolls along and make sure we are in good stead. I'd obviously love for both operating and capital funding to be high, but it's not the worst thing in the world for capital to be the high one.

REVELEY III: Yes, the capital funding was, in my experience, quite generous and crucial to our efforts to renovate aging but elegant buildings and build new ones. The campus when I became president had acute needs on both scores, which we were able to take giant steps toward meeting. When I would launch into my frequent sermons about the utter necessity that William & Mary build its endowment and drive up annual giving, because the commonwealth supported its public universities less than the national norm (only 12 percent or so of W&M's operating budget, down from 43 percent as recently as 1980), I always hastened to add that the commonwealth was very generous with funds for bricks and mortar. We were able to renovate and build at a speed and on a scale that would have been impossible if we'd had to fund the projects completely with private donations.

Now if I had a magic wand and could change William & Mary's relationship with the commonwealth, I'd say, "Keep us in mind when you're handing out funds for capital projects, but don't give us any more operating money. Give what we've been getting to other state schools who need it more than we do. On the other hand, let W&M have a self-perpetuating majority of our board of visitors, with only a minority named by the governor. Leave us alone when it comes to how many out-of-state undergraduates we enroll, so we can bring in more very able students, paying out-of-state tuition, which should help us with the budget while increasing the number of in-state kids who'll be warmly welcomed at the other universities in the commonwealth. Give life to the reality that William & Mary was a private university from 1693 to 1906. Private is its natural state."[9]

I sang this song all over the place, on the campus and with alumni, legislators, and administration officials when making talks off-campus. Few took me seriously since it all seemed too pie-in-the sky. Someday, I believe, this pie will come down to Earth.

REVELEY IV: There would be jubilation. The General Assembly, to its credit, increased the appropriation to Longwood and all other public institutions far more than inflation through the teeth of the COVID pandemic and in subsequent years.

REVELEY III: But there are also the escalations in the state-mandated costs of health care, retirement support, and pay increases for faculty and staff, two-thirds of which, in William & Mary's case, have to be funded by the university. I used to say, "You gave us more operating money with one hand but then took it back with the other by increasing our health care, retirement, and salary costs." This wasn't acknowledged in Richmond. Rather, there would be back patting for the biscuit given and dead silence about the biscuit taken.

Reveley IV: Alas true: the state gives us a dollar and we turn around and give close to fifty cents right back to subsidize health care and retirement benefits for the state's entire employee base.

Reveley III: A different part of my drumbeat was the matter of our official name: The College of William and Mary in Virginia. W&M has been a university at least since December 4, 1779, when the board of visitors approved a law school on campus.[10] We've long had significant PhD programs and professional schools alongside our glittering undergraduate program. But very few people inside the commonwealth, much less outside it, seem to know that William & Mary is a significant research university, not simply a great undergraduate institution. When your name leads with "The College," this is the fruit you reap. So when the state hands out money to help fund research at its universities, W&M often has to run behind the wagon yelling "Hey, wait for us, we're a university too."

Both TR3 and TR4 value the role that the State Council of Higher Education for Virginia (SCHEV) plays.

Reveley III: Virginia, unlike North Carolina, Florida, and many other states, has a decentralized system of public higher education. There is no overarching state governing board to create severe trouble for its captive campuses if it's under the sway of the right wing or left wing—or, more normally, to just sprinkle sand in our wheels. SCHEV, especially when it has a strong, able leader and board, has a useful convening function for the public institutions in Virginia. It's adept at bringing the presidents together to discuss common concerns. It can help convey to the legislative and executive branches the views and needs of the schools. And it can bring legislative and executive perspectives to the university presidents.

SCHEV is also the instrument the state uses to impose certain requirements on the universities and to approve, or not, certain new programs each university proposes. But its writ in these regards is modest. If the state were to abolish SCHEV, as has been threatened from time to time, it's hard to see how the public universities in Virginia could keep evolving as successfully as they have, with boards of visitors and presidents remaining free, as they are now, to focus on how best to realize their schools' potential.

REVELEY IV: It's a very Virginia-specific creature that I think helps us avoid a North Carolina–style, consolidated Stalinist system of central planning, by serving as a circuit breaker preventing unmediated partisan or ideological action with regard to higher education.[11] So when a higher education question first arises, the General Assembly reflexively thinks, "That is SCHEV's domain, with its long and extensive policy expertise." Democracy works because of mechanisms for reflection in the cool of the day, which helps keep the partisan fray of the hot moment away.

REVELEY III: Even so, if the academy doesn't get a grip on how it's perceived on many scores, the political costs could be chilling. Take tenure. It's got a lot of problems, some real, some imagined. Tenure could be gone in a generation, I fear, if it's not better explained and its grim impact on the availability of professors for teaching undergraduates isn't remedied. What used to be de facto tenure in large law firms and corporations is now dead as a doornail. When I joined my old law firm over fifty years ago, once someone got to be a partner, de facto tenure set in. The partner's pay might suffer for underperformance, but a seat in the firm would remain. Emphatically not true anymore. Or when a blue-collar employee of a corporation was doing a good job, that worker would usually have a spot at the company until retirement unless the business failed. Long gone.

So there is real resentment that tenure still burns brightly in the academy. At some point legislators may end it at public institutions. That would be a serious loss. Tenure does contribute to the creation of new knowledge, even if there is no immediate practical use for it. It does protect the expression of a wide range of views by the tenured. It does build a sense of community among those who have it and may encourage senior people to remain with their schools. It may even hold down the compensation of the tenured, strangely enough, lest they jump ship and not be able to regain the sort of tenure they left behind.

REVELEY IV: The fact that Virginia is a purple state politically was something very familiar to both of us when we became presidents. What that means is that you've got to cultivate leaders in both parties so that when divisive social issues arise that may have implications for higher education, you're less likely to get stranded without friends on one side or the other. For presidents who come to Virginia from other states that are monochromatically red or blue—which is all but a handful of states nowadays—they often don't know how to walk that walk, at least at the start.

The Media

Boards, parents, and (partly as a consequence) politicians are sensitive to what is being said, written, and posted about colleges and universities in the media, both in general and at the institutions they especially care about. As a result, both TRs emphasized the good and harm that media coverage of their universities can do.

REVELEY III: As president I fervently hoped and wanted the media to pay attention to William & Mary but only if they reported the facts accurately and stated their opinions fairly. We needed our story to be told. The *Virginia Gazette*, the hometown paper in Williamsburg, paid attention to W&M when I was president, but its staff came and went, without much understanding of higher education or us. Even media in cities like Richmond and Norfolk rarely have the funds any longer to hire reporters who specialize in higher education or to station a reporter or two in a small city like Williamsburg, as used to be the case. So to get fair attention to William & Mary, the context of the matter at hand, nuance, even the facts right side up—lots of luck.

On the other hand, if something happened on campus that looked salacious, or might be salacious, and thus interesting to a large audience, the media could descend like hungry dogs, coming from near and far. Once reporters had a taste for blood, it was hard to wean them off it. At times you had to deal with the media like they were vials of nitroglycerine prone to blow up at the slightest provocation. And when social media join in with newspapers, radio, and TV, the results can get really wild.

But, of course, the media are a fact of life, and they can be very helpful in explaining your school to the larger world and in testifying not just about its problems and failures but also about its glories and triumphs. As a rule, you're better off responding to reporters than trying to ignore them. And it's essential to try to anticipate when a media storm might be about to hit.

The university has to have experienced communications people. They know the demands and deadlines reporters face and which hounds of media occasionally cover the school. They know which reporters have difficulty getting even basic facts straight and need to be given them in writing as well as orally. They also know how to deal effectively with reporters who're smart, know something about higher education, and are careful with the facts, even when what they write or say isn't how you would have put it.

One of the main initiatives while I was president was what we called the "William & Mary Promise." It had many mutually supportive elements, all designed to strengthen the university's financial base. The most politically risky element, and its most vulnerable one in the media, was a sharp uptick in the tuition charged each new class of students from Virginia whose families could afford it, with substantially more financial aid for those who couldn't.[12] The Promise to students and their families was that tuition would then remain unchanged until they graduated four years later. We worked quietly to reach political and media leaders to explain the Promise and why it would be good for our students, the university, and the commonwealth. It was important not to surprise these leaders and to be sure they understood what we were about to do and why.

The moment of truth came one morning when the board of visitors, with reporters in the audience, voted to begin the Promise and significantly increase tuition for incoming Virginia freshman and then freeze it for their time on campus. Holding our breath, we waited for the first headline about what had just been done. It soon came over the internet: "William & Mary Holds Tuition Flat for Next Four Years." Not "William & Mary Goes Nuts with Tuition." The Promise got a whole lot of good, satisfying media attention far and wide.[13]

REVELEY IV: It took a similar effort to cultivate media buy-in when we announced that we were reopening the Longwood campus to students in the fall of 2020, at a time when deep uncertainty about COVID was still causing a lot of schools and universities to keep operating remotely. I think we were fairly successful in persuading the *Farmville Herald* and other state and local media that having students on campus was the right way to go because we could do contact tracing, quarantine those who needed to be quarantined, and then, as the months proceeded, do the community some real good by deploying our nursing education program to distribute the vaccine. (*See the prologue and chapter 7 for a fuller account.*)

I've also been open to being more of an ongoing presence in the media than my dad, who somewhat followed the approach of Bill Bowen in offering public comment only on issues that directly affected his institution.[14] I have felt a slightly broader ambit, in part because Jerry Baliles helped persuade me that it was important for college presidents to be in the public square on matters concerning not just Longwood and Farmville (which I've done my share of) but on broader matters relating to higher education. In fact, whether it's for the *Herald*, the *Richmond Times-Dispatch*, or national publications like the *Wall Street Journal* and *Time* magazine, I've probably written at least as many op-eds as any other college president in the state since I took office, about a couple a year on average, and there aren't too many higher ed leaders nationally who have done more.[15] It's allowed me to trumpet Farmville's important place in history, for example, as well as to make the case that living in a dorm with fellow students is one of the most real-life diverse experiences that people are ever likely to have.

I feel that in this moment of flux and even crisis in American higher education, it's important to give voice to the things that can make it thrive in the coming decades, especially concerning what I regard as the deepest purpose of higher education, which is to be a bulwark of democracy. It's complicated—this is a role you have to go about very carefully and very adroitly. The key is to do it in ways that are relevant but not partisan.

Town-Gown

Relations between campus and community are intrinsically both affectionate and antagonistic. On the one hand, the college or university provides employment for townspeople and customers for local businesses. On the other hand, tensions are bound to arise over mundane matters such as zoning and right of way and important matters such as tax exemptions and rowdy or merely unconventional student behavior. For presidents, the challenge is to accentuate the positive and diminish (if not eliminate) the negative.

REVELEY IV: Williamsburg is famously the colonial capital of Virginia and a major tourist destination because of all the wonderful efforts that have been made over the years to restore its original buildings. And as my dad often points out, William & Mary not only overlaps with the restored colonial area but can make its own claim to being the nation's oldest university, Harvard being less ranging in its scope in the early days.

Farmville's claims to fame are different but also impressive, and I've made a concerted effort to highlight them. Some caveats aside, it has the claim to being the oldest two-college town in all of America, and with some local encouragement the General Assembly passed a resolution celebrating that. And even though in the 1950s Farmville shamefully reacted to the Supreme Court's *Brown* decision by closing its public schools for several years, on the positive side of the ledger it was the site of the first student protest that helped to set that groundbreaking case in motion. The cooperative relationship we've forged between Longwood and the Moton Museum has really helped the town embrace the inspiring aspects of that chapter in its history.

REVELEY III: William & Mary sits cheek by jowl with Colonial Williamsburg, and the university's ties to the CW Foundation have always been strong. The campus also abuts, or is very near to, a number of single-family residential neighborhoods. Absentee landlords began buying houses in these neighborhoods and renting them to students, some of whose nocturnal and partying habits jarred the sensitivities of their neighbors. Beer cans and trash in the yards didn't help.

At my urging, the city and the university made a real effort to make peace. We created a Neighborhood Relations Committee to pursue it. We leaned on carousing students to clean up their act. We urged them to introduce themselves to their neighbors and let them know when a party was planned. My message to the students was, "If you want to live in a neighborhood, you've got to be a good neighbor. Otherwise, find a habitat not in a residential neighborhood." The city was less helpful than I'd expected, mostly because its capacity to lean on absentee landlords renting to unruly kids proved to be discouragingly modest. This was a town-gown issue of continuing moment, but not because we disagreed about what should happen.

REVELEY IV: The William & Mary campus itself is both beautiful and wonderfully open to the town. When we developed a master plan for Longwood, we really embraced the New Urbanism philosophy of doing things on a walkable scale and making the campus and the town porous to one another. For instance, we redesigned our two high-rise dorms to make them feel like an entryway into campus that invites people walking along Main Street to come in, as opposed to their previous incarnation, in which they were literally walled off from the town. I've worked constantly to reinforce and strengthen the connection between Longwood and Farmville, which had somehow become rivalrous and antagonistic over time. So that, for example, the relationship between our campus police force and local law enforcement has been harmonious instead of full of tension, which it sometimes is in the higher ed world. With regard to all this, it was wonderful when after two centuries of Hampden-Sydney alums being mayors of Farmville, a Longwood alum, David Whitus, was elected soon after I began.

TR4 was hailed as "a champion of New Urbanism" in a 2023 issue of *Traditional Building*. "New Urbanism," he said, "in some ways is simply elaboration on common sense—it's good to be able to walk around, meet people, enjoy public spaces and the bustle. I grew up in a great neighborhood in Richmond, the Fan, which sprang up in the early twentieth century. Knowing from experience that great neighborhoods, built not that long ago, exist and can work, I've been a longtime advocate."[16]

REVELEY III: Like Taylor, during my presidency we worked hard to have close, cordial, productive relations with the City of Williamsburg. The mayor, city manager, one or two members of my cabinet, and I met monthly to talk through pending and anticipated issues. This made for good will, avoided surprises and misunderstandings, and provided easy means of engaging difficult issues. It helped, for instance, in 2013 when William & Mary bought the Hospitality House, a hotel directly across from the campus, and in 2016 bought the Days Inn motel a few blocks away.[17] This took both of them off the city's tax rolls. As a public institution, the university didn't have to make a payment in lieu of taxes to the city, but we agreed to begin a small one to soothe the city's angst at losing two tax-paying businesses.

6
Reforming the Curriculum

During the half century that spanned TR2 becoming president of Hampden-Sydney in 1963, TR3 becoming president of William & Mary in 2008, and TR4 becoming president of Longwood in 2013, the nature of the undergraduate general education curriculum—the course of study required of all students—was an ongoing topic of conversation and controversy in American higher education.[1] Sometimes thought of (by faculty) as a purely faculty matter, curriculum is of intrinsic presidential concern as well because it "puts its stamp on your students and its intellectual effects are carried into the world by your graduates."[2] Each of the Reveley presidents began his administration with curriculum reform in mind, in part because the "gen ed" requirements at his institution had become stale with the passage of time and in part because each had strong ideas about what sort of curriculum would be better.

The curricula the Reveley presidents inherited at the outset of their administrations were each problematic in their own ways. Hampden-Sydney required every undergraduate to study ancient Greek or Latin, a legacy of the standard college curriculum during prior centuries that by 1963 was found at few institutions. Unlike truly classically based institutions such as St. John's College, however, Hampden-Sydney no longer had a coherent, four-year curriculum built on that classical linguistic foundation. As for William & Mary and Longwood, each had a roughly two-decade-old set of distribution requirements that, however much sense they may have made at the time of their adoption, had devolved into a sort of "one from column A, one from column B"–style menu of mandated choices that served the enrollment interests of the institution's academic departments without embodying anything resembling a coherent educational philosophy. Students commonly characterized these requirements as obstacles to remove from their path toward their major, as courses to "get out of the way."

141

Reveley IV: Several questions keep reemerging every three or four generations: What do we teach? How do we teach it? And how do we pay for it? For all the continuity that exists in American higher education, there have been strikingly different answers to these questions at different times. And without any doubt we're in the midst of one of those periods right now where the questions are once again very much alive and very much contested.

Essentially what we saw from the earliest days of American higher education through to the Civil War was the traditional classical curriculum—the Latin and Greek curriculum. And then it became contested and moved in lots of different directions, including ample room for choosing electives, before recentering on the liberal arts as the basic tie that binds in the wake of World War II. That's the period that set the basic framework that endured until recent years, and, like any framework, it also began to fray eventually.

Broadly speaking, the answer that emerged from the post–World War II era to the question of what to teach was: a liberal arts–based general education curriculum combined with a somewhat vocational focus in a major. How to teach became fairly settled too: a residential campus with in-person instruction, including the sort of 150-person-style large lecture course that was less typical of how American higher education had been transacted before. As for how to pay for it, until twenty or thirty years ago it was widely assumed that the government, federal and especially state, would provide the money in great measure, directly to public institutions and indirectly to private ones through grants and student aid of various kinds.

Now all three of those questions feel like they're being raised again at full tilt. Online education is becoming a more prevalent way of teaching. Government funding of colleges and universities has been shrinking. And the liberal arts gen ed curriculum has lost its moorings. It feels like a check-the-box operation that doesn't have any philosophical coherence.

Democracy—preparing students to become citizen leaders—strikes me as the North Star that should guide us out of this confusion. Along those lines, a body of work that doesn't get as much attention as it should these days is the report of the Truman Commission, which President Harry Truman set in motion after the crisis of democracy posed by World War II.[3] Its purpose was to examine all the ways that American higher education ought to buttress democracy. It was a fairly high-profile endeavor in its day. American government at the highest level was committing itself to the proposition that the liberal arts were vital for the nation's future. And then in 1957 the Soviets launched *Sputnik* into space, and the focus shifted to emphasizing the hard sciences and workforce preparation—the so-called "things that really matter."

Liberal arts came to be seen as a kind of frolic. And deservedly so, to some extent. They lost their focus on preparation for citizenship and democracy and became refocused on self-actualization. You now were encouraged to read great works of literature, study history, ponder philosophy not to gain a sense of perspective on life together in a democracy but to achieve an elusive sense of self-fulfillment. That doesn't do much for democracy, and over time it lost its purchase on the marketplace too, as underscored by the collapse in the number of humanities majors across the country.

TR2 and Hampden-Sydney

TR2 came to Hampden-Sydney from Rhodes College. His experience teaching in Rhodes's twelve-credit Search course (initially called Man in the Light of History and Religion), an innovative multidisciplinary humanities program, was one he wanted to share with Hampden-Sydney students. Like the Truman Commission, the Search course was in large measure a response to World War II and the issues it raised about how securely rooted democracy was in the Western world.[4] TR2 was not alone in his desire to bring Rhodes's wide-ranging approach to general education to other colleges. In 1961, two years before TR2 became president of Hampden-Sydney, Davidson College hired one of his closest friends and colleagues on the Rhodes faculty, Dan Rhodes, to introduce Search to Davidson. Other southern colleges followed suit with their own variations on Search, including Sewanee, Eckerd, Millsaps, and Hendrix.[5]

Hampden-Sydney's curriculum was a hodge-podge when TR2 arrived ahead of the fall 1963 semester. On the one hand, it required proficiency in an ancient language of all students, a carryover from the pre–Civil War era of American higher education that nearly all colleges and universities had long since abandoned. On the other hand, it did not include sociology or political science, the latter omission a major turnoff to TR3 when he was deciding where to go to college. Instead, the remainder of the curriculum was an accretion of requirements and electives that reflected what the small existing faculty was capable of teaching, and was substantially unrelated to Greek or Latin.

REVELEY III: Just random. Little or no coherence. The worst of both worlds, in a sense. But some of the old guard, in particular, were deeply disturbed by the prospect that Greek and Latin would be given short shrift.

As a way of laying the groundwork for what he wanted to do at Hampden-Sydney, TR2 invited his mentor, President Peyton Nalle Rhodes (after whom the college was later renamed from Southwestern), to give the main address at his inauguration as president in April 1964. At this point, TR2 hoped the college would launch not just its own version of the Search course but a similar multidisciplinary course in the natural sciences.

PEYTON NALLE RHODES, LETTER TO TR2, FEBRUARY 19, 1964: Please look the [enclosed draft of my address] over. . . . Does it dovetail fairly well with what you anticipate?

TR2, LETTER TO RHODES, FEBRUARY 22, 1964: It states precisely the point which seems to me to need emphasis; namely, that the liberal arts demand both the humanities and the natural sciences.

REVELEY III: Daddy's challenge was to rally the faculty's Young Turks who were restless for change and eager to help shape it, and then to get on with deciding exactly what to do. And to do so without alienating the older, long-serving professors who had sustained the college over the years, many of whom were the salt of the earth. The overall size of the faculty increased during TR2's first few years as president, while the ranks of those who were Hampden-Sydney alumni and generally inclined to preserve the old ways went down. These trends continued during his fourteen years in office.[6] He launched a college-wide self-study soon after he got to campus. As he hoped and expected, it recommended a core curriculum of multidisciplinary courses to replace some of the traditional departmental courses.

The faculty committee charged with developing a new sequence of multidisciplinary general education courses in the natural sciences was not able to come up with a proposal. But with the Search model in mind, along with TR2's experience teaching in the course at Rhodes, the humanities committee was more successful. In 1965 the faculty approved the committee's recommendation for a new Western Man program, a four-course sequence (two of them double courses) that was required of all freshmen and sophomores. The program replaced departmental courses in religion, philosophy, English, and history.

As in Search, the idea was to weave all four disciplines into all four semesters, with a strong emphasis on primary texts rather than textbooks. "We looked at the programs at Southwestern [Rhodes] and Davidson," recalled Hampden-Sydney classicist John Brinkley, "but it was the Southwestern syllabus that had the most influence on our program."[7] In 1968 the faculty also voted to replace the ancient languages requirement with a broader foreign language requirement. Brinkley, who taught Greek and Latin, was bitterly disappointed.

JOHN BRINKLEY: Worse, a full-page advertisement (prepared in February 1968) that touted the distinctiveness of Hampden-Sydney's ancient language requirement—"You mean I have to take GREEK?"—appeared in the 17 May 1968 issue of *Time* magazine.[8]

The reformed curriculum did continue to require Bible-related courses of all students, which reflected TR2's commitment as a Presbyterian minister leading a Presbyterian college.

REVELEY III: Daddy was a child of faith, with earnest veneration for the Good News. He also was moved by the fact that Presbyterians had created Hampden-Sydney to provide an academically rigorous undergraduate education on a campus where being a Christian was perfectly acceptable—the norm through the eras and decades—and where students had a chance to think seriously about the possibility of faith. This required knowing something about the Bible in the tradition of mainline Protestant thought, not fundamentalist dogma, and knowing something about the history of Christianity. It also meant an opportunity to learn about other religions.

In general, he wanted Hampden-Sydney to keep its ties to the Presbyterian Church. But he returned to Hampden-Sydney when such ties were falling from favor, or had long since fallen, at great universities with strong Christian origins such as Harvard, Yale, and Princeton. Daddy was anachronistic when it came to church ties. He was Hampden-Sydney's last president to be a Presbyterian minister or any kind of clergy, at least to date.

TR3 and William & Mary

As was the case at Hampden-Sydney, when TR3 became president of William & Mary in 2008, the curriculum needed renovation. General education was grounded in distribution requirements for a specified number of courses in the social sciences, humanities, natural sciences, foreign languages, and so on—nearly all of them offered by individual departments.

REVELEY III: As soon as I became interim president, I began pushing for a fresh look at our undergraduate general education curriculum. It had been in place for twenty years and grown long in the tooth. Though perhaps innovative when created, it no longer effectively grounded undergraduates in the liberal arts. While some departments enjoyed being fed students by these distribution requirements, this wasn't a good enough reason to let it keep limping along, though it was the basis for opposition to change.

Worse, our undergraduates had long since learned how to game the system. Kids with the academic chops to get into William & Mary usually arrived with strong AP (Advanced Placement) or IB (International Baccalaureate) credentials.[9] They had taken AP courses in high school, often many of them, and gotten top marks. One of the first things they did on reaching W&M was figure out how they could use their AP credits to satisfy our general education requirements. Some freshmen were able to avoid all of them. The others finished the few college courses they had to take as quickly as possible. Then they began specializing in the disciplines that became their majors or minors, often majors and minors.

By no stretch of the imagination were AP courses in high school comparable to those taught in the flesh by William & Mary professors to classes of smart, high-achieving undergraduates. Something had to be done.

Our provost, Michael Halleran, and I, with a strong faculty cohort, wanted general education elements in all four years of an undergrad's education. We did not want to allow AP or IB credits to satisfy any of the gen ed requirements. There needed to be more emphasis—effective emphasis—on learning to think and write, plus an obligatory international component, whether abroad or, failing that, on campus. For each senior, not just honors students, there should be a project pulling together, to the extent feasible, their academic experiences on campus. And we wanted to organize families of disciplines, with each family developing cross-disciplinary courses or seminars for underclass students.

As this rich mix of desiderata evolved over countless departmental and faculty meetings, discussions in offices and halls, and step-by-step votes—sometimes two steps forward, one step back—much time passed. I was appalled by how long it was taking and how close the faculty votes often were. Michael, our provost, soothed me: "That's just the way these things go. This is moving along at its own pace. We'll get the votes when we need them." He was deeply immersed in the process, along with a core of devoted faculty colleagues.

On December 12, 2013, the faculty approved the new College Curriculum—dubbed COLL—by a clear but narrow majority: 101 to 83.[10] All students were required to take one of a number of COLL 100 classes their freshman year followed by COLL 200 sophomore courses and COLL 300 junior courses, culminating in COLL 400, a senior project. All were designed to be interdisciplinary, with an emphasis on reasoning, problem solving, globalism, writing, and other forms of communication. The curriculum launched in the fall semester of 2015 for students in the class of 2019.

REVELEY III: I was determined that the process succeed and protected its flanks from any off-campus challenge. A group of alumni became concerned about what they were hearing from campus sources unhappy with how the new curriculum was taking shape. These alums argued we were going to dumb down our cherished academic rigor, that no longer having a specific requirement that a course be taken in the English Department or that a stand-alone writing requirement be met, would do great damage. They feared William & Mary, a traditional bastion of demanding instruction in hard-core liberal arts, was going soft, trendy, squishy, left-wing. They wanted a chance to deliberate with the faculty, a seat at the table. Using social media, they rallied others to their cause and created concern on the board of visitors about what was afoot. I spent time explaining, rebutting, soothing, and pointing out that, in the end, the curriculum was the province of the faculty.

Significant curricular change in a school is a matter of passion. I think most faculty members in arts and sciences understood our general education regime needed to change. But what this change should be was another matter. Each department scrutinized every twist and turn in the debate to see how it might affect them. Small departments in particular worried about losing students.

Woodrow Wilson was president of Princeton during a crucial effort to reform an ossified undergraduate curriculum, and at one point of frustration, he famously exclaimed: "You never know how many friends the dead have until you try to move a cemetery." Right!

We got there. To breathe life into the new curriculum was going to take many faculty members doing many new things. We created a center expressly designed to support faculty as they innovated. The Mellon Foundation gave us a large grant to help get the center up and running. They believed our new general education curriculum was so inventive, with such potential, that they urged other liberal arts schools to take a look at it and learn.[11]

The Mellon Foundation also gave William & Mary a significant grant late in my presidency to help us deal with the need for more focused education in leadership, particularly servant leadership. Thomas Jefferson and George Wythe had created legal training at William & Mary in the late eighteenth century expressly to educate lawyers to work for the greater good, especially in politics. This became the concept of the "citizen lawyer," which I stressed and taught while dean of the W&M Law School.[12] The need for the university to grow its strong commitment to service and citizenship was among the emphases of my final years as president. I became particularly involved with the idea of an expected, though not obligatory, year of service for young people at some point between age eighteen and twenty-eight.

TR4 and Longwood

Like his grandfather and father, TR4's interest in curriculum reform ran deep by the time he became president of Longwood. Unlike them, he benefited from an extended search and transition process prior to taking office.

REVELEY IV: I started at Longwood in 2013, fifty years almost to the month after TR2 started at Hampden-Sydney, but in my case with some lead time that neither he nor my father had before taking office. Curriculum reform was an idea right there in my mind even during the search process. It helped that Longwood's gen ed curriculum—the course of study outside one's major—was about fifteen years old, which in recent generations has been about the life cycle of a curriculum before it gets reformed. People at Longwood were already beginning to think about this.

Apart from the felicity of timing, curriculum had been a real interest of mine throughout the arc of my own education and career, in part because it's been a focus of interest for the Reveleys through the generations, including at Longwood when my grandmother and her sisters were students there, and their mom before them and their dad as a professor.[13] And what I knew about Longwood was that before its momentum was disrupted by its resistance and Farmville's resistance to school integration in the 1950s, it was widely considered to be one of the twenty best women's colleges in the country. The liberal arts were at the core of that standing. Longwood obviously isn't a women's college anymore, but I wanted to recapture that emphasis on the liberal arts.

Any curriculum is highly guarded turf on a college campus, and departments and individual faculty members feel very protective of their own pieces of that turf. But over time a curriculum loses coherence and, for students, comes to feel like a sequence of hurdles they need to clear that doesn't make a whole lot of sense. So when I sat down with Ken Perkins, our provost, Lara Smith, Ken's eventual successor, and Justin Pope, my chief of staff, during the summer of 2013, Lara's very wise view was, "We're in this for the long haul. Let's take our time and do it right." I would help set the basic parameters and secure board support for those parameters, but the faculty needed to be and feel deeply involved in the process.

The most fundamental parameter we set was that democracy itself should be the gen ed curriculum's North Star, a phrase we kept using. The board felt good about this, and an adroitly constituted faculty committee, meeting weekly, really worked at it for three years, from 2013 through the fall of 2016. As I learned in a very different context during my experience at the Miller Center with the National War Powers Commission, if you bring together people from across the waterfront, people who have some actual sway, then the group really does have the ability to get something done and the stature to go forth afterward and make a case to those with whom they are in good standing.

I also benefited from my father's recent experience at William & Mary, which enlivened my mind to the pitfalls and complexities and politics that would be involved in any curriculum reform that was worth doing. I understood, just from our shop talk with one another, that it would not by any stretch be a straightforward process. It would require some real attention and political sensitivity throughout.

Allowing the process to unfold over a stately period of years rather than an accelerated period of months worked well. It helped foster a broader spirit of cooperation and buy-in across the faculty than we otherwise might have gotten. Of course, as we got closer to the finish line, it naturally became clear that some oxen would be gored, which produced anxiety in various departments. But because of the care and deliberateness of the committee, the resistance wasn't angry or even particularly dramatic.

The basic idea—again, the North Star—was to focus on democracy across the whole body of the curriculum. Which is to say that rather than just Biology 101, it would be Biology 101 with a flavor of the public policy challenges related to biology. A Shakespeare class on *Othello* would include attention to the responsibilities of citizenship and the pitfalls of power in the twenty-first century. And so on.

The name of the curriculum—Civitae, pronounced Civi-tay'—came to mind on campus near the end of the process. I had long felt and advocated that giving it a name would foster a sense of vibrancy and specificity as opposed to something that had a bureaucratic air to it like "general education curriculum." Civitae, a late Latin word, basically means "things relating to citizenship," and just hearing the word kind of conjures that meaning so that students are reminded constantly throughout their years in college that they are preparing to become citizens.

Civitae was approved by the faculty and then the board in 2016 and launched in 2018. Almost all faculty at Longwood are engaged with Civitae in one way or another. The chemistry professor is regularly talking with the English professor about how to help students find natural connections between their subjects. And we encourage professors to actually teach some of their courses together if they see a way to do that. The progression culminates in what we call Symposium, a senior-level course which requires focused work by students on a particular set of public policy considerations. And once each semester we hold a Symposium Day at which all the seniors who are taking Symposium at that time come together for a sequence of discussions about the basic ambit of the coursework they've been doing. It can really harmonize across campus when students in different majors see that they are looking at similar issues but through different lenses.[14]

One other virtue of calling the program Civitae is that it hits the ear and eye as something unique and specific to Longwood, which it is. In higher ed writ large, attention to civic involvement often drifts toward volunteerism, so that being a good citizen is equated with, say, helping build a house for Habitat for Humanity. It certainly is that, but it's not only that. The thrust of Civitae is to encourage students to engage in public affairs while they're in school and forever after, whether that comes in the form of actual government service or just being a very engaged citizen who is thoughtful about the issues and involved in the political process.

The vice presidential debate in October 2016 became a source of real momentum for Civitae just around the time the faculty and board were voting to adopt it. It was an occasion to pilot some courses of a kind we hoped would be part of the new curriculum. And because we didn't have Donald Trump and Hillary Clinton here, but instead had Governor Mike Pence and Senator Tim Kaine, two mainstream figures in American politics, we could treat it as a celebration of democracy—perhaps the last such moment of its kind since then. Then, after Civitae launched in full cry in 2018, it wasn't long before we were dealing with the challenges of COVID. So it wasn't as if we were trying to get students to think about democracy and citizenship at a time when these were dry and hoary concepts. Instead they were visceral and real.

One of our hopes is that Civitae will serve as a beacon to other institutions, just as the Search course at Rhodes was to Hampden-Sydney and Davidson and elsewhere. Consequential national organizations and leaders in higher ed have taken a real interest in it, including the Teagle Foundation.[15]

Computers, Online Education, and AI

All three Reveley presidents led institutions that place a premium on in-person, residential education. In recent years online teaching has become technologically feasible and, at least during the COVID shutdowns that began in March 2020, necessary as a practical matter. TR2 brought the use of computers to Hampden-Sydney in 1967, and the pace of change has accelerated ever since.

Reveley II, President's Report to the Trustees, August 2, 1967: The enthusiasm with which faculty members on campus received the news from the Executive Committee of the Board that it would be possible to secure a computer almost overshadowed that of the NSF [National Science Foundation] grant! This is a significant step for all the sciences. At this point our plan is to use the computer for educational purposes. As time goes on we shall probably be able to employ it also to help in administrative functions.

Reveley II, speech, January 1972: [An] Orwellian glimpse into the future probably does more to frighten contemporary academicians with the specter of blinking, whirling, giant-sized computers gradually engulfing the campus than it does to document the educational validity of computer techniques. Perhaps the most important aspect of the irrational fears aroused by the computer on campus is the witness of those fears to the tremendous importance of this new instrument of modern technology.

Reveley III: Several decades later, there was a moment while I was president when it became highly fashionable among universities to have a MOOC (Massive Online Open Course), or, even better, a herd of MOOCs, lest you be left behind in the scramble for relevance and cost-effectiveness. So we sought to create one about the American Revolution in conjunction with Colonial Williamsburg and took serious steps toward it. But before we reached Valhalla, the fever broke, and MOOCs lost their glitter.

Undeterred, our interest in thoughtful online education in general remained strong. The Mason School of Business was the pathfinder at William & Mary. It did a great job of launching an online MBA and an online master's in data analysis. I became convinced online education had real potential for us in certain spheres, and urged our various schools and programs to explore its possibilities. I can't imagine it ever replacing in-person instruction for those students who value the campus experience and live professors, but I can see it reaching countless other students who want William & Mary caliber-teaching but can't spend time in residence for any of a host of reasons. There's nothing simple, or cheap, about cracking the online egg, however. It takes significant resources and expert guidance.

REVELEY IV: There are certainly all sorts of useful online endeavors at Longwood on the graduate student side. And we did plenty of that for undergraduates during COVID. But we've honestly tried to roll those back so that we're squarely focused on the in-person undergraduate experience.

Obviously, the question of online education is going to hang over higher education for generations to come because of its convenience and lower cost. But at a time when people are becoming more and more tribal in where they live and vote and go to church and so on—more isolated from people who are not like themselves—the residential campus is more important than ever. And that's true not just of the face-to-face learning that takes place in classrooms. It's true too of the experience students have living in dorms, which almost certainly is the most genuinely diverse experience they've ever had in their young lives and may be the most experience with real-life diversity they'll ever have. For whatever number of years they live cheek by jowl with roommates and hallmates and everyone else in their dorm, they have to learn how to coexist and even thrive through daily interactions with people who are not like themselves. So as important as Civitae is for fostering democratic engagement, dorm life may be just as important.

LONGWOOD BOARD OF VISITORS BRIEFING MATERIALS, MARCH 2023: At the end of the spring semester, Longwood had its first known artificial intelligence (AI) academic integrity violations; to date, five students have been charged with alleged violations involving AI.

REVELEY IV: How will learning work as the AI revolution gains momentum? My kids have grown up with a helpful robot in the kitchen to answer questions, Amazon's Alexa, well before they could read or write. And Marlo has spent her career focused on the cutting edge of technology and now AI. I don't know the answer with clairvoyance, but I think some old verities will hold. People will crave being around each other and learning from each other in a personal way. The habits of democracy will still require attentive development. And torrents of information and misinformation will require that much more wisdom and discernment.

7
Enhancing the Student Experience

As discussed in chapters 4 and 5, presidential leadership in higher education affects (and is affected by) multiple constituencies, including trustees, faculty, the media, government officials, and others. But none is more important than the students whom colleges and universities are charged to educate. This is especially true of residential liberal arts colleges like Hampden-Sydney and residential liberal arts universities like William & Mary and Longwood. Curriculum, the subject of chapter 6, is an important part of that education, but not the only important part.

The range of student-related issues with which a president must deal is so vast that no book chapter can treat them all with the thoroughness they deserve. The approach in this chapter is to take deep dives into two such issues—athletics, a matter of ongoing challenge and consequence, and the COVID pandemic, a crisis of transcendent importance for as long as it lasted—and then offer a sample of other student-related issues, more to illustrate their variety than with any pretense of treating them comprehensively.

Athletics

Uniquely in the world of higher education, athletics are a prominent feature of American colleges and universities. In varying degrees, all three Reveley presidents were student athletes in college and believed they benefited from the experience. They carried that belief with them into the institutions they led. In TR4's case, he also carried it into leadership positions in the wider college athletics community, including chair of the Big South Conference and member of the NCAA's Division I board.

REVELEY IV: My dad rowed crew for Princeton for two years and I played football when I was there. But my grandfather was clearly the leading student athlete among the three generations: a Hall of Famer at Hampden-Sydney who, among other things, threw a no-hitter for his sequence of great baseball teams. His success in sports, enjoyment of sports, was an ambient part of my upbringing. So it always felt natural to me to be involved in sports, and to think of sports as part of the fabric of college life. That was probably true for both my father and me.

REVELEY III: Yes, it was. Daddy played three sports in college. As soon as he finished one, he'd start the next one. He was unusually good at baseball and basketball, not unusually good at football, but he played it. He coached football and baseball when he was teaching at Rhodes, and continued to play a lot of basketball and handball. Sports and physical activity mattered enormously to him. I always liked that about him, and while playing all these sports he did other things, like being class president and then student body president. When I finally did something in organized athletics myself, rowing on Princeton's lightweight crew for two years, he was pleased, though we didn't talk much about it and he was never able to see me race. Crew pushed me to my physical limits, but I got real satisfaction from it and learned a good bit about how teams do their thing.

Working with coauthor James Shulman, Bill Bowen, friend of TR3 and well known to TR4, published a widely discussed book in 2002 called *The Game of Life: College Sports and Educational Values*. In it Shulman and Bowen argued that, on balance, college sports were more in conflict than consistent with educational values, not just in large state universities, such as the University of Alabama and the University of Kansas, but also in the elite New England liberal arts colleges and Ivy League universities on which their study focused.[1]

Part of their argument was that student athletes no longer have the time to do the range of things that TR2 did in the 1930s: play three sports and be involved in student government or other campus activities. But their main critique was that the athletes were not as strong academically as their fellow students and took little advantage of the rich intellectual and cultural opportunities their schools laid before them. Bowen himself was an athlete, a champion tennis player in high school and college who played long thereafter and enjoyed watching athletic contests.

Reveley IV: As he was for my dad, Bill Bowen was a model for me in many things. For example, when he was president of Princeton, he taught Econ 101 as a way of staying in touch with a wider range of students than those who actively demanded his attention on behalf of one cause or another.[2] I also taught a course each year with Longwood professor Bill Harbour on the American presidency until he retired.

But on one matter I probably disagree with the great Bowen and, for that matter, with any number of voices that over the decades of American higher education have thought college athletics is an alien endeavor and the educational enterprise would be purer and better if it was not tainted by intercollegiate sports. To me, to all three of us, the parallel question to "What are these athletes like as students?" would be "What are they like as forty-year-olds"? Because the academic record is not the pure barometer of what someone has gained from their college experience.

Reveley III: It's certainly not the sole barometer. No question you can learn a whole lot about how to live successfully for the rest of your life from being on a team and competing in intercollege athletics. But Bill regretted, and I do too, that being an athlete these days takes so much time and energy that there's little left except to eat, sleep, and meet basic academic demands. Three-sport athletes like Daddy are scarce as hen's teeth these days, and it's hard to find even one-sport athletes who're able to take part in a broad range of campus life. Being on a team, in season and out, has become more all-consuming than it used to be, even in small liberal arts colleges.

Reveley IV: Fair enough. But weighed in the balance, I think the gains from participating in college athletics more than compensate for the losses: the mental toughness to persist, the spirit of teamwork, the deep understanding of how mind and body are connected, and so on.

And if you play a sport in front of crowds, you learn another skill that's pretty hard to learn otherwise: how to perform well when lots of eyes are trained on you.

Reveley III: Well, the gains from participating in college athletics may more than compensate for the losses for many athletes, but not for those who never graduate, or who learn little or nothing from their classes, or who make no friends off the team, or who leave campus with no sense that their school cares about them apart from what they do on the playing field.

Still, it was certainly my experience at William & Mary that alumni who had been Tribe athletes, compared to the alumni body as a whole, were unusually prone to help sustain the university. They led, they gave, they brought to bear what they learned about friendship, loyalty, and teamwork while on their teams. Often, too, they had the means to give significantly because they had gone into business or finance and thrived.

REVELEY IV: One thing I can convey to the student athletes at Longwood is that I really, in my bones, understand the pressures and rhythms of their lives. I actually know what it's like to be bone-tired and a little beaten up and try to work your way through a hard class the next day. And I can convey to professors who may feel frustrated that the jocks in their class seem inattentive that it's not for want of willpower or interest, it's just that what they're doing is really hard.[3]

The scale of Longwood helps with this, because athletes make up a fairly significant share of the student body. They're not a breed apart from the rest of the campus and, as professors have learned from experience, they include many of our best students. It helps that all of the schools in our conference—the Big South—are in either Virginia or the Carolinas, which has all sorts of bearing on how much class time team members miss from traveling to away games. They're a bus ride away rather than a complicated set of connecting flights.

The Supreme Court's decision in 2021 authorizing student athletes to benefit financially from allowing others to use their names, images, and likenesses—the NIL decision—created a good bit of alarm in higher ed circles, not unlike the kerfuffle a few decades ago when professional athletes were allowed to compete in what had previously been the all-amateur Olympics.[4] Plenty of people worried then that this would be the end of the Olympics. It obviously wasn't.

I think the same will become apparent once the NIL regime is digested. A few hundred college basketball and football players may well command consequential amounts of money, but that won't be the case for the vast majority of the 100,000 or so Division I athletes, let alone the 400,000 college athletes in Division II and Division III. At schools like Longwood and William & Mary, a player might get a kind of in-house deal with a local barbecue joint to appear in some print or online ad in return for free food, but it's not as though all of our basketball players, let alone cross-country runners, are somehow going to be getting hundreds of thousands of dollars on the open market.[5]

All that said, the NCAA is under increasing duress, with legions of detractors and grifters pushing it into extremis. What too few people keep in mind is that in a very organic, Tocquevillian way the NCAA since its founding over a century ago has come to serve as the tie that binds for most of higher ed—the 1,200 institutions across America where parents drop off their kids as freshmen and come back a few years later to celebrate them as seniors walking the stage. Remarkably, there's no other organization or association of any kind that mainstream colleges and universities as a set belong to. The U.S. Department of Education, by contrast, deals with all 6,000 "institutes of higher education," in its parlance. The regional accreditors each have a slice of that 6,000 under their purview, and other associations all have their subsets and swaths.

The staying power of the NCAA is important well beyond athletics. It was reactive, permissive, and—honestly—greedy for decades. I hope it can begin to act with genuine foresight, and enlist Congress ultimately to help craft a durable framework for the future.[6] Longwood has been lucky to have a good duo navigating all this—our savvy finance VP, Matt McGregor, and our athletic director, Tim Hall, who has decades of experience and a deep network across all of Division I. The NCAA was born in a difficult moment for college sports—at the turn of the twentieth century, when football needed far better safety measures—and I am actually hopeful that it will keep navigating forward. History often counsels optimism.

REVELEY III: The pressure on the NCAA was already growing when I began as president in 2008. The pressure is immense now. Many across the academy view it very warily.

REVELEY IV: I'm one of only ten, maybe fewer, presidents of Division I schools who were DI athletes themselves. There are very few people in the presidential hot seat who really understand athletics, and that produces the temptation to sort of outsource the big decisions and let the athletic department run itself. It also means that a lot of the pressures on student athletes are a bit alien to the typical university president, and that these presidents may not be as alive as they could be to the powerful virtues of college sports for their institutions.

One of those virtues is that there's nothing like sports to promote esprit de corps and excitement among alumni. We saw that at Longwood with March Madness when our men's and women's basketball teams made it into the NCAA tournament in 2022 and the men repeated in 2024. Another virtue is that sports connects what is in its nature an elitist enterprise, academia, with a tumultuous populist democracy. Basketball and football especially are primary pulls in this regard for people all across a state or region, whatever their educational background. Supporting the teams enables them to feel a strong bond with the campus, which might otherwise seem far apart from them. That's unique to American higher education, and I think it's an altogether good thing.

As a former DI athlete, I also have a feel for the excitement that college sports can generate among the other students on a campus. Basketball has certainly done that for Longwood, especially with the great momentum under Griff Aldrich, our men's coach, who has garnered a national spotlight. If you've got a really compelling basketball program, men's and women's, then you've got at least a couple dozen home games a year that get students excited and also bring alumni and townspeople onto your campus. We made a point of building our new arena—the Joan Perry Brock Center, the JPB—right in the heart of things. It's adjacent to our two freshman dorms and readily accessible to downtown Farmville.

REVELEY III: Football, in particular, provides a special rhythm and excitement to the campus. Football games are occasions for communal gatherings and feedings, for cheering and celebrating when the team triumphs, for collective gnashing of teeth when it doesn't. Football afternoons and evenings have a pageantry about them that's equaled only by the rites of commencement.

REVELEY IV: Our alma mater, Princeton, despite all its football glory and tradition over the years, has begun to let that wane. Once the old habits atrophy, it's hard to build them back. A similar issue hovers for schools that don't play football. As Justin Pope often wisely notes, it's easier to have a football team than to start one or restore a program and all its trappings to full cry.[7]

College athletics is more than just the teams on the field or the court. It involves a whole range of related matters with which presidents must deal. As two examples, TR3 described the choosing of a new mascot for William & Mary and TR4 discussed the demise of the university golf course at Longwood.

REVELEY III: Coming up with an acceptable, successful mascot for W&M was a trackless wild when I became president. Native American students figured prominently in William & Mary's early life in the 1700s.[8] Much later, when schools began having mascots, W&M picked "Indians," called itself the Tribe, and had an undergraduate dressed as an Indian riding a pony around the football stadium as its mascot.

Feathers figured in the mix. William & Mary phased out the rider in the late 1970s but kept two feathers as our mascot, plus an unloved entity called Colonel Ebirt (Tribe spelled backward). The colonel was a shapeless green blob wearing a tricorner hat. He had no fan base. After a while, the NCAA proscribed Indian feathers. I've often wondered what the NCAA would have done if W&M had said, okay, our feathers are actually quill pens like the ones our alumnus Thomas Jefferson used to write the Declaration of Independence.

I insisted we make another run at coming up with a mascot that would be a unifying, morale-boosting, fun presence in the university's life. There was serious concern, especially among athletic administrators, that another attempt at mascot-making would be divisive and feckless, a mission impossible. It proved to be the opposite. Led by our highly respected athletic director, Terry Driscoll, the search was a howling success. None of the five finalists swept the field.[9] Driscoll and the selection committee then said it was my presidential duty to break the deadlock and pick the winner. Lucky me, I thought.

The new mascot—the Griffin—was introduced to the campus during a mass gathering in the basketball arena. In a video made for the announcement I picked up the phone on my desk and shouted, "Get me the Griffin!" As soon as the winner began weaving and dancing down a long flight of steps onto the arena floor, cheers broke out. Hallelujah!

My pick, like all griffins, was an eagle on top, a lion on the bottom. The lion evoked William & Mary's creation by English monarchs and our strong ties to England through most of the 1700s, and the eagle recalled the powerful role of our alumni in the country's revolutionary and founding eras. From time immemorial, griffins have guarded precious treasure, and what's more precious than William & Mary? It all made sense once you got the concept. But I had to spend a good amount of time explaining our Griffin to alumni.

The Griffin was a hit on campus. We bought a couple of first-rate griffin suits. The undergrad who was our inaugural Griffin had all the right moves. He was athletic and had experience as a cow in a Chick-fil-A commercial or some sort of commercial.

There was some early concern on campus that the Griffin wasn't wearing pants. I pointed out lions don't wear pants.

REVELEY IV: Well, now for a less euphoric topic—the golf course. Longwood had a really beautiful nine-hole course and a tradition of great success in golf, but by the time I walked onto the scene in 2013, it was very clear that we were spending a lot of money—half a million dollars a year—maintaining a course that was very lightly used by our students. A relative handful of grown-ups, though, were devoted users.

It was a real challenge justifying that kind of expense to the state government in Richmond when we were trying to get money for other things that, unlike a golf course, really were core functions of the university. Our golf teams didn't even practice there very often. They primarily used a quite good eighteen-hole course a couple miles down the road.

I decided to close the course but maintain the land so it could still be used for cross-country meets and other purposes. It wound up being an object lesson in how hard it is to stop doing anything that has a vocal constituency, however small it may be. A few avid users literally dressed in black shook their fists outside Longwood House. They protested to the board of visitors, a rare occurrence since I became president. Then the more zealous did their cause in by calling the *Richmond Times-Dispatch* with the idea that once this watchdog learned about the egregious sin that Reveley was committing against golf and golfers the newspaper would expose it. Suffice it to say that the paper did not paint them or their cause in that light.[10] And the story actually prompted some officials in Richmond to raise fresh questions about having spent any money at all to maintain the course. So I closed it in 2016. I still hear about it almost every week—that's maybe shifting to just every month.

COVID

As an aspect of campus life, the COVID pandemic may seem on first inspection to have posed an entirely different student-related set of problems (and, in some ways, opportunities) to college presidents than athletics. In most respects it did. But in certain important ways, handling athletics and handling COVID turned out to be interwoven challenges when the pandemic struck campus, community, commonwealth, nation, and world in early 2020 and beyond.

TR4's urgent communication to his fellow Virginia public university presidents in early April 2020, written after consulting the retired TR3, was described in the prologue. But the story of how Longwood responded to the COVID pandemic began three months earlier.[11]

REVELEY IV: I started paying attention to COVID on New Year's Day 2020. Some scattered news reports from China activated the old pandemic-sensitive antennae that I'd developed while working with hospital clients as a lawyer at Hunton & Williams. That was in 2003, when the possibility of a SARS pandemic became a matter of national concern. I kept monitoring the COVID situation throughout January and February, just keeping an eye on it, and I distinctly remember a Council of Presidents meeting in late February when, just as we were wrapping up, I thought, "I ought to say something about this." But people were literally packing up to go, and so I decided, "Well, we'll be together in a month and I'll bring it up then."

On Thursday, March 5, as a matter of great good fortune, I'd already scheduled a retreat for the Longwood vice presidents in Lynchburg during our spring break. Just as a table-top exercise to stress test our campus operations, we'd set aside three or four hours to talk through a COVID scenario: how it would be likely to play out, how we'd respond, and so on. Not that we were predicting that would happen, but it turned out to be an in-the-cool-of-the-day opportunity to think things through in advance that proved really valuable for us when it did. Add to that the muscle memory our team had developed from managing the complicated campuswide preparations necessary to host the 2016 vice presidential debate.

It was just a few days later that things really began to go south very quickly. At that point I knew—again from my earlier law firm experience with the hospitals and SARS—that (1) as serious as it was, for younger people the underlying pathogen was not the Black Death, and (2) state governments were not well equipped to provide authoritative guidance about what was really happening. I also worried that in the strange political environment at the time—the unreliable Trump administration, the adversarial Democrat-controlled House of Representatives, the 2020 presidential campaign—the truth was going to become a football that our national leaders would kick around.

Students came back after the break on March 9. We found out the next day that we had the first case of an infected student on a college campus in Virginia. Unlike many schools, which immediately ordered their students to evacuate and leave for home, we did not. Instead we swung into gear to provide that student with safe quarantine space and quickly began the arduous process of contact tracing and moving our classes online while letting students remain on campus if they chose to do so. To us it did not seem prudent, from a public health standpoint, to take twenty-year-olds who might be vectors of the disease but not particularly in harm's way themselves and send them home to parents and other older people who really would be in harm's way if they were infected by their children or grandchildren. But eventually the pressure from outside to close the campus became too great to withstand, a lot of it grounded in a genuine lack of scientific knowledge about the parameters of COVID, but a lot of it also from people who lacked the background to understand what knowledge there actually was.

Then began the long cycle of semiprosaic but intensely complicated decisions that we and campuses everywhere had to make. Figuring out refunds. Deciding who needed to come in to work and, if they didn't need to, whether they'd get paid. What to do about graduation. What to tell people about the fall semester. What to tell high school seniors who were in the midst of deciding what to do about college, with all the attendant financial considerations for their families.

It became clear to me that if we didn't find a way to reopen safely in the fall of 2020, higher education—maybe not the Ivies with their multibillion-dollar endowments, but the rest of higher education—was in actual peril.[12] And in a real sense, so was this generation of students. Being in Farmville, I knew from the experience of Prince Edward County closing its public schools in the late 1950s—of course, under utterly different circumstances—that when students are denied the opportunity to actually be in school, the aftershocks just ripple out for them and for the community for decade upon decade.

Beyond that, what we were hearing from students during the spring and summer of 2020, when they were banned from being on campus, was how deeply they yearned to be together. So much of what makes a campus community sing are its informal habits, its traditions. If those break, it's hard to rebuild them. Having that sense caused us to redouble our commitment to being open in the fall, in large measure so that students' nonclassroom learning and experience could resume. But I was in a lonely spot for a while. Reopening was not an idea that had a lot of immediate purchase in other minds. The fog of war was a real thing.

The first thing I did, starting in late March 2020, was to talk discreetly with the governor, Ralph Northam, who was a doctor. He understood and resonated with the case I was making that morally as well as financially, we needed to be open in the fall and could do so safely if we took the right precautions. That was step one.

Step two was to look through the financial statements of all fifteen Virginia public universities and, on our next emergency call, point out that we were all in hot water if we didn't figure out how to reopen. And just because we're talking about money doesn't mean the question is somehow removed from morality. If we can't proceed, it means our employees and their families will suffer. The communities that depend on us will suffer.[13] Our students are going to be deprived of the lifelong benefits that in-person education provides.

Eventually—and you'll remember that email I drafted to the other presidents in consultation with my dad—these arguments got through to them. On July 24, we got word from Richmond that SCHEV and the Virginia Department of Health approved our COVID preparedness plan. Longwood and Virginia's other public universities reopened in the fall. Everyone wore a mask. There were oceans of hand sanitizer everywhere. There was social distancing. For Longwood, some classes—but by no means a majority—were online, but we were unusual in how in-person we were. Our faculty were remarkably brave—not without lots and lots of care on everyone's part.

One other way Longwood was different involved COVID testing, even though that became the holy grail at most other places. Because the supply of tests was still limited, we didn't think it was ethical to do test after test after test on a population that skewed young. A second consideration was what came to be called the Hamptons effect, where people would test negative and, even though that test was only valid for the nanosecond they took it, go out and party on the assumption that they'd been certified as invulnerable.

We certainly tested symptomatic people and then quarantined them if they tested positive. And having done that, we put the full force of our effort into contact tracing so we could find out who they might have infected or been infected by. And I'm confident that the trust we placed in our students and they placed in each other to be responsible about these matters will repay dividends over the arc of their lives because they learned to get through the crisis relying on each other instead of fearfully facing it alone.

I was insistent that we hold a timely in-person graduation for the class of 2020, and we did that in October—not in the usual way but instead over about fifteen or so ceremonies in one day broken into batches of about two dozen students with two guests apiece. We did it on the spacious back lawn and side of Longwood House, the president's home.

Pia Trigiani, a longtime board member and eventual rector, and I officiated. She has a wonderful flair for ritual moments like these. The precautions and the logistics were incredibly intricate. Pia and I went literally from dawn to dusk.

The following spring we held a more normal in-person graduation for the class of 2021 on campus. Some schools were still doing virtual graduations even then.

Sometime during the course of that COVID year, Justin Pope said, "Navigating this crisis really has called on all the elements of a liberal arts education." That deeply resonated with me. On the one hand, there was the "hard science" core of the problem, as in, how does COVID spread? And then you had to think through all the aspects of communicating clearly and persuasively to a wide range of people, and figure out the complex riddles of human nature when it's under pressure and dealing with uncertainty. In the meantime, there were the crucially important but very complicated governmental dynamics playing out that called on your understanding of law and federalism and the U.S. presidency. Each day brought at least one interwoven problem from the hard sciences, the social sciences, and the humanities.

In my role as chair of the executive committee of the Big South Conference and as a member of the NCAA's DI board, I was also a voice on the inside encouraging football to proceed in the fall. I may have been overthinking this, but I worried that if college football didn't figure out a way to come back, that would be one more aspect of national life that would be frayed. If something that important to the American psyche was further strained, it just might break.

That was a hard argument to win because the Ivy League just completely punted in the fall of 2020. That was still presumed to be the safe and fashionable thing to do, and so the weight of inertia was heavily in that direction. I was by no means the only voice to the contrary, but it took plenty of cajoling and diplomacy to get the NCAA to push for a posture that would allow schools to safely play sports in the fall. But it happened, and I think it helped enormously in getting America kick-started again, and helped Americans realize that there was, with protocols and care in place, a way they could begin to restart normal life.

Varia

The sampling of student-related issues offered below makes no pretense to depth or comprehensiveness. It is offered as a way to illustrate the broad range of immediate and longer-term considerations that presidents face in leading their student-centered institutions. The issues range from the mundane (condoms in dorms) to the profound (beauty as an aspect of campus life).

Encounters

REVELEY III: Unlike TR4 or me, Daddy had been a student at the college he later led. He had a deep feel for its ways and its precincts. He and Mother lived in Middlecourt, the stately home for Hampden-Sydney's presidents, planted right between a freshman dorm and the college's dining hall. There was a lot of student traffic between the two, with freshmen sometimes passing close by the front windows. This was one of many ways Daddy readily encountered the full range of students, not just those representing student organizations or pushing causes.[14]

As was true when I was dean of the law school, as president I thoroughly enjoyed the students and liked seeing them. I made a habit of speaking to everyone when walking around the campus and was always glad to stop for a picture. Despite the vast gulf between our ages, it was easy to relate to them. When I left the law school for the main campus, Helen's and my fourth child had just gone to college, our daughter, Helen Lanier. We'd already had three undergraduate sons by then, one following another with little intermission, Everett and Nelson after Taylor. Back in my law firm days, I'd chaired the firm's recruiting committee at one point and was awash in young lawyers. And while I served on Princeton's board of trustees, I chaired its standing committee on Student Life, Health and Athletics for seven years; this entailed a good bit of traffic with students. So though I was long in tooth when I was president, students were not a distant or forbidding form of life for me.

Reveley IV: My sister being in college from 2008 to 2012, my dad's first four years as president of Wiilliam & Mary, made it much more natural for him to feel at ease with students. And it helped me feel at ease with them when I started at Longwood in 2013 because they were essentially my sister's age.

When it comes to meeting with student groups, just the speed and straightforwardness of scheduling have greatly increased over the years, and it makes a difference. To get the president to meet with a group twenty or thirty years ago involved moving all sorts of paper around within the group to notify its members and then go back and forth trying to schedule a time with the president's office. Nowadays a group can email the president, offer a range of dates, the president's office can settle on one, and the group can instantaneously tell its members, "This is the time and place to materialize." By the same token, I can instantly send a message to the entire student body via email, whereas not that long ago the sheer mechanics of communicating would have required stuffing all their mailboxes with pieces of paper and hoping they'd see it in some reasonable time.

Conduct

Reveley III: Daddy's presidency coincided with the high-water mark of student resistance at Hampden-Sydney to traditional limitations on personal conduct: frequent mandatory chapel, no alcohol on campus, no female visitors in the dorms (which, of course, were all-male), and so on. These were revolutionary times on campuses across the country, fueled by concern about the Vietnam War, especially among draft-eligible young men. Student tolerance for their schools acting in loco parentis was over.

Daddy made strategic retreats. Much less chapel, a pub on campus where near beer was on tap, greater dorm access for invited female guests, and heaven only knows what else. He had to persuade conservative trustees that the sky would not fall if these changes took place, and he had to reason with Presbyterian churches in the region that were dismayed by them. He responded faithfully and kindly, though it must have struck him that their desire to govern behavior on campus was not matched by a willingness to help fund the academic enterprise. Presidents know this sort of disconnect all too well. The changes were welcomed by the students, deplored by some outspoken alumni, and accepted as one more bit of evidence about the waning influence of college administrators.

REVELEY II: It is a perplexing world for adults. Experience has shaken the foundations of assurance. Things aren't what they used to be and we are not always sure what will happen next. But we doubt we shall like it. . . . Seriously, it is amazing how adults fail in understanding youth and foul up in their treatment of them. . . .

Allowing alcohol on campus and opening the dorms to female visitors on weekend afternoons were the greatest confrontations. They were issues that had the entire student body united. But even this was done with some sense of responsibility and did not get out of hand. They proceeded through all the appropriate channels. . . . The college is fortunate to have a small student body with the consequent possibility of maintaining open communication between student and administration-faculty leadership.[15]

REVELEY II, PRESIDENT'S REPORT TO THE BOARD OF TRUSTEES, APRIL 1970: All of you have read in *The Tiger* or elsewhere the current student appeal for changing the social code at the point of extending the hours parents and dates are permitted to visit residence hall rooms. . . . Apparently feeling that little success would be achieved by taking their requests to the executive committee of the faculty, the students have indicated their intention to present a petition to you.

Let me say only at this point that I urge you to approach this matter with sympathetic interest. By that I mean please do not interpret their request as cut from the same cloth as most of the student unrest about the country. These are fine young men. Some of them may present a far more shaggy appearance than your taste or mine enjoys, but they are not radicals bent on destruction. . . . I do ask that you suspend judgment until you have heard them fairly. I believe you will find that you can be proud of them even when you may disagree with them.

MARIE EASON REVELEY: Taylor disliked the buildup of tedious regulations governing student behavior which had occurred in the preceding years and pushed the young men to assume more responsibility for their own actions. . . . He remembered his college days as being unencumbered by a plethora of rules.

REVELEY II, LETTER TO A. L. RICHARDSON JR., MAY 22, 1969: We concluded that the presence of nonenforceable regulations tended to increase those actions they proposed to abolish.

Reveley IV: In loco parentis waned from the late 1960s forward, but something like it has been burgeoning again over the past decade or two, in new contours and on new fronts, which keep our longtime general counsel, Cameron O'Brion, duly prepared to innovate. He's had to wrangle with a variety of emotional support animals, for instance, encompassing a wide range of sizes and demeanors. If the old in loco parentis, whether successful or not, or helpful or not, was maybe aimed at the well-being of the soul, there is a new, still forming and growing set of expectations that in its own way is perhaps similarly geared to protecting mental health, as well as health and safety more broadly.

Reveley III: One issue I ran into at William & Mary that Daddy was spared concerned machines in the dorms to sell condoms. Students petitioned for condom machines. Our Office of Student Affairs leaned on me to allow the machines to help prevent sexually transmitted diseases and reduce unwanted pregnancies, though we weren't having a wave of either.

In my mind's eye, I could see the parents of freshmen helping move their daughters (or sons for that matter) into the dorms only to come face-to-face with condom dispensers in the halls. Not a happy vision. It took me a couple rounds of "No, let's not do that" before the condom campaign subsided. There were too many other things we were trying to accomplish that required political support or acquiescence in Richmond for us to provide the General Assembly an easy way to beat us about the head and shoulders. Anyway, as I pointed out, it wasn't as if condoms weren't readily available. Bowls of them were open to all who wanted them in the campus center and the infirmary. "Just go pick some up, put 'em in your pockets, plan ahead!"

Some issues were sufficiently important to William & Mary's values to take political heat to defend our positions. A good example early in my presidency concerned the rights of gay and lesbian students. We had adopted a policy making clear they were to be treated exactly like other students. Pressure came from Richmond, the incumbent state attorney general in particular, to do otherwise. I refused. He may have had the better argument as Virginia law then stood, but our position was that whatever might happen elsewhere, on William & Mary's campus, we were one Tribe, allowing no discrimination against our gay and lesbian students.

TR3 issued a statement that "William & Mary neither discriminates against people nor tolerates discrimination on our campus. . . . This is not going to change." Soon afterward, Governor Robert McDonnell announced that the commonwealth's public universities were free to establish their own policies, overruling his fellow Republican, Attorney General Ken Cuccinelli.[16]

REVELEY IV: You hear a lot today about cancel culture, about students shouting down speakers because they don't want certain ideas even to be heard on campus. The intense protests in spring 2024 on so many campuses concerning Israel's military campaign against Hamas may exemplify that sensibility. Longwood didn't experience major disturbances, perhaps in real measure because of the spirit of discussion and engagement we've worked constantly to foster. More broadly, in some sense, what we're experiencing now in higher education is the right saying, "Don't teach certain things," and the left saying, "You've got to believe certain things," and students saying, "If we don't like it, we'll cancel it." But this isn't as new a problem as many people believe. During the McCarthy era of the 1950s, there was a lot of flak over what you could say and couldn't say about communism on campuses, and during the Vietnam War there was a great deal of student-led shouting down of speakers. And looking farther back, campuses were hubs of protest during the American Revolution too. So plenty of antecedents, and we've always managed to work through them. Free expression is—must be—a crucial feature of academic life.

REVELEY III: In late September 2017, I was away from Williamsburg speaking somewhere when Claire Guthrie Gastanaga, the head of the American Civil Liberties Union of Virginia, came to William & Mary, invited by a student group to talk about why the ACLU had helped an alt-right group get a permit to demonstrate in Charlottesville the previous month.

As the ACLU speaker began her remarks, she was shouted down by a group of student protestors. They were given an opportunity to read a statement, which they did, and asked to let the speaker continue. When she tried, the protestors again shouted her down. And when some students from the audience gathered around her on stage to try to talk informally, the protestors formed a circle around them and shouted them down too.

All this was utterly alien to my experience at William & Mary and to my understanding of how protests ought to take place on the campus. We identified as many of the protestors as we could and took disciplinary action against them. I revisited for the community our rules governing speech and comity and reminded everyone that violations would result in sanctions that could entail suspension or expulsion, depending on the severity of an offender's actions and their prior disciplinary record. We invited Gastanaga to come back and speak on campus, which she did some months later, successfully. And we began providing event organizers with more guidance as they planned speeches on campus, giving more support for events likely to be controversial.

I also wrote this to the campus: "Silencing certain voices in order to advance the cause of others is not acceptable in our community. This stifles debate and prevents those who've come to hear a speaker, our students in particular, from asking questions, often hard questions, and from engaging in debate where the strength of ideas, not the power of shouting, is the currency."[17] I also quoted an old friend for whom I have great respect, Hanna Holborn Gray, president emerita of the University of Chicago. She cut to the core when she said that "education should not be intended to make people comfortable. It is meant to make them think."

Whether it's coming from the right or the left, when a cancel culture takes root in classrooms, faculty meetings, venues for speakers, or simply in conversations among members of the campus community, it does terrible damage. And it does nothing to prepare students for life outside the academy, where the argument that some speech must not be heard lest it harm sensitive ears gets short shrift.[18]

The Cost of College

Reveley IV: The issue of college cost is a real one, a pressingly real one. If costs continue to escalate—net cost, adjusted for inflation—the way they have over recent decades, it is inescapably true that college will not be affordable for middle-class families.

I don't think we've reached that inflection point yet., but it's coming. The federal government's inept rollout of its new FAFSA form (Free Application for Federal Student Aid) going into 2024 has exacerbated and accelerated sensibilities about the problem. The inflection point we definitely have reached is that the escalation in cost has promoted legitimate political concern all across the spectrum.[19] One of the things I'm proudest of at Longwood is that we've often managed to raise tuition by a smaller percentage than any other public university in Virginia, by less than the rate of inflation whenever possible.

If colleges and universities can manage to hold the line on cost going forward, as Longwood has, that will have beneficial consequences for the issue that tends to get even more attention in the political arena: student loan debt. The truth is that a significant majority of the trillion dollars–plus of student debt is a function of for-profit institutions taking advantage of people. That sector has done a remarkable job of classic lobbying at the federal and state levels to obscure its predominant role in the problem, which is that the for-profits lure people into borrowing lots and lots of money to finance a so-called education that generally doesn't lead to much of anything.[20]

The average debt for a Longwood graduate is relatively typical of the great majority of public universities in America—somewhere in the mid-$20,000 range. That's not a crushing amount to incur in the course of getting a strong degree. It's about on the level of debt they'd incur buying a good but not exorbitant used car.

All that to say we haven't reached a moment of apocalyptic reckoning for our public universities yet. We still have time to forestall it. And if we can slow down the increases in the cost of college and treat the for-profit sector as the problem it is, the student loan issue will become much more manageable.

Beauty

Reveley IV: So much of what a university president does regarding students involves meeting their immediate needs or dealing with issues that instantly arise. But it's never far from my mind that, as is the case at Rhodes and Hampden-Sydney and Princeton and William & Mary, nearly all Longwood students live on or adjacent to the campus. We're a very residential community. And the physical aspects of that community—the buildings, the landscaping, the statuary, the relation of the parts to the whole—profoundly affect the lived experience of its members. They can either enhance that experience or detract from it.

Reveley III: Too often, seriously unattractive, brutish buildings get built on the assumption that this is necessary to meet the state's construction requirements or budget limitations. In the service of the least expensive alternative, it's been felt that this is the way it has to be. There are now a host of buildings dating back to the sixties and seventies and eighties that are especially awful.[21]

REVELEY IV: That is the con job. At Longwood, we've proven that you can build beautiful buildings for the same price as ugly ones. Proportion is free, for starters. Decorative elements that once would have cost a lot because only highly skilled craftsmen could make them can now be easily machine-tooled or even 3D printed.

Beauty is something that matters fundamentally. It's good for the soul. It helps elevate the spirit of endeavor. I'm no great admirer of that archmodernist, Corbusier, but one of his phrases captures the essence of what a college campus should be: "a temporary paradise."

REVELEY III: Stately buildings matter to the beauty and feel of a campus. There needs to be constant effort to keep them stately. I also deeply believe the grounds matter too, sometimes even more than the structures. William & Mary is blessed with 1,200 acres, half of them woods, rolling terrain over much of its reach, bodies of water, a great variety and mass of trees and shrubs, and a large grassy expanse called the Sunken Garden just west of the oldest part of the campus. Landscaping and gardens, like buildings, take constant attention.

Helen and I believed strongly that a beautiful campus lifted people's spirits and drew them closer. So we pushed in that direction. The university's limited budget for campus beautification got tapped for all it could fund. I was my mother's child in all this. I watched what she did at Hampden-Sydney to bring beauty to its campus on a landscaping and gardening shoestring.

REVELEY IV: Landscaping, urban planning, campus planning, architecture—these are longtime passions of mine. And when I became president I had a keen sense that Longwood once was really beautiful, remained really beautiful in parts, and could very well be that way in full measure again. It had been a meaningful interval since Longwood had a master plan for the campus, so it was a good moment to breathe some life into that type of work. We issued a standard RFP—request for proposals—and Cooper Robertson, a firm I had dealt with at the Miller Center, worked its way through the process and we were able to secure their services.

Once we developed a plan, I was able to go on the hustings to donors and the General Assembly and, say, persuasively, "We've thought this through very carefully, and here are the pieces we need." With the nearly $400 million in capital funding we've been able to secure over the ensuing years we've built or are building new and redesigned dormitories, a new university center, a new admissions building, several new academic buildings, a new basketball and convocation arena, and more.

I don't think it's too much to say that the best American campuses are a lot like the cathedrals of Europe in the intensity and centrality of activity that surrounds them. And so, at a deep level, just being in that kind of setting can't help but enhance the student experience.

Taylor Reveley II greets Robert F. Kennedy during the attorney general's visit to Prince Edward County and Hampden-Sydney College in May 1964 as the county's public schools were moving toward reopening after closing for several years to avoid racial integration. (Photo courtesy of Hamden-Sydney College)

Taylor Reveley II, Marie Eason Reveley, and their children, Taylor III and Chris, at Middlecourt, the Hampden-Sydney president's home, during TR2's first year as president. (Photo courtesy of Hamden-Sydney College)

Taylor Reveley II, a Presbyterian minister as well as a college professor, dean, and president, preaches at the National Cathedral in Washington, DC, as part of Hampden-Sydney's bicentennial celebration in 1976. (Photo courtesy of Hamden-Sydney College)

Three generations of Reveley presidents: Taylor Reveley III, Taylor Reveley IV (age two), and Taylor Reveley II, along with TR3's wife, Helen Reveley, and TR2's wife, Marie Eason Reveley, shortly before TR2's retirement as president of Hampden-Sydney in 1977. (Photo courtesy of W. Taylor Reveley IV)

Taylor Reveley III, former Virginia governor Gerald L. Baliles, former secretaries of state James A. Baker III and Warren Christopher, University of Virginia Law School dean John Jeffries, and Miller Center managing director Taylor Reveley IV after a meeting of the National War Powers Commission, which concluded its work shortly after TR3 became president of William & Mary in 2008. (Photo courtesy of W. Taylor Reveley IV)

Taylor Reveley III on the hustings, as he frequently was after launching William & Mary's $1 billion For the Bold fundraising campaign. (Photograph by Steve Salpukas, © William & Mary 2018)

Taylor Reveley IV speaks at his inauguration as president of Longwood University in 2013, with Governor Gerald Baliles and TR3 looking on. (Photo courtesy of Longwood University)

Taylor Reveley III and Taylor Reveley IV meet with their school mascots, William & Mary's Griffin and Longwood's Elwood. The Griffin, with its eagle's head and lion's body, was W&M's eventual response to the NCAA's requirement that mascots and team names avoid Native American imagery. (Photograph by Steve Salpukas, © William & Mary 2018)

Former Princeton University and Mellon Foundation president Bill Bowen and Taylor Reveley III at the 2015 dinner celebrating TR3's more than two decades of service on the foundation's board. (Photo courtesy of W. Taylor Reveley IV)

Taylor Reveley IV addresses a national television audience just prior to the 2016 vice presidential debate, which he persuaded the Commission on Presidential Debates to hold on Longwood's campus. (Photo courtesy of Longwood University)

Taylor Reveley III strolls the William & Mary campus with the college's longtime chancellor, former secretary of defense and Texas A&M University president Robert M. Gates, class of 1965. (Photograph by Steve Salpukas, © William & Mary 2018)

Former Virginia Supreme Court justice John Charles Thomas and Taylor Reveley IV celebrate Longwood's convocation in 2021, its first since the COVID pandemic. (Photo courtesy of Longwood University)

Taylor Reveley III and Taylor Reveley IV outside William & Mary's Wren Building, the oldest college building in the United States. (Photograph by Steve Salpukas, © William & Mary 2018)

8

Engaging Diversity

Contemporary visitors to the Princeton University campus may be surprised (in ways TR3 and TR4, graduates of Princeton from the 1960s and 1990s, respectively, were not) to learn that the letters DEI, which appear on Princeton's shield and are carved into the stone of its older buildings, spell the Latin word for "God," not the American initialism for "diversity, equity, and inclusion." Yet it is new-style DEI, not the much diminished emphasis on God in mainstream higher education, that has become an important concern among contemporary colleges and universities, posing a range of challenges and opportunities to their presidents.

Diversity—the "D" in DEI—was the first of these qualities to become a prominent goal, especially in connection with race and ethnicity. It arose in connection with a landmark Supreme Court decision—*Regents of the University of California v. Bakke*.[1] The plurality opinion of the court was written by Justice Lewis Powell, who, like TR3 and TR4, was a former member of the Richmond-based law firm of Hunton & Williams. In his opinion, Powell argued that institutions of higher education were free to take the racial identity of applicants for admission into account, but only because all students on a campus benefit educationally from being part of a "diverse" student body. (He offered "a farm boy from Idaho" as well as a "a black student" as examples of how Harvard might diversify.) In practical terms, however, the decision linked race and ethnicity with diversity in the minds of college administrators as a matter of both law and policy.

Like many transformations in the history of American higher education and of race relations more generally, the post-*Bakke* emphasis on racial diversity, especially recruiting more "students (and faculty) of color," sparked a reaction. In 2023, the Supreme Court effectively overruled its earlier affirmative action decisions, and several mostly southern and western states soon passed legislation aimed at reining in diversity initiatives, including two of Virginia's bordering neighbors, North Carolina and Tennessee.[2] The legislation took a variety of forms, such as eliminating mandatory "diversity statements" from the public university hiring process, forbidding the teaching of "divisive concepts" concerning race and ethnicity, and abolishing campus DEI offices (which prompted some to rebrand themselves as did the Division of Access and Opportunity at the University of Oklahoma, for example).[3] Virginia's Democrat-controlled General Assembly stymied such legislation, but Republican governor Glenn Youngkin's education secretary, supported by most of his board of visitors appointees, successfully pressured George Mason University and Virginia Commonwealth University to abandon plans for required courses called Just Societies and Racial Literacy, respectively.[4] Supported by a state attorney general's opinion, he also stressed to the visitors that they were legally accountable to the state rather than to the university on whose board they served.[5]

All three Reveley presidents dealt extensively with issues of diversity, which presented themselves in various forms. By the time TR3 became president of William & Mary in 2008 and TR4 became president of Longwood in 2013, most legal barriers to racial diversity were in abeyance. That was not the case in 1963 when TR2 became president of Hampden-Sydney. TR2 also faced a diversity-related issue that his son and grandson never had to—namely, whether the all-male institution he led should admit women as students and become (in the parlance of the day) coeducational.

TR2 and Hampden-Sydney

In 1963, when TR2 became president, nearly 250 American colleges and universities included only men in their undergraduate student bodies. Another group of about 230 colleges admitted only women; indeed, Longwood University was thought of as Hampden-Sydney College's "sister" institution when TR2 was a student at Hampden-Sydney and Marie Eason Reveley was a student at Longwood. As late as the 1960s, the ranks of men's schools included nearly all of the Ivy League universities, dozens of mostly private liberal arts colleges, and all of the publicly funded military academies, including Virginia Military Institute. To Yale President Kingman Brewster, being all-male was consistent with his university's core mission: to fill the nation's leadership ranks, which also were virtually all-male.[6] But he, along with the presidents and boards of Harvard, Princeton, and other elite colleges and universities, came to realize by the end of the decade that not only did women want to attend their institutions but also that current and prospective male students now wanted them admitted as well.[7] By 1977, when TR2's presidency ended, the vast majority of all-male institutions had changed their policies and practices (including West Point and Annapolis but not VMI) by deciding to admit women.

To this day, Hampden-Sydney is an all-male liberal arts college, now just one of three such institutions; the others are Wabash College in Crawfordville, Indiana, and historically Black Morehouse College in Atlanta, Georgia. But the issue of whether Hampden-Sydney should go with the flow and become coeducational was very much up for grabs during TR2's presidency. He and the college were torn by the issue, with most of the faculty (eventually) on one side and most of the more conservative trustees and alumni on the other.

MARIE EASON REVELEY: On the issue of admitting women students to Hampden-Sydney, Taylor kept an open mind. His personal belief was that in a country as large and diverse as America, there was room for different types of colleges, one of those types being single sex. But if it had become necessary to admit women to Hampden-Sydney to fulfill the enrollment quotas he would have done it. . . . Taylor did not push for coeducation but neither did he lead a rah-rah cheer for keeping it all-male.

REVELEY III: Daddy believed deeply in coeducation, which was not his experience as a student but was very much his experience as professor and admissions dean at Rhodes. But he played the hand he was dealt on all-male education because he had far bigger issues to deal with, especially race. I think if he had been president for thirty years, he would have done what Harvard, Yale, Princeton, and ultimately Washington and Lee did because he thought it was good for men and women to go to school together. He also realized that the Hampden-Sydney applicant pool had shrunk because all-male schools had gone so totally out of fashion. It's one thing to be single-sex when most of the really good schools are single-sex. It's different when that's no longer true.

By 1970, midway through TR2's tenure, the presence of women students in Hampden-Sydney's classes was no longer unknown. Joining with other single-sex colleges in Virginia and North Carolina, he had created the College Exchange Program, which brought a handful of students from all-female Mary Baldwin College and Randolph Macon Women's College onto Hampden-Sydney's campus, where they lodged with faculty members.

REVELEY II, *REPORT TO THE TRUSTEES*, APRIL 1971: It may be wise for the Board to appoint a special committee to study carefully the pros and cons of coeducation.

REVELEY II, *SUMMER REPORT TO THE BOARD OF TRUSTEES*, AUGUST 1971: Without usurping the role of the Board committee to be appointed to study the question of coeducation at Hampden-Sydney, I believe that we could follow a lead set by Davidson [College]. They have announced their intention to permit wives of students as well as wives and daughters of faculty members to enroll as degree candidates.

By May 1972, a faculty committee, acting on its own initiative, recommended that "the Faculty go on record as favoring coeducation in this institution." The recommendation was approved by the faculty as a whole.

REVELEY II, *PRESIDENT'S REPORT TO THE FACULTY*, OCTOBER 2, 1972: Despite the excellence of the committee report passed by the Faculty, I continue to be "hung" on the need for diversity in educational patterns and hope that we can continue as a men's college.

Led by TR2, Hampden-Sydney did open the enrollment door to student wives and faculty wives and daughters. He successfully pressed for the hiring of the college's first women professors and the election of its first women trustees, both of which were achieved in 1973. But he renewed the "commitment of the college to remain a college for men," once again invoking "diversity" in service of this commitment.

REVELEY II, *REPORT TO THE TRUSTEES*, OCTOBER 1973: Its rationale comes from the need to preserve the diversity of educational experience present today. The preservation of this diversity represents no antiquarian impulse but a belief that a men's college remains a desired pattern for many young men. That many others desire coeducation, indeed the majority, does not destroy the need for retaining single-sexed colleges.[8]

Reveley IV: An aspect of the deliberations was Title IX, the landmark federal legislation from the early seventies that has been a focus of higher education ever since. It became clear pretty quickly that Title IX allowed Hampden-Sydney, because of its long history as an all-male institution, to remain essentially all-male. But the spirit of gender equality that animates Title IX began to change the country and campuses everywhere, driving access to education, intercollegiate athletics, and more recently, an important emphasis on preventing and punishing sexual misconduct. Its passage soon required Longwood, as a public institution that had at times admitted male students, to become fully coeducational by 1976. TR2 would not be surprised to know that interpretation and jurisprudence around Title IX—on a range of subjects and issues, some perennial and some new—remains at the forefront for higher education.

Coeducation was an issue that TR2 was able to deal with over time as a possible course of action for the college. He reconciled himself to all-male education as a political reality at Hampden-Sydney as well as in service of his understanding at the time that diversity in higher education meant providing students with a wide range of choices in deciding what kind of college they wished to attend.

In contrast, issues of race and, in the modern sense of the word, diversity cried out for his immediate attention.[9]

REVELEY III: When Daddy and Mother arrived at Hampden-Sydney in July 1963, the racial climate in Prince Edward County, where the village of Hampden-Sydney is located, was incandescently hot. It was intense on campus too between those who believed in segregation forever and those who strongly felt an end to segregation was morally, socially, and politically essential. That included young faculty who had school-age children.

Daddy listened to both sides and felt no need to engage in virtue signaling. But he was determined to get the college to desegregate and kept pushing for what he believed was morally and practically compelling.

REVELEY II, "HAMPDEN-SYDNEY COLLEGE ANNUAL REPORT," 1965–1966: Four professors . . . resigned from the college in order to accept positions elsewhere. Their loss is most regrettable for each of these men is an outstanding teacher and a fine Christian man. Their leaving underscores the difficulty the college faces in its location in Prince Edward County, for despite the virtues of the good people of Prince Edward County (and they are many), their embattled reluctance to provide any appropriate pattern of integrated public school education, perhaps even more their insistence upon maintaining an avowedly segregated pattern of education, [is] a heavy burden.

MARIE EASON REVELEY: The board of trustees, reflecting the views of students, parents, alumni, and a few staff and faculty, were not yet ready to admit black students.... We would be outvoted in every instance, but there was still persuasion.

REVELEY III: Daddy's insistence on desegregation came close to costing him his job before it had meaningfully begun.

OWEN NORMENT: Taylor served as president in a period of extraordinary racial upheaval in Prince Edward County. With moderation and sensitivity he guided the college community through a time of tension and difficult family adjustments involved with the reopening of the public schools, always standing in the forefront of the growing push toward easing the grip of racism and insuring civil rights in the county.[10]

External forces strengthened TR2's hand. Foundations and other potential major donors were increasingly unwilling to support segregated institutions. The Presbyterian Church U.S. with which Hampden-Sydney was affiliated stopped "dragging its feet," in TR2's phrase, and pressed for integration.[11] Even more important, with the enactment of powerful civil rights legislation by Congress, colleges were forced to sign an Assurance of Compliance with the Civil Rights Act of 1964 in order to remain eligible to receive federal funds. Grudgingly, Hampden-Sydney's board agreed to sign the assurance in 1965.

REVELEY III: It wasn't just a matter of getting the board of trustees to vote to desegregate the college and then to begin recruiting Black students and Black faculty and welcoming them to the campus, though that was the heart of it. Racial issues came up in all sorts of ways, such as whether to invite Attorney General Robert Kennedy to visit the campus in May 1964 and whether or not to allow an integrated kindergarten to be created and operated on campus.

When Kennedy came to Prince Edward County to express his support and concern for the Black students whose public schools were closed, he was not invited to visit Longwood because it was a state school and the state government was still dead set against integration. So Daddy invited him to come to Hampden-Sydney, where he was warmly greeted by the students and faculty who showed up to listen to him speak. The rest of the campus community, a few of whom definitely viewed Kennedy as an instrument of the devil, simply stayed away. Daddy knew he would get flak from the segregationists. He was not disappointed. He believed it was important to welcome the attorney general of the United States.

Then there was controversy over having an integrated kindergarten on campus. Mother had been heavily involved in its creation and early operations, and she felt strongly it needed to include Black children as well as whites. Again there was incoming fire from the segregationist wing, including some on the board, since the kindergarten was on college grounds in a college building *(see chapter 4)*.

As challenging as racial issues have been for TR4 and me, we've never confronted the discord and animosity Daddy faced early on for taking steps pretty much everyone eventually acknowledged were the right steps to take. Had he not returned to Hampden-Sydney so highly acclaimed for his undergraduate years on campus, and had there been any serious doubt that he was devoted to the good of Hampden-Sydney as he understood it, his presidency would likely have crashed on racial rocks.

REVELEY IV: Fifty years later, when I was trying to forge a closer connection between Longwood and the local Black community, it carried some weight that I bore TR2's name and that as early as 1966 Rev. Francis Griffin, the great civil rights leader for Prince Edward County and well beyond, had described my grandfather as his "yoke-fellow in the Gospel."

TR3 and William & Mary

REVELEY III: I learned a lesson in the importance of diversity as a campus flash point at the very beginning of my time as interim president. I was asked whether I'd cochair the university's diversity committee, as my predecessor had done. At that time I was totally absorbed in trying to deal with all the issues stemming from his very sudden, very angry resignation as president. So I asked some of my senior people if cochairing the diversity committee was something I needed to do right at that immediate moment. The answer was no, given all the pressing demands afoot, your time is better spent elsewhere. So I begged off.

Talk about being politically out to lunch! Declining to cochair the committee was taken to mean a lack of commitment to racial progress, against a background of concern among many on campus that my predecessor's departure would inexorably mean serious backsliding on racial matters. Immediately some members of the diversity committee resigned in protest, and a tempest began gathering steam. I got on the phone promptly with the members who'd quit, said I would cochair the committee, and urged them to stay on and help William & Mary keep moving forward. Most, not all, did. The tempest blew over.

This experience strengthened my conviction that when you make a real mess, it's best to admit it quickly and take remedial action, rather than try to motor on hoping the passage of time will save you. Usually that would just make it worse.

More important, this experience underscored what I already knew from my time as dean of the law school: making racial progress had to be, and should be, an important part of William & Mary's life and of my presidency. It was. And progress would be measured in substance as well as symbols.

As to the diversity committee, I very much hoped it would be able to do more than just have a lot of meetings, hold badly attended events that largely preached to the choir, and layer diversity process on top of diversity process in the various arts and sciences departments and professional schools, without much demonstrable progress being made. We worked at it. The results varied.

A crucial matter, and one that had a great deal of student involvement, was the need to come to grips with William & Mary's history of slavery and Jim Crow. The university needed to understand that history, to dig out all the facts that could be dug out about it. We needed a sustained effort of recollection and reconciliation. We needed to chart a forward course of remembrance involving not just the campus but also the local Black community.

In 2009, drawing on ideas from the diversity committee and the broader campus community, I proposed a course of action to the board of visitors, which adopted it. The project we launched was named for an enslaved man called Lemon who had been prominent on campus and in the community during the eighteenth century. Our Lemon Project had a faculty leader and organizer, with financial support from the university, and was among the first efforts by any university in the country to get serious about its racial past. The Lemon Project grew into a multifaceted program of research, teaching, and outreach to the local community. It's still going strong.

I found it very helpful to create task forces to tackle certain especially difficult issues on campus, racial and otherwise. I tried to staff the task forces with people knowledgeable about the full range of facts and views, and to get them in gear and productive before concern about these issues reached the point of real angst and outright protest on campus. After a whole lot of information gathering, discussion, and thought, each task force produced a written report, including concrete recommendations for me, which I then engaged together with either the chair of the task force or the whole group. Some of these recommendations, invariably, made really good sense and were immediately feasible (the proverbial low-hanging fruit). Some were desirable and practical but would take a while to implement, and the rest would have required funds and staffing of a sort that was simply out of reach. Sometimes a few of the recommendations seemed off the wall to me, even if funds and staff had been available. We'd get on with grabbing the low-hanging fruit, start moving on the intermediate practical steps, and talk about why the rest couldn't make the cut, given everything else the university had on its plate—the eternal conversation about trade-offs.

One of the most important and hard-working of these task forces engaged racial issues, focusing on the Black experience on campus. To help gather information, this task force held a series of town hall–style meetings. What kept happening was minority faculty, administrators, and students would attend, along with some white administrators and a few white faculty members, plus some white undergraduate women, but either no white male undergrads or just one or two. On one occasion, a Black student stood up and asked—really exclaimed—"Where are the white guys?" Well, I had a pretty good idea they didn't want to come and risk being bashed for being white and male. It still distresses me how hard it is to come up with ways for white and Black students to sit down together and trust one another enough to talk about what's on their minds and start building bridges to each other. It's just really hard.

Even so, I felt William & Mary was making serious progress racially. We worked doggedly to combat any remaining vestiges of racial harassment or discrimination on campus, and we also worked hard to recruit minority faculty and students. The diversity committee provided continuing focus on the mission and took steps toward achieving it. The Lemon Project gained momentum year on year, making a serious difference for the better, including William & Mary's outreach to the Black community in Williamsburg.

We renamed two of our buildings, one for Lemon and the other for W&M's first Black senior administrator, Carroll Hardy. We removed all remaining Confederate iconography from public display on campus and did so before it became the subject of protests.

There was significant discussion about, and planning for, a large, freestanding memorial to William & Mary's enslaved people while I was president, and the board of visitors approved having one, which came to fruition after I retired.[12]

And during my final months as president, the board formally apologized for William & Mary's involvement in slavery and Jim Crow, using a resolution I drafted. In my view, creation of the Lemon Project in 2009 and its subsequent life had constituted unmistakable acknowledgment of the university's complicity and regret, but it became apparent that a more express apology was also important.[13] So we did it.

Removal of the last public vestiges of William & Mary's years in the Confederacy required the most extensive discussions with members of the board of visitors of any of our racial initiatives. I involved them at every step in what proved to be a long process of decision-making. Objections to our ultimate course came largely from well-intentioned members who felt it was a mistake to remove aspects of W&M's history. I made progress with some of them by talking about my own deep roots in the South and my own strong commitment to history and tradition.

The university's great silver ceremonial mace, carried on Charter Day, commencement, and other occasions of high moment, included images of the flags and other symbols of the various governments under which William & Mary had existed since 1693, including the Confederate States of America. Ever since becoming president, I'd been telling the students who carried the mace to keep the Confederate indicia pressed tightly to their chests as they marched, lest someone take a picture of the CSA items and all hell break loose. It was hard to retool the mace as a matter of artistry (what new images to create in place of the old ones?) and craftsmanship (how to get the old ones off and the new ones on without doing in the mace?). But the mace survived in its redeemed form, and it no longer had to be carried on ceremonial occasions with one side pressed tightly to the body of the bearer.[14]

We addressed an issue in the Wren too. A major passageway leading into the Wren Building is lined with plaques commemorating William & Mary alumni who have fought for their colony, state, and country, especially those who died in combat. One of the largest plaques listed the students and faculty members who left the campus when the Civil War broke out to join the Confederate Army. This plaque meant a lot to many even as it offended many more, a growing number. My initial plan was to send the old plaque to the archives and replace it with a new one that would include no Confederate symbols and would list all the alumni who fought in the Civil War on either side. This included Winfield Scott, the commanding general of the Union Army at the beginning of the conflict, who devised the "Anaconda" strategy that ultimately strangled southern ports. Scott also tried to persuade Robert E. Lee, a fellow Virginian, to take command of the federal forces.

So we had the new plaque made. It took a powerful effort to identify all those whose names should be on it. The result was a magisterial bronze record of a telling and tragic period in the university's life. But there were only six or seven names of Union soldiers on it, so I had the names of all who fought listed alphabetically, the many for the Confederacy and the few for the Union, with the federal troops identified as such. I then asked one of our senior Black administrators, a man of really good judgment, can we hang this one on the wall of the Wren? He looked at me, smiled, and just shook his head. I was disappointed, but I concluded he was right. So we put the plaque in a little museum in the Wren devoted to William & Mary and the Civil War and put the old plaque in the university's archives where to see it you have to ask.

I hope we will learn how to repudiate slavery and all its works without denigrating and blotting out all other aspects of what took place at William & Mary and in Virginia during the awful war years. They had a profound effect on the university and came within a hair's breadth of killing it.

These were all important, tangible actions that needed to be taken. But schools seem to be less effective these days at bridging cross-racial and cross-cultural divides than they are at creating cloistered havens for various identity groups, especially those for minorities. These havens meet deeply felt needs, but they don't build much cross-racial empathy and understanding.

Reveley IV: It is hard, and I've gotten a sense in a way of what the experience could be like for minority students. I happened to mention to a Virginia state official that I am an enrolled tribal citizen of the Cherokee Nation, through my mother's side of the family, and all of a sudden I became the font of wisdom on all things Native American. So I can see how it feels when, proverbially, a professor turns to the only Black student in the class, and asks, "Tell us about your experience." The assumption being that you're less an individual than a spokesperson for an entire race or ethnicity.[15]

Reveley III: When that happens, it can certainly be chilling for the purported spokesperson for "your people." But on those rare occasions when it arises naturally and spontaneously, it can lead to meaningful discussion in the class. We need to have more conversations going on campus, conversations that get into what people actually have on their minds and in their hearts and what they'd like to learn about others and what they'd really like to say about themselves. This would take a measure of trust and a willingness to take risks that are hard to come by.

Reveley IV: Of diversity, equity, and inclusion, inclusion is definitely the hardest to achieve. It's not just a matter of having people of different backgrounds. It's a matter of how they actually come to feel a sense of esprit de corps. Athletics helps. The members of a team feel an intrinsic solidarity with one another, whatever their backgrounds. And for the rest of the student body, the residential college experience can make a true difference because students of different backgrounds in the same dorm are obliged to find a way to live together and share experience in the fulcrum years of college.

Reveley III: As I've already mentioned, I whiffed at the very beginning of my presidency by making a bad call, quickly corrected, about cochairing the diversity committee. To my lasting regret, I whiffed again near the end of my presidential run on another racial matter.

A couple of students involved in a Black Lives Matter conference at William & Mary contacted my office and asked to come see me to give a quick report on how the conference was going. The afternoon they wanted to come was fully scheduled, but I invited them to stop by briefly, fifteen minutes or so. They came, not just two students as I expected, but in force, filling the room. One of their number immediately began live-streaming the event from an iPhone, without asking if this would be okay, and their leader jumped right in, declaring "these are our demands" or something to that effect.

I knew full well what I should do, just say: "Thank you for coming to see me. We will give your demands thoughtful consideration. I do think we've made a lot of racial progress at William & Mary, but there is always more that can usefully be done. I wish I had more time to spend with you right now, but I've got a stuffed schedule this afternoon. I'll be happy to talk with you again on another occasion."

Instead I fecklessly said: "You know, at William & Mary we really don't deal in demands with one another. We make requests, and we back up our requests with substance, with explanations as to why our requests make sense. But we don't go around demanding things."

The conversation went downhill from there, and I let it go on for an hour, blowing my schedule and making the situation worse with each passing minute. I kept trying to explain all that William & Mary had done to atone for our past racial wrongs and to do better going forward. I talked about how different life was now compared to when I was growing up during the dying days of enforced segregation and Jim Crow. None of this got diplomatic recognition from my visitors. They just got angrier and angrier. I, too, began to get mad. Meantime, the live-stream ground along, providing grist for carefully selected social media snippets designed to depict me as a complete troglodyte. Finally, much too late, I called it quits.

Of the innumerable meetings and conversations I had as president, this is the one I would most like to do over.

I got a lot of loud flak for being inadequately gracious and understanding with my visitors, plus some sotte voce "What were you *thinking?*" from my troops. On the other side of the scale, I got an outpouring of thanks from people tired of "demands" and tired of the failure to acknowledge how much racial progress has been made, even though more is essential.[16]

It was a point of pride for William & Mary when, based on data from 2013, the *Journal of Blacks in Higher Education* reported that W&M ranked first among "prestigious" public universities in the narrowness of its gap between Black and white graduation rates.[17]

Reveley III: Let me mention something that doesn't often get much attention when the subject is diversity on campus. Pretty late in my presidency, some Asian American students asked to schedule a meeting with me. About a dozen showed up at the appointed hour. Their message was essentially this: "Everyone thinks we're all the same. We're not. Our family origins are Korean, they're Thai, they're Malaysian, they're Filipino, and more. We're not homogeneous. And everyone assumes we're doing well. But actually we're not. We do make good grades and take our academic work seriously. We don't stage protests or drink too much. But we're unsettled and sad." They pointed out that William & Mary had no program or even a course on the Asian American experience in the United States. Plenty of courses on the history, politics, and culture of different parts of Asia, but nothing about how Asians in all their complexity have come to the United States, how they were treated once here, how they were fitting in or not. They said W&M wasn't reaching out to Asian American students in ways comparable to what the university was doing for our other racial and ethnic minorities.

I asked each of the students to talk about his or her experience not just on campus but in the United States generally, and if they'd visited the country from which their family had come, and how that had gone. I particularly remember one young woman saying she'd visited South Korea where her family had roots, hoping she would feel at home and comfortable there, but was instead viewed as an American. She wasn't feeling comfortable in the U.S. either and wondered where she did belong.

William & Mary got on the stick and created a new program called Asian American and Pacific Islander Studies, focused on the Asian experience in the United States in all its diversity. I'm glad of that.

TR4 and Longwood

In a real sense, one of TR4's primary goals concerning race and diversity at Longwood picked up where his grandfather's had left off. TR2 inherited the situation that arose in Prince Edward County from a series of events originating at the county's Robert Russa Moton High School: first a walkout by the school's all-Black student body; then a Supreme Court case inspired by the student walkout that, as part of the *Brown v. Board of Education* litigation, mandated an end to legally imposed segregation; and finally the county's decision to keep its public schools closed for five years, until specifically ordered by the Supreme Court to reopen. By the time TR4 arrived at Longwood a half century later, the Moton School had become the Robert Russa Moton Museum, a widely recognized historic site but one that faced challenges relating to its financial and organizational sustainability. He quickly identified the opportunities for both the museum and Longwood that could arise from a partnership between the two institutions, one unlike any other in the country.

REVELEY IV: One of the first things that happened after my appointment as president was announced in March 2013, even before I took office, was that the then-president of Hampden-Sydney, Chris Howard, invited me and my dad to speak in April at what Hampden-Sydney episodically called the Reveley Lecture, named for my grandfather. I introduced my dad, and he devoted his lecture to the topic of civil rights and Prince Edward County. One of the other speakers that evening was Lacy Ward, who was at the time the director of the Moton Museum and a member of Longwood's board of visitors. The occasion helped crystallize my focus, which had already been forming, on Longwood's need to try to do justice about its sins of commission and omission in the past and the possibility of a deeper relationship with Moton. After much initial work on this front, in June 2014, at the end of my first year, our board of visitors committed to the idea of exploring a formal partnership with the museum.

That began a sequence of community discussions, often held at the museum, in which members of the Black community expressed their honest and deeply held wariness of Longwood because of their living memory of things Longwood had done and failed to do. I was right in the thick of those discussions, and they included visceral expressions of the hurt that was still very much there. I realized that to have any chance of moving things forward, Longwood needed to issue a formal apology for "the real and lasting offense and pain" it had caused to the local Black community during the Massive Resistance era.[18] The board issued that apology in September 2014, the start of my second year as president. The partnership could then move forward.[19]

Reveley III: Longwood apologized relatively early in what became a wave of university apologies. This was quite wonderful.

Reveley IV: It had to happen, and the adoption of that resolution had a galvanizing effect on the spirit of trust in the community for Longwood. There were some older white people in Farmville who were not happy about it, but only a few. And even they weren't arguing in some arch-reactionary way that the world was fine or even better during segregation, but instead just: Do we need to keep talking about this? The trust that the apology established was a necessary precondition for our ability to formalize a partnership with Moton.

One advantage of the partnership for Moton was that Longwood could provide professional assistance with philanthropy. Previously, the museum had made its way in a very uplifting fashion, early on raising money literally through bake sales and five- and ten-dollar donations just to keep it together. Clearly there were limits to how far that could take it. It had a burst of corporate and community support, but it needed more.

Another thing was to help with Moton's back-end operations—HR and benefits and the various administrative functions that need to be performed but that soak up a lot of time and money. A third was that Moton could benefit from the university's experience seeking grants, in this case for efforts to marry aspects of what the university is working on with aspects of what the museum is working on. For instance, the Teagle Foundation gave us a grant for the Civitae curriculum that centers on collaborating with Moton. The partnership with Moton has also done enormous good for the spirit of diversity at Longwood among students.

And then there's the unpredictable kinetic energy that has arisen out of the partnership. When Longwood hosted the 2016 vice presidential debate, the story of Barbara Johns and her leadership of the Moton student walkout jumped strongly to statewide and then national recognition, such that in 2020, when the Commonwealth of Virginia decided to remove Robert E. Lee's statue from Statuary Hall in the U.S. Capitol, it chose to replace it with a statue of Barbara Johns, to go alongside George Washington. That's a poetic and profound thing that it's hard to imagine would have taken place but for the strength of the Longwood-Moton partnership.[20] In fact, the debate itself surely would not have occurred at Longwood if we and Moton hadn't somewhat dispelled the cloud of Massive Resistance that hung over everything for so long.

To this day, the Longwood-Moton partnership is the only one of its kind in the country—a university partnered with a civil rights museum. As for our students, dozens and dozens of them have a really intense relationship with Moton, whether of an academic research nature or a volunteer nature. And our student body in full has an inspirational relationship with the museum, where they see a vastly important American story that has unfolded right here in Farmville.

Addressing issues of race and diversity will continue to be a defining challenge for America, and certainly for higher education. This is more and more at the forefront for courts and legislators at all points on the ideological spectrum, and the intricacies of law and policy add to the complexity. My own sense is that there is a widespread yearning for harmony and good will that's sometimes, or maybe typically, obscured by rhetorical posturing and partisan positioning. But viewpoints are passionate, and stumbles are easy. Stumbles are maybe even intrinsic to the work, as much difficulty as missteps and miscues can cause.

My dad's experience with the students in the Black Lives Matter group at William & Mary was definitely forefront in my mind when a similar situation developed at Longwood several years after that, as the world and grassroots activism were hitting fresh, full stride again in the fall of 2022, after COVID, the George Floyd murder, and a host of other upsetting events. Plenty of divisive national politics was still in the atmosphere, something rarely in short supply nowadays.

The situation began when a student group issued demands (that word again) to the university and administration on various issues related to diversity during a regular Student Government Association meeting. And this very, very hotly boiled my blood when it came to my attention, not least because I already had a meeting scheduled with the group in the days ahead. Why didn't they just wait and talk to me? Were they just trying to embarrass me or others? Or just trying to get "likes" or "follows" on social media? How, I fumed, could anybody disregard the strong steps Longwood has taken?

Late that night, probably past midnight, I dashed off a stern draft of an email I wanted to send to the group. I sent it first to Cam Patterson, our wise vice president of Student Affairs, whose previous role was as executive director of the Moton Museum and who just that summer had started as vice president, succeeding Tim Pierson, a longtime and much loved campus leader. Tim and I had worked through similar, if less heated, situations any number of times, but this was new for Cam. By morning, I had cooled down, which is my more natural barometric state. Cam cooled me further, and counseled patience for these twenty-one-year-olds working to find their voice—something that's always good to keep in mind, and which I usually do. I didn't send an email.

When I then actually had the scheduled meeting with the group several days later, they were still impassioned and full of spirit, maybe even more than before. As the meeting unfolded, I worked to keep my dad's BLM experience emblazoned on my psyche. This was not the time for sweet reason, I knew and kept telling myself, though it's endlessly tempting to go down that path in moments like these. I listened, as best I could. And after their opinions had been thoroughly aired, I concluded the meeting by saying I would consider everything we had discussed.

I took counsel with TR3—as much to grouse as to get actual advice, knowing what his advice would be: calm and dispassion. I took counsel with Mike Evans, the board's rector, whose career had been in social services at the local and state government level and who had given me my first real job twenty-five years before with the City of Richmond. And I spoke with another splendid board member, Cookie Scott, Longwood's first Black alum, class of '72.

The three of us—Mike, Cookie, and I—met with the group again, shortly before Thanksgiving. Mike and Cookie spoke with the students about their own college days long before, and about their subsequent careers. Mike and Cookie also spoke with the students about the progress Longwood had made in recent years. I did so as well, partly because the disruptions of COVID had broken the transmission and student memories of a number of steps we took prior to 2020. This moment, this meeting had a different tenor and different spirit from the earlier meeting. We all agreed to take sound, student-centric steps.

There is never perfect harmony, but on this front, in this moment, greater harmony followed.[21]

9
Advancing Fundraising

When it comes to funding, the contrast between private and public institutions is not as great as it once was. In 1963, when TR2 became president of Hampden-Sydney, nearly all the college's funds other than tuition came from private sources in small amounts: donations by friends and alumni of the college, income from the college's endowment, and support from the Presbyterian Church. In the same era, William & Mary and Longwood, as public institutions, derived the bulk of their nontuition income from the commonwealth. In return, the state government insisted that its public institutions not only charge lower tuition to Virginia students than to students from out of state, but also that they reserve at least two-thirds of the places in the undergraduate student body for Virginians.

Much had changed by the time TR3 became president of William & Mary in 2008 and TR4 became president of Longwood five years later. On the positive side of the ledger, federal funding for student loans and scholarships, faculty research, buildings, and other campus functions had grown exponentially since the mid-1960s. This development benefited private institutions, including Hampden-Sydney at TR2's initiative, and public universities like the ones his son and grandson later led. More than offsetting this trend for William & Mary and Longwood by the time TR3 and TR4 took office, however, was the decline in state funding, especially for operations. TR3's first two years as president coincided with the financial crisis of 2008–2009, which prompted a 32 percent reduction in state funding and led him to tell the university community, "We must increasingly fend for ourselves."[1]

Nearly two decades after that crisis, public universities in Virginia are still expected to fund most of their own operations while maintaining the minimum two-to-one ratio of Virginians to non-Virginians. As a consequence, the challenge facing TR3 and TR4 as presidents of public institutions came to resemble the challenge faced by TR2 as president of a private one: to persuade potential donors to make substantial gifts in order to advance the university's mission.

The Need

When TR2 became president of Hampden-Sydney in 1963, the need was great for, at a minimum, a new science building and dormitory, but the college's endowment was a trifling $4 million. The board of trustees felt little sense of urgency.

MARIE EASON REVELEY: What Taylor could see was that unless the college could take a quantum leap forward in prosperous times it would find itself lagging far behind during a period of recession.... [Yet] he was encouraged to run the college, to keep things on a steady course, and to leave the fund raising to the board....
[The alumni affairs director] urged Taylor to speak in reassuring terms at alumni meetings all over Southside Virginia.... Taylor was so good at reassurance that after a meeting at Halifax I remonstrated: "Enough of reassurance. Tell them Hampden-Sydney needs a science building."

By spring 1970, the need for TR2 to focus on fundraising became acute, leading him to tell the board that he was "relinquishing much of the immediate involvement in the daily routine of conducting college affairs in order that I may spend more time being involved in the development program of the college." In 1973, he reported, "fully eighty-five percent of my time is being spent in this quest."[2]

As presidents of public universities in an era of declining state support, the fundraising demands on TR3 at William & Mary and TR4 at Longwood, though usually less all-absorbing, were as least as great as those on TR2. And, as former University of Texas at Austin president Peter T. Flawn has written, "No matter what institutional arrangements you may make, the president is always the chief development officer."[3]

REVELEY IV: In today's environment, university presidents are in a way rivaled only by U.S. presidential candidates in the fundraising expectations that are on them.

REVELEY III: One of the professors who taught me in law school used to say, "Money isn't everything, but it's everything else." Money certainly isn't everything. It's not love or integrity or any of the other cardinal virtues. But money makes progress possible that is otherwise flatly beyond reach.

A university's goals, especially its grand ambitions, are just so much flapdoodle if the schools don't have money to realize them in the first place and then sustain them. While I still was dean of the law school, I remember a meeting at which one of the university's vice presidents drew an analogy between William & Mary and an airport where many planes loaded with wonderful ideas landed but few took off, for lack of fuel. Perfect analogy, I thought, for my life at the law school. This became even more true during the Great Recession that began with the financial crisis in my first year as president.

My drumbeat focused relentlessly on the need for us to take steps beyond simply carrying our alms cup to Richmond and rattling it. I drove home that because the state would not, could not, provide adequately for us, William & Mary must increasingly see to its own financial salvation. To this end, all parts of the university community had to pull their fund-generating oars—administration, staff and faculty, board of visitors and foundation boards, students and parents, alumni and friends. No part of our whole could stand on the sidelines waiting to be fed.

This did not mean we would stop seeking help from the state, especially for bricks and mortar. The state was, in fact, extremely helpful with funds to renovate and build at a time when William & Mary badly needed to breathe new life into its physical being.

I was less willing than the average bear to accept the view that when the state didn't provide what we needed, we should reflexively cut the budget, as opposed to finding other ways to generate revenue.

I leaned hard on the state to let William & Mary take more high-paying out-of-state students, something some public institutions in the rest of the country were beginning to do. This proved politically infeasible while I was president, but it's beginning to get some traction in the commonwealth now. It makes powerfully good sense on so many scores.

Governments have an insatiable desire to impose regulatory requirements on schools, with attendant costs. Meeting the health and wellness needs of students, especially their mental health needs, has become extremely costly. Technology, security, athletics—the list goes on ad infinitum, all requiring staff, facilities, and operating funds. The explosion in knowledge also calls for ever more sophisticated academic responses. Need-based financial aid for students and competitive compensation for faculty and staff are major consumers of cash. Each center of expense has its own constituency jealously guarding the ramparts, with scant regard for the trade-offs essential in any enterprise. Sometimes it feels like the only friends trade-offs have are the president and provost.

Reveley IV: The political climate hasn't been favorable either. The right for almost a generation has been dyspeptic about higher education. The left talks about corporatization. They both complain about cost. And those complaints have a lot of commonsense appeal, which is why they resonate politically. But simple stories of administrative bloat do not describe what's really going on.

Health care costs, for example—Longwood today spends millions of dollars more each year just on health care for our employees than we did ten years ago, on essentially the same total employee base. That's a staggering amount that, unlike, say, a new building, has no effect on people's perceptions because it's not resulting in anything that looks or feels different.

Reveley III: When people complained about our costs of operation, I'd start by asking, "What would you like us to eliminate? IT? Campus safety? Our diversity efforts?" If they had an answer, I'd probe it until they contemplated the possibility they might be mistaken. I'd point out that some of our freshman dorms were not graced with air conditioning, for example.

Building an Operation

Fundraising (later relabeled in higher ed–speak as "development" and then "advancement") is the furthest thing from a one-person operation, although the president clearly stands at its center. When TR2 became president of Hampden-Sydney, not a single staff position was devoted to raising money. If anything was done, TR2 did it until finally he was able to create a small development office.

Reveley III: The obstacles Daddy faced were enormous. There was campus resistance to creating a development office because it would cost money when money was badly needed on every front. The alumni body was tiny and included few alums with major resources. Alumni were not accustomed to giving much to the college, if they gave at all—they hadn't really been asked because there was no development staff to ask them. Foundations and corporations were not drawn to Hampden-Sydney because it was so small; again, there was no development staff to educate and pursue them. The Presbyterian Church no longer was a meaningful source of financial support. And the college didn't yet accept federal money because that required taking racial equity steps the more conservative members of the body politic, including some on the board, were unwilling to take. Early in his presidency, Daddy got that to change.

TR2 had a lot of ecclesiastical and athletic experience, knew teaching and academic administration very well, had years of dealing gracefully with all sorts of people, and knew how to keep a thousand balls in the air at once. But he had to learn the mysteries and rhythms of serious fundraising. Even if he had been a veritable wizard at it going into the presidency, Hampden-Sydney was not a fertile field for fundraising in the 1960s.

MARIE EASON REVELEY: Right from the start, Taylor saw the need for a development office as paramount. One of his recent predecessors as president, Dr. Joseph Robert, had attempted to instigate a development office, but the young man he brought in soon fled to greener pastures. His efforts were perceived by a nucleus of Hampden-Sydney men as a threat to the "real" Hampden-Sydney.

Because of the covenant relationship between the Church and the college, which Taylor thought was important, the splendid ministers and laymen elected to the board had only limited access to those foundations and individuals who might bestow significant funds on the college.

REVELEY III: During a $2 million campaign for the two Presbyterian-related colleges in Virginia, Daddy went from church to church preaching, urging congregations to put Hampden-Sydney and Mary Baldwin College in their budgets. The yield on this effort was modest compared to the time and energy required.

MARIE EASON REVELEY: Taylor did manage to persuade a major prospect to visit the college and hoped he would assist in funding the construction of a new science building. Afterward the man wrote Taylor to say that he'd prefer to give his money to students and institutions that were actually in need. He based his judgment on the number of cars he saw on campus and on Hampden-Sydney's failure to seek government funds, which he interpreted to mean that Hampden-Sydney and its students must have all the money they needed.

The same thing happened when Charles Dana of the Dana Foundation visited. When someone began telling him about Hampden-Sydney's famed proportion of men who were listed in *Who's Who,* Mr. Dana cut him off. "I'm not interested in that," he stated bluntly. "Hampden-Sydney students are capable of paying more than they are paying and the board members and alumni must contribute more than they are contributing. And they don't want to seek government funds."

Taylor, in his low-key way, was able to persuade the board . . . to consider accepting government funds, with all that acceptance implied. Government dictates would include actively seeking black students, a belief which Taylor had held for some years.

Reveley III: He persuaded the board to desegregate the college, and it began admitting Black students. This was crucial to Hampden-Sydney's future, and its soul. It opened the door to federal funds the Johnson administration had flowing from Washington. A Hampden-Sydney development office was created, staff hired, and an annual giving program launched. Daddy and Mother worked doggedly at fundraising, planting seeds that drove prosperity for decades ahead.

In 1974, TR2 told the board of trustees, in connection with the college's planned bicentennial celebration in 1976, that they needed to help in specific ways.

Reveley II: Make no mistake: the receipt of federal funds is no unmixed blessing. Just the multiplicity of paperwork has frightened many a business office. Yet when private support is so inadequate, assistance from federal sources becomes necessary in the competitive struggle for faculty and facilities.[4]

Reveley II, *President's Report to the Board of Trustees,* 1974: Each trustee will receive the names of two or three prospects whom we want him to cultivate and secure a contribution and/or pledge to the 1976

Bicentennial Fund.... If by more careful cultivation a ten thousand dollar gift can be a one hundred thousand dollar one, or a half-million can become a million, then please do not hurry.[5]

TR2's efforts bore fruit. By the time he retired in 1977, the college's endowment had more than doubled to about $10 million. Federal funds had been secured. The college experienced the greatest period of new construction in its history. The science building and dormitory were built, along with more faculty housing, increased athletic facilities, a library expansion, a new infirmary, and more.

REVELEY IV: His dogged work produced notable results in their day. In his closing year in office the college received the largest gift by far in its history to that time—roughly $14 million in present-day dollars, adjusting for inflation.

By 2008, when TR3 became president of William & Mary, the need for an extensive advancement operation was crystal clear at all institutions of higher education. Once the dust settled from the financial crisis that tanked the economy that fall and sent it spiraling into recession, he set the wheels in motion that eventually become the For the Bold campaign.

REVELEY III: William & Mary had very recently finished a campaign for $500 million. My first idea was, let's take a run at $250 million for student aid. But as we meditated, the conclusion was, "not worth the effort." A consultant then took soundings and reported we might raise $600 million, but it would take enormous effort and still might run aground.

To head the advancement phalanx, I recruited Matthew Lambert, who was then at Georgetown University and already a master fundraiser, despite his tender years.[6] We got another consultant report. With trepidation, it said a billion dollars was conceivable though mountains would have to be climbed.

At that time, no public university without a medical or engineering school had ever raised a billion dollars. William & Mary had neither a medical nor an engineering school. Nor had any public university our size, about 8,400 students, undergraduate and graduate. There was serious concern about even trying, lest failure take a real bite out of the university's morale and momentum. Matthew was unphased. I remember him saying something to the effect of, "We gotta be bold." We got agreement from our alumni leaders and the crucial boards, named the campaign "For the Bold," and blasted off.

"Six hundred million doesn't get the blood flowing," TR3 told the *Washington Post*. "A billion, on the other hand, is a round number with some body and flavor."[7]

Reveley III: The campaign required quickly growing a very large development staff, staging countless high-quality events in Virginia and around the country, and committing a whole lot of money to the mission. In our case, this meant taking funds from some other attractive initiatives and drawing on our reserves. That was a political call I had to make, with support from the board of visitors and the William & Mary Foundation Board. To better staff the effort we created fundraising offices outside Williamsburg in the District of Columbia, New York, and California. Matthew and I were on the road continually, along with our indefatigable campaign chair, Sue Gerdelman, an alumna. Development staff were on the road even more.

For Matthew and his people, a crucial step was deciding who we needed to see on each road trip, getting appointments to see them (a task not for the faint of heart), and working to bunch them reasonably close to each other geographically. When there were interludes between visits, we'd go to a Starbucks or some other watering hole, whip out our computers, and try to catch up on the work stacking up back at the ranch. Usually there was also an alumni event of some magnitude at which I would speak and press the flesh with as many people as possible. We did that over and over again.

Early on we developed For the Bold materials keyed to particular needs. There was heavy emphasis on funds for people, not buildings, especially financial aid for students. But our appetite for gifts was omnivorous. If somebody said, "I'm not interested in giving to anything on this list but I would like to give this bit of bricks and mortar," you certainly took the money, so long as the donor's intent was compatible with the university's interests.

For the Bold was a howling success, not just in the funds raised but in creating a powerful development office, ready to do great deeds in the future. It also built broad-based financial support for the university, especially among alumni. Our percentage of alumni who give annually to alma mater became the highest of any public university in the country and remains one of the highest. For the Bold brought the Tribe together for elegant, rousing, confidence-building parties across the country. These events continue. The campaign was living proof that William & Mary increasingly can rely on itself to feed itself. By the time I retired, we had raised slightly over $800 million. My successor, Katherine Rowe, raised the remaining $200 million and more, finishing just as COVID hit in early 2020.

Reveley IV: There's an extent to which a proud alum knows, when the president comes to visit—they know why you're there, and it feels like an imprimatur and a rite of passage. "I've really made it, haven't I? The old place is coming to get my help."

Reveley III: Even faculty can be a resource for fundraising when they have ties to former students. I pushed for a while to get departments and programs to figure out which of their graduates they might productively engage. Some tried, and some individual professors were crucial in securing funds. But faculty in general, like most mortals, are reluctant to ask other people for anything so crass. They're afraid they'll tarnish their cordial relationships with former students by talking about money. We probably didn't provide enough development staff to that part of the effort for it to realize its potential.

Many people on campus, including some faculty, didn't get that most gifts to schools these days are given for specific purposes and this is all they can be used for. Or that gifts made in bequests aren't available until the Grim Reaper reaps. And even gifts made without conditions while the donor is aboveground are often paid over a number of years. I kept hearing, "We're raising a billion, where's the bread?" So I wrote a message to the campus community laying out how all this works and beamed it out as an email attachment. It didn't generate robust conversation.

The private foundations that support various aspects of the university played meaningful roles in For the Bold. The William & Mary Foundation, with its university-wide focus, pulled the strongest oar. Its board members were extraordinarily generous and useful. Matthew Lambert and I worked hard to be sure this foundation was heavily engaged.

An important by-product of For the Bold was its impetus to do something thought to be politically infeasible at William & Mary. This "something" had long been regarded as the third rail of campus politics—deadly if touched. It involved mating the alumni and development offices to create an integrated advancement whole, devoted to both nurturing ties to alumni and raising funds from all corners. Our alumni leadership, though able and vigorous, had long operated on shoestrings. Their effort to raise funds to build a badly needed addition to the Alumni House on campus was lagging. Development, in turn, needed their know-how to help galvanize and delight the alumni. After hard negotiating, the deed was done. It proved enormously successful.

REVELEY IV: And of course, when I became president of Longwood there was a lot of shop talk with my dad about how to make an advancement operation really sing, because he was in full cry doing that at William & Mary. Similarly at the forefront for me were all the hard-charging efforts with Governor Baliles at the Miller Center because we were working the high art of philanthropy there every day, every week, every year.

Longwood, by contrast, needed to shift into a higher gear at that point with fundraising, and was eager to do so, building on strong efforts in recent years, because the future was not one of more and more state support but one in which universities would rise and fall increasingly on their own efforts. Building up our operation was a mix of adopting new approaches and relying on Longwood's experienced and veteran staff. Courtney Hodges, who had already been in our advancement office for almost a decade when I started, quickly stood out as a leader who could drive our efforts to the next level. The juggernaut began to roll.

Annual Giving

REVELEY III: In most of my board memberships, I've been involved in raising money, especially in sounding the trumpet for annual giving. "AG," in my view, is the queen of philanthropy because everyone can participate, not just fat cats. Even the smallest gifts count. Donors can get started when they are very young, develop the habit of giving every year, and then, as their resources increase, become larger donors. Annual giving is a garden in which major gifts often grow. It also provides immediate fuel for operating budgets and does it dollar for dollar, unlike endowments, which take a while to begin producing and contribute a very small percentage of their assets each year to the operating budget.

Despite annual giving's virtues, it isn't an emphasis for most development vice presidents. It requires recruiting and training many volunteer helpers and doesn't have the career-enhancing gratification of major gifts. I sang AG's virtues loudly at William & Mary until it was firmly rooted.

I would tell young alums, starting while they were still on campus, especially as graduation approached, your gift to William & Mary, whatever its size, matters because you matter to William & Mary. If it's $10, we'll take the $10 cheerfully. Once you get into the habit of annual giving, your small gift can grow as you prosper. If you become an enormously fat cat, you can make a huge difference for the better. But however large or small your annual gifts prove to be as the years roll by, making them is a way to stay in touch with William & Mary and keep nurturing her. Your annual gift is a vote for alma mater.

I would usually add that a degree from W&M is one of your assets. Like assets generally, the value of your degree keeps appreciating or depreciating. For lots of reasons, appreciating is better, and this hinges, in no small measure, on alumni support for the university. Then I'd add the "Ah!" or "oh" test. When asked where you went to school and you reply "William & Mary," you want to hear an "Ah!" not an "oh."

I really was an apostle of annual giving. Through endless labors, we got the alumni participation rate up to 30 percent, a stratospheric number by public university standards.

REVELEY IV: One thing we've found, or perhaps confirmed, is that students are really the superpower from an annual giving standpoint. When a loyal alum gets a call from a current student or a note from a current student, that has a powerful effect.

Major Gifts

As TR3 and TR4 agree, one virtue of inculcating the habit of annual giving, however small the amount, is that it may form a lifelong habit that, as time goes by, can result in the sort of major—that is, large, often multimillion-dollar—gifts that can truly transform a university. Annual gifts donated one year help fund operations the next year. Major gifts are long-term assets, either money for the endowment or buildings for the campus. In 2022, more than 80 percent of the $60 billion donated to American colleges and universities came from 1 percent of all donors.[8]

REVELEY IV: Out of the gate I focused on major gifts so that we could communicate to the campus and the larger world that Longwood was ready to be a serious player in the philanthropic world. It's very tempting to think that all wealthy institutions were always wealthy, but that's not so. Princeton in particular, arguably the wealthiest, pound for pound, institution in America today, was not wealthy a hundred years ago.[9] It wasn't impoverished, but it was a little bit less wealthy than Longwood is right now. It then made the decisive turn to start raising money and perfected the art. Inflation obfuscates everything, but it wasn't until the 1960s that Princeton's endowment reached $100 million, which is about where Longwood's is.

All of which is a long way of saying that when I was first really thinking about Longwood from a presidential standpoint during the search in 2012–2013, it was very clear that it could make real strides. We especially needed to overcome the long and vexing sense around campus that, although you could raise money for buildings now and then or for athletics or for certain quirky things, it was just impossible for Longwood to raise money for the direct heart of the academic enterprise. We disproved that theory, more than doubling the endowment, and only then began focusing on tuning the annual giving agenda, which is so important for all the reasons my dad mentioned.

REVELEY III: The relationship you forge with a prospective donor is key, and the relationship has to be nurtured and cultivated. It helps enormously if you come to have genuine respect and affection for the donor, if you truly like the person, and if he or she truly cares about you. Still, you are leaning on them to part with significant resources, which they know perfectly well. You have to be willing and able to look them in the eye and make the ask, especially if it's for mega-bucks.

REVELEY IV: The presidential visit usually is not the first step when seeking a major gift, although it can be in occasional circumstances. Not unlike in political fundraising, at consequential levels the principal is not wheeled into motion until things are really primed for that.

Reveley III: The way the donor mating dance typically begins is, the research arm of your fundraising staff seeks to divine whether a potential donor has serious means. That's step one. If so, the second question is whether there are signs the person is willing to give money away and does so. The research people can help again. Third, if the results are promising on these first two scores, is there reason to hope the person might be interested in helping your school? Well, there's always hope in life; at times hope may have legs, and further research may find out. Finally, if the person is prosperous and philanthropic, is he or she already supporting other worthy causes and firmly committed to them? Finding out usually takes visiting the prospect for live conversation.

During For the Bold it was distressing to talk once with an alumnus in a city far from Virginia who loved William & Mary, had serious means, gave generously, but was already committed to institutions in his community. Turns out William & Mary had never talked with him about the possibility of a major gift to alma mater. We came to the party too late. There is compelling merit to timely development research.

Bonds of trust and affection are often so very important between donors and the president and senior development people. It takes time to build these bonds, many visits, much conversation, many meals shared. Real, lasting friendships can result. So, often, does a continuing stream of significant support.

When it was time to talk money, I always put in a plug for unrestricted gifts. Unrestricted endowment is worth its weight in gold, because it can go where funds are most needed. These days donors have little appetite for unrestricted gifts. They want to specify how their gifts will be used. Often, however, they are very open to suggestions about which specific purposes those gifts might support. We would usually suggest several, after trying hard to first find out where the donor's interests lay.

A well-conceived, really large gift can be dynamite, and not just for the school. Giving can be exhilarating for those making the gift as well as for those receiving it. Seeing cheerful givers delighting in what their largesse wrought was one of the most marvelous aspects of my time as president.

Reveley IV: When the time comes to make the ask for a major gift, if it's being done adroitly, no one gasps at the mention of high six figures or really seven figures and above. Instead it's like a complex business transaction where nobody's surprised at the end by what's under discussion.

It's tempting for people to think that the art of raising money is a mystical exercise in which the fundraiser somehow performs exotic feats of psychology to persuade people to do things they don't actually want to do. In reality, strange as it may sound, you are helping the donors as much as they are helping the institution. They often find that making a major gift is one of the most meaningful things they do in their lives. They—at least many of them, in my experience—view their great wealth as an intense and significant responsibility, and they are eager to find ways to fulfill that responsibility fruitfully and meaningfully. And you can help people think that through.

REVELEY III: You begin to plumb such details as the timing of the gift—while the donor lives or later in an estate? If the latter, I would usually tell them, only partly in jest, that, at least in William & Mary's experience, making an estate gift would extend their life by fifteen years or more.

For some truly major gifts, closing the deal can take a long time. A lot of concerns must be addressed, sometimes more than once. A lot of reassurance must be credibly offered. Presidents need to be patient and pastoral. You cover the same ground over and over, as often as needed. I found some major donors feared that these days, universities spend money profligately and so they don't really need more funds—not unlike what Daddy heard from a couple of major prospects when he was president of Hampden-Sydney. And so you try to demonstrate with data (in one crucial instance, an exhaustive amount of data) that this isn't true of William & Mary.

Marvelous gifts do sometimes simply drop out of the sky. But, as a practical matter, you might as well count on the Easter Bunny as count on that.

REVELEY IV: The stars sometimes align to drive momentum. A month after we hosted the vice presidential debate in 2016, we finalized and announced the then-largest gift in Longwood's history, $5.9 million from the great Joan and Macon Brock to endow our place-based learning initiative, courses we call Brock Experiences and which involve intensive travel within the United States rather than abroad. Our philanthropic engine really took off from that point forward. An exclamation point a few years later was the $15 million lead gift for the Joan Perry Brock Center, our convocation center now gleaming in the heart of campus.

Reveley III: Giving responds much more readily to reports of success than to cries of doom. To plaintively (or angrily) cry that the state has failed to provide vital support, the university barely has one nostril over the waves, so please come to alma mater's relief—to say all that is not very effective. Far better to trumpet that William & Mary's juggernaut is rolling, so come get behind it and help push alma mater to ever greater glory.

10
Leading

How to lead a college or university is a matter all three Reveley presidents have thought about seriously. In an era in which the average presidential tenure has fallen below six years, the ability of each of the three to lead for a decade or more and leave at a time of his own choosing is remarkable. All of them led successfully not only on their own campuses but among their peers in the commonwealth. During their presidential tenures, TR2 was elected to chair the Virginia Foundation for Independent Colleges for 1970–1972, TR3 to chair the Virginia Council of Presidents (formally the Council of Presidents of Colleges and Universities in Virginia) for 2016–2017, and TR4 to chair the Virginia Council of Presidents for 2023–2024.

In the course of reflecting on careers and life paths that led them to their presidencies and the variety of issues with which they dealt in office, the Reveley presidents sometimes reflected on leadership more generally. The leadership challenges facing TR3 and TR4 as college presidents resembled those facing TR2 by the end of his tenure in 1977, challenges very different from those that greeted him and other presidents of his generation at the time he took office in 1963.

OWEN NORMENT: Taylor began his presidency under an older model and concluded it fourteen years later with crucial elements of a newer model firmly in place, establishing lines along which future developments would occur. In the older presidential model, the president is largely concerned with internal management of the college and closely oversees faculty and other administrative areas. In the early years of his presidency, for example, Taylor chaired faculty meetings and certain college committees and was closely involved with faculty hiring and curriculum development. There were relatively few administrative officers and little staff support.

In the newer model, and with Taylor's guidance, the administration became fully professionalized with new and needed positions added, such as an office of development and a director of counseling and career services. The academic dean gained more authority over curricular development and faculty recruitment and began to chair faculty meetings. With this administrative evolution, the president's attention could be directed more generally, to broader institutional needs, especially external college relations and long-needed financial stability.[1]

By the time TR3 became president of William & Mary, the newer model of presidential leadership was fully established in American higher education.

Reveley III: I remember when I first went into my office in the Brafferton and my new executive assistant gave me a notebook labeled "President Reveley's Schedule." All of a sudden you are "Mr. President" and people defer to you in ways different from other jobs you've had. Some of them don't always tell you what they actually think as opposed to what they believe you want to hear. That's an occupational hazard you have to look out for assiduously. I first began experiencing it while managing partner of a law firm, and then as law school dean, but it took even more vigilance when I became president.

Being called "Mr. President" did fall sweetly on my ears, I gotta admit. I told myself that's silly. There are a whole host of academic presidents in the USA. But I liked it, though I responded cheerfully to anything, and when asked what to call me, said "Taylor." That's the way I signed my letters, "Taylor," on most of my communications to the campus and alumni, not "President Reveley."

Still, on your own campus, being the president is a big deal. I'd seen that with my father at Hampden-Sydney. Within the confines of your institution, you are the Big Enchilada, so long as you are doing well and seem to be hanging on to the mandate of heaven.

I'd seen how satisfying it was for TR2 to leave Hampden-Sydney in far better shape than he found it, pretty much across the board. When you take a ship that's heading for the rocks and get it turned around and sailing in accord with its mission, that's enormously satisfying.

Reveley IV: Not that we haven't faced challenging times, to say the least, but his years at Hampden-Sydney from 1963 to 1977 were obviously among the most fraught in American history. From the civil rights movement to the various assassinations to urban riots to Vietnam and all that the war unleashed at home—just to mention some of the obvious highlights and lowlights of that period, all of them with seismic effects on college and university campuses, which were at the epicenter of the nation's shift in mores.

REVELEY III: Daddy's experience and example helped me grasp a reassuring reality about higher education, at least for schools with deep roots in their communities and the affection of their alumni. They're probably the most indestructible industry in the United States. It's really hard to kill them, which means they survive presidents who are ineffective, or worse, and thrive anew with really able presidents.

REVELEY IV: It's true. If you look at the Fortune 500 of American companies, you will not find many that are even a century old. By contrast, if you constituted a Fortune 500 equivalent of American colleges and universities, you would find many, like Longwood, that have been there since the nineteenth century and a few from before that, including William & Mary and Hampden-Sydney.[2]

Which isn't to say that leading a college or university is the same now as it was then, or from era to era. With regard to the power to get things done, there is command authority, on the one hand, and persuasive authority on the other, and different sectors of life have different balances of the two. In the military, command authority is at a premium, but persuasive authority still matters enormously. In the corporate world, command authority is not quite what it is in the military, but it's still consequential, as is persuasive authority. In government, persuasive authority matters more, but there's still plenty of command authority. But in academia, college and university presidents have far less command authority than most people assume—and much less than a century or so ago—but they do have enormous standing to exercise persuasive authority. A president needs to comprehend that "You will do this because I am telling you to do it" won't work for very long or for many things, but "I think we should do this for these good reasons" has a really good chance of succeeding.

REVELEY III: Well, true, though it seems to me you can direct quite a bit, especially when getting things started, even with the board of visitors and the faculty. And the administrative wing of a university, which has become quite large and important, is a sphere where the president has a lot of command authority. But even when in command mode, it would be very unwise to speak in command terms, and I didn't. Far better to direct the orchestra with as much grace and empathy as you can muster. Treat people as colleagues—that's everyone, junior staff included, perhaps especially them. By the same token, however, when I asked that something be done, or made a decision about what to do, I expected it to happen, unless those charged to act came back and explained why another course might be preferable and I agreed they were right.

REVELEY IV: It's been interesting hearing you say this, because I often feel that the only thing I can just unilaterally decide is what I'll have for breakfast. Everything else is a function of cajoling in one way or another. But that constant stream of negotiating is easiest when you keep the best interests of the institution at the forefront, the common good. It's also easiest when there's minimal focus on who gets credit in triumph or red marks in defeat.

Within the metes and bounds of a college or university, there is a far more complex kind of British constitution–style governance situation than in other walks of life—shared governance with the faculty, a volunteer board, parents and students, the town-gown dynamic. So you constantly find yourself dealing with the ambiguity of which barons are paramount, so to speak, as well as which need primary attention at a particular moment.

If you distill what a president has to be good at, it's, to begin with, decision-making, which sounds straightforward, but the simple act of making decisions takes some fortitude and willingness to deal with the flak that usually comes with them.

REVELEY III: Flak is going to come sooner or later, and at times it may seem relentless. Even when the flak is deserved, it may be stated in vile terms and, with social media, be instantly delivered, grow enormously, and wander farther and farther from reality. If you can't take it—can't control your anger, can't stop thinking about it even in the middle of the night—it's time to think seriously about laying down your mantle and letting somebody else lead.

REVELEY IV: You also have to be good with words, written words, spoken words. You have to be good with money in practical terms—how to find it, track it, disperse it—and also understand its powerful psychological dimensions. Then you have to be good with people, and have the finesse and ease and ingenuity with them to resolve situations that don't lend themselves to textbook solutions. And if you're not good at all those things, you can easily find yourself wandering on winding paths in the deep woods.

You also need the perspective to realize that presidents of the United States at their zenith know that 40 percent of the country is not with them, which is something that academia can lose sight of. Academia gets very tempted to operate by veto rules so that if a particular faculty member or trustee or other stakeholder objects, that's enough for everybody else to say, "That obviously can't happen now that Bob or Sally doesn't want it." The fact is there's always dissent and as long as you steel your soul and go about things in a principled way, dissent is an aspect of the process as opposed to a defect.

REVELEY III: It really helps if you care about people, and they know you care, especially when you're telling them things they don't want to hear. One of Daddy's salient characteristics was he wanted to help people succeed. He was not looking for reasons that a young professor should be deemed a failure and thus ripe to be driven off so that someone more glittering could be brought in. That just wasn't his worldview. If a staff member was having trouble he would often basically do their work for them to get them jollied along, sometimes to an extreme when really it was the wrong person for the job.

MARIE EASON REVELEY: Temperamentally, Taylor was a mediator. His forbearance, patience and nonjudgmental characteristics helped.... [He] controlled his desire to excoriate those who blocked or aggravated him.

Sports had taught him to take his lumps. His training and work experience had routinely placed him in positions which required self-control on his part while guiding some who displayed an absence of that quality. He did not complain to me of the behavior of others.[3]

REVELEY III: I think one of the hardest things is to deliver bad news to people and tell them no. It's really hard to do that. But the farther up the chain you go as a leader, the more you have to make decisions that disappoint some people, and the more you sometimes have to make really wrenching decisions to advance the best interests of the university. And even as you're in the throes of making a hard decision, or have just made one, you've still got to move on with the schedule, and if the next act is an event that is supposed to be cheerful and fluffy, you've got to be cheerful and fluffy.

Hard decisions come with the territory of being a leader, and that's why, when push comes to shove, I believe a lot of people really don't want to lead. They may be extremely good at what they otherwise do. They may have strong views about what their school ought to be doing. They may express their views freely, even vociferously. But they are not actually inclined themselves to get in the arena and see what they personally can get done. And on those occasions when they do get in the arena, they find there's a lot to learn to lead effectively, and they may also find that doing it isn't as satisfying for them as what they used to do, for instance, teaching, research, writing.

Early on, when I was young and began getting involved with organizations, I started feeling like, if I'm going to be spending time on this, I might as well be the lead dog. This was especially true if things I cared about weren't progressing.

Reveley IV: The impulse to not see things get screwed up is probably highly correlated with the impulse to seize the wheel.

Reveley III: You need a leader, first of all, to set priorities. There are always a large number of worthy things that might be done, but you don't have time or energy or resources to do all of them. So you have to pick and choose, and it's really hard to pick and choose unless someone takes the lead. Every day people are coming to you, over the internet, in writing, in person, saying, "William & Mary needs to do this or that" or "this is a big opportunity or a big difficulty you've got to focus on next." You can easily, every day, end up spending most of your time dealing with what's come in over the transom as opposed to the core issues that you are pushing forward. Really hard to stay focused on those core issues, but if you don't you're not going forward.

Then you've got to rally the troops to move in that direction, to persuade people to follow you. The question is, how and when should the persuading take place? It obviously depends on the circumstances. For small matters, it may suffice simply to ask people to do what you think necessary. Major matters are different.

I am not a great devotee of explaining everything in advance to the whole body politic, seeking comprehensive understanding and buy-in at the outset of big initiatives. It's often better in my view to do that initially with the small cohort of those who must act to get things rolling. If you and they can then move the initiative through its fledgling stage to early success, that success will have persuasive power for the rest of the body politic, even those who would have strongly objected to the initiative on its merits or for fear of failure. I know this grossly oversimplifies the complex dynamics of getting people moving toward important goals, but it does seem to me if you wait for everyone to be on board before moving out, you may never move out, or you'll do it late, allowing people too much time to tie themselves to the mast of passionately articulated objections.

Part of persuasion is inspiration. The leader, particularly when it's a hard road to travel, has to keep inspiring the troops with a galvanizing vision of what lies ahead—without creating unrealistic, unachievable expectations. That's very hard to do. It's awfully easy to end up veering too much toward either undue optimism about how splendid it will all be or undue pessimism, grim and dour, about the difficulties of the road ahead and how many wolves lie in wait.

It sure helps if you can stand on your hind legs and talk in a way people want to hear. You hope they will look forward to listening to you, not groan, "Oh Lord, he's approaching the podium, heaven only knows how long he'll talk or how many times he'll repeat himself this time." Presidents need to talk in winsome, compelling ways. Standing up and babbling, with little or no forethought about what to say, doesn't cut it.

When I was practicing law, it was hard for me initially to do the amount and type of public speaking required for litigation. I started out shy. But if you have to learn, you learn.

You've also got to deal with the internal conflicts that inevitably arise as you go forward. It's crucial to make midcourse corrections when necessary, or even abandon an effort that proves feckless. Acknowledge that, and move on to something else.

It's hard to admit it when you make mistakes. You've got to avoid the impulse to put your head down and mush on, hoping no one will see the mistake, or bob and weave, blame malign fate or other people, anything but yourself. Instead you need to say, early on, I whiffed, I goofed, I blew it, I'm sorry and I won't let it happen again.

It helps if you surround yourself with good people, nurture them, delegate to them, and then leave them alone to do their jobs. Got to draw fully on their talents. If you don't, if you constantly hover over their shoulders or do their jobs for them, you'll burn out while getting little done that you need to do.

Above all, you have to want to lead. If you don't want to lead, it's very hard to do it effectively.

Reveley IV: A college presidency is a field of temptation to just wander in any of a thousand directions because there are ten thousand interesting things going on at any college campus. And they're all worthy in their own way. And if you don't stick to what really needs to get done, you can easily delude yourself into thinking that you're doing important things.

Reveley III: It's not worth fighting every battle. Particularly when core values or basic operational issues aren't at stake. Sometimes it's just a garden-variety disagreement, even though passions may run high. Presidents have a finite amount of political capital. You have to decide how much you're willing to spend to prevail on this or that matter. It's always prudent to keep in mind what the consequences of winning might be for future effectiveness. It's not good if people feel dragged behind your chariot wheels.

Reveley IV: But the wheels have to churn, and do keep churning relentlessly, and with such pace. Once upon a time, pre-Longwood, if somebody had asked me what I'd be doing three Thursdays from now, I would have quite readily been able to tell them. Whereas now I essentially wake up in the morning and look at my phone calendar, and discover what those who are able to add to my schedule have put there. Sometimes that will change in the midst of the day, as other people add to it. You're in charge in one regard, but in other regards you have to just let it flow and go where you're supposed to go.

Then you add the events that seize the psyche—Charlottesville in 2017, the George Floyd murder in 2020, the Israel-Gaza conflict starting in 2023—and come with shock or unforeseeably. They almost always arise from somewhere else, but given social media, they land on your campus too. And they will consume your attention just by their very force, as will a sudden and awful event within the campus community, like the death or disappearance or arrest of a student. And you have to deal with those matters in real time without much opportunity for perspective to build.

On one occasion in our interviews, TR4 reviewed the complicated reality of a somewhat typical day in his life as president.

Reveley IV: Faculty and others periodically wonder, what does a president even do? So here's how I spent Wednesday, September 15, 2021, a day in the office and not out on the hustings or far afield for fundraising or legislative work. It was also a day that did not involve public speaking or making the rounds on campus, but not unusual in the range of focus it required. The issues of that workday were:

- Meeting at length with key folks about the complex riddle of admissions against the tides of changing demography.
- Meeting at length with a core set of people about the dynamics of all the key personnel considerations around Longwood and how to keep everything moving.
- We had a student die very tragically several days before. And without any rival, that is the hardest thing that this job brings to you. It was unclear what, exactly, happened. Possibly a stroke. It's very complicated, and each death has its own set of complications.
- Considering the fanfare and substance around this being the year we'll graduate our first class to have fully gone through our new core curriculum, Civitae.
- Then planning the dedication ceremony for the research facility that we're naming after Jerry Baliles next month, the complex hydraulics of who in the diaspora from a beloved governor's administration gets invited to what and when, and who speaks, etc.
- Then a meeting with six or seven people about Longwood merchandise—baseball caps and tee shirts and the like—and how that licensing works. That's on the order of a million dollars a year in merchandising, sales.
- Then naturally some of the folks from that meeting, including the athletic director, went into some discussion about the athletic department and some considerations that she has right now, trying to keep a key member of her team.

- Then turned to talking with our finance brain trust about a very complex nine-figure deal related to energy efficiency and sustainability that we'd been working at for almost a year.
- Which then led to a different but germane thing, which was talking about our live-on-campus requirement for students, how we want to handle that, going forward.
- Which then led to a phone call from the mayor of Farmville to talk about the Afghan refugee situation. Fort Pickett is relatively close to Farmville, and that's where several thousand Afghan refugees are right now, and there's been some discussion of whether many might come to Farmville and what role Longwood might play. Very unclear who exactly is in charge at the state level or the federal level. So we were attempting to demystify that, which led to just some inside-baseball discussion of town dynamics.
- I then turned my attention to the HVAC system in the sorority dorm, which has not been working over the last week when it's been very hot. This sounds like it would be small potatoes but it resulted in lots of angry calls from sorority parents.
- And then I closed out the workday with a meeting with the executive committee of the Longwood University Foundation, which needed to hire a new executive director. After the meeting, I had several follow-up conversations with various folks about who the executive director might be.

And that was it, a mix of ballet and improv that's really only possible—and this is likely true of any presidency that's trundling along well—because of the gifts of my assistant, which is too light a title, Kay Stokes. She gracefully weaves it all, and that is vital.

This was a hard and varied day, but not one of the hardest or more varied, or even unusual. So you add it all together, and there are very few days when it's just calm and you feel like you're able to push your agenda forward easily. Even so, knowing that whatever challenges a college president might face, they are not the challenges that FDR or Lincoln or Washington faced—that can give you some ballast.

REVELEY III: There is conflict between all that comes at you every day, some scheduled and some random, and the need to keep on pushing toward major goals. I found that to do both took a huge amount of work, during the day, at night, on weekends, with splendid help from Michael Fox and my executive assistant, Cindy Brauer—or earlier, Cassi Fritzius at the law school, or still earlier, Fran Minner at Hunton. Experience teaches you how to let people help you.

Leadership is a collective matter. It's crucial for presidents to surround themselves with very strong, capable, independent lieutenants who are committed to the good of the university and are leaders themselves. Some of them will probably be in place when you become president. Others you will recruit. In every instance, you want to help them grow in their abilities and capacity to do great deeds. I was young when I became managing partner of my law firm. I wasn't accustomed to delegating much. It quickly became apparent: either start seriously delegating or start failing to get done all the firm needed done. I developed a profound appreciation for delegating.

I inherited some splendid senior administrators at William & Mary upon becoming president and brought in others. A couple of them were barely out of the cradle, especially compared to me, and are now meeting new challenges—Henry Broaddus, leading Virginia's Episcopal Church Schools, and Jeremy Martin, now president of Florida Southern College. They all had powerful work ethics, liked and respected their colleagues, and worked well together. All, too, were willing to tell me what they thought. Once decisions were made, even if not of their choosing, they jumped to, without whining or backbiting. I was blessed. This emphatically isn't how it is for all presidents. But when it is, you can make extraordinary progress.

REVELEY IV: You cannot lead in isolation. Leadership always occurs in a crowd. I have yet to surround myself with people in really consequential positions that I didn't enjoy being around, at Longwood or before. And I also often have this military phrase in mind: "Can they hold a command?" Do they have the ability to rally their troops to get the job done?

There's also an extent to which temperament and judgment are arguably more crucial for a college president than pure analytical capacity. If a leader is too purely analytical, too reliant on their sheer intellectual firepower, that itself can be a stumbling block. Inherent in the art of leading others is being able to discern which other people to rely on and which to trust.

REVELEY III: Some aspects of leading, I think, you learn by watching other people lead successfully and unsuccessfully. You see what you think works and what doesn't work. Other aspects, probably most of them, you learn by experience, by actually doing the job, and developing your own ways of leading. There is no one way. A good bit depends on taking advantage of your comparative strengths and steering clear, to the extent feasible, of your comparative weaknesses. And having a constant appetite for learning how to lead better.

Of course, there are also aspects you can be taught—for instance, to mention a mundane matter, how to run a meeting that doesn't drive people nuts, or leave them feeling left out, or take forever to work its agenda. It's surprising how many otherwise able people have no idea how to run a meeting.

REVELEY IV: How to run a meeting, for sure. Public speaking. How to write for a public audience. How to raise money. These are technical skills that can be taught. But some of the things I know how to do I learned through essentially an apprenticeship model: my dad working with me on writing things, or thinking about a particular problem with Governor Baliles. Helping them as they were doing something consequential and in the process seeing how it played out and then, in the fullness of time being allowed to work on consequential things myself under their guidance.

Some other aspects of learning to lead came from studying the American presidency. First is realizing that in many cases even the president of the United States cannot divine what is going on in a particular situation. Strangely, that gives you some confidence when you're dealing with the haze and chaos and uncertainty that are intrinsic aspects of decision-making. The same is true when you've seen people you deeply admire when they're tired or angry or worn—that also gives you some fortitude when you're dealing with big things in trying circumstances.

Another is accepting the fact that you're constantly choosing among competing goods, and you often have to pick just one. And if you let that gnaw at you too much, it will be debilitating. I don't like having to do that, but it comes with the territory.

REVELEY III: When you study U.S. presidents, you see that good things rarely come easily for them. Even more than for most other leaders, incoming flak is constant, and they need to have the resilience to deal with it. Now that doesn't mean they like the flak, and it's perfectly okay to complain to the dog and say whatever it is they want to say. They can even write angry letters and then tear them up. But they've got to be able to not be done in by the flak, and the same is true of university presidents.

Luck, good or bad, weighs heavily too. Being POTUS is tough. Still, they have to keep making decisions, either by actually deciding or by failing to decide, and whatever they do, they'll be second-guessed, criticized, and at times soundly beaten about the head and shoulders. Recognizing all this provides useful perspective for academic presidents. To say the obvious, leading a college or university isn't nearly as tough as leading the USA, and you still get your portrait painted. You have to keep on trucking, making decisions, and counting on history to be the ultimate arbiter of how you did.

Another POTUS thought: often when a governor, senator, or even a vice president gets elected president, I imagine they think they have a reasonably good handle on what the job will entail and are reasonably prepared for it. Emphatically not so.

I thought going from a deanship to the presidency would be pretty much business as usual. That wasn't my experience. Sure, there were some similarities. But the scale and complexity of a college presidency are materially greater. So is the cast of characters with whom you deal, a lot more of them off campus. Your immersion in fundraising and in navigating political waters is far more intense. You deal with many more boards, one of which hired you and can fire you. You and your verbiage are much more closely scrutinized, and typically you live on campus in a house that doesn't belong to you and is highly visible.

Also, your perspective on certain matters shifts. To pick a minor example: what I thought as dean about the large parking fees and the even larger athletic fees imposed on law students at William & Mary evolved when I had to keep the university afloat financially. I saw that the fees were badly needed to help pay bonds issued to build a parking deck on the main campus and to help our athletic budget keep its financial nose above water.

Reveley IV: The act of communicating is at the heart of holding sway in these jobs. And if you can strike the right balance, where you're realistic, not overly high-flown but at the same time aspirational when appropriate—that's a hard balance to strike, but it's the approach people respond to best, I think.

You've also got to be able to "gear shift," as I call it, depending on who you're communicating with. You can start the morning talking to three members of a legislative committee in Richmond, and then motor back to campus to talk to the basketball team, and then have lunch with a faculty group, and then make a phone call to an important donor. You then shift to a written communication to one of the accrediting bodies we're accountable to, making sure that things are in good order, and then give a keynote address to several hundred people at an event that night. That would not be an unusual day. That would be sort of a Wednesday.

REVELEY III: Communicating is a two-way thing. I saw how Daddy listened. He made time for people who wanted, and sometimes really needed, to tell him something, often at great length in ways that could truly try one's patience. He was always gracious. Near the end of his presidency, there was concern among the most able and committed people at Hampden-Sydney that his patience was admirable, but he needed to crack down more on those who needed to do better or were obstacles in the path of progress.

I took from him that listening is important, and it has at least two dimensions. One, actually hearing and absorbing what's being said to you, and, two, letting the person who's talking to you know you've heard and understood what's being said, maybe repeating the guts of what they've said and showing some real empathy for them.

I had to work hard at taking the time, and making the effort, to listen carefully, especially with people who came with advice. Not always successful. I did better at trying never to shoot the messenger, even when the message was unwelcome.

And then as I've said before: mistakes, messes. When you make a mess, communicate, even though the normal human instinct is to hope the mess won't be noticed or the dog did it—anything. The odds are that's not going to happen. My experience has been that the best thing to do is claim the mistake right away, express regret, take remedial action, say you'll learn from the experience and then do so.

REVELEY IV: The constant art, as my dad says, is to find ways to keep advancing the things that matter in the face of the events that keep coming. And a mistake that's left unaddressed will just elevate the degree of difficulty in doing that.

REVELEY III: You don't get bored much if you're the president. Dealing with your mistakes certainly isn't boring. Being the president of an academic institution these days is a remarkably hard job to do well. The range and intensity of the matters coming your way are greater, I believe, than those confronting most CEOs of major corporations.

To pick just one example: the politics you've got to engage are wild and crazy—campus politics in all their teeming, conflicting profusion. Alumni and donor politics coming from all directions. If you're a public institution, the complicated, shifting politics of your owners and partial funders in the state capital. The federal politics aimed at higher education. The intimate politics of the jurisdictions in which you're located. The politics of the athletic conference to which your school belongs. I could go on, but the picture is clear: lots of politics. You've got to take all this, and much more, seriously, and try to figure where it's going and how best to deal with it, lest you ignore it and let it take a bite out of your school and you personally.

REVELEY IV: The range of issues is itself a field of peril for many people in the job because you have to have the wisdom and the judgment to know what to focus on and what not to focus on. And another thing that contributes to the challenge is the range of actual business functions that are part of a college or university. You're operating a complex physical plant with all of its intricacies, a residential enterprise, a dining enterprise, a complicated athletic enterprise, as well as the core instructional enterprise.

REVELEY III: And you've got more and different constituencies than in just about any other job besides governor of a state or president of the United States. You've got students, you've got faculty, you've got staff. You've got the athletics axis. You've got the whole donor complex, actual and potential. The media will take an unhealthy interest in you if things aren't going well, and conversely you have a fervent desire that they'll cover the triumphs. You've got all sorts of boards. That's on top of the alumni and everyone else who cares about your institution.

And everyone is not focused in the same fashion or with the same purpose. Sure, everyone will say they're operating for the good of the school. But it's not always so. They're operating in their own spheres, with their own interests. It's usually not a matter of bad faith. It's mostly differences of perspective. So it's up to the president to figure out how to hold it all together, how to navigate among the phalanxes and keep pushing the place forward.

I think the relatively short tenure of most presidents these days is a testament to the job's potential to chew you up and spit you out. For it to be meaningful and satisfying, you've got to be doing some real good for the university, pushing it forward, not just going through the motions to no particular effect, or beating your head against a stone wall of opposition. You have to believe you're making a serious difference for the better.

If those stars align, then being president can be one of the best jobs in the world. That's how I found it, most days, a tremendously exciting and meaningful undertaking. But it still takes a toll on you as the years roll by, especially if you begin the journey when you're sixty-five.

Sleep helps. But getting it wasn't always easy for me when things were moving at warp speed, big decisions loomed, or something bad had happened. Then my mind could refuse to take a break.

REVELEY IV: Ambition and the desire to serve aren't always easy to neatly sort out, but if you acquire power for purposes other than trying to do good with it, it can be a very dispiriting thing for the institution and also for you. And even a president with the right motives and the right skills needs to find ways to recharge. For me and my dad, who are probably more introverted than extroverted, stretches of unjostled time are profoundly important. Time with family—the holiday season surrounding Christmas and then interludes in the summer—can be times when you can regroup and think productively about the long haul, although you can't necessarily count on the pace of events outside campus allowing that. Church itself, graced with good liturgy, apart from its other profound virtues is a rejuvenating thing. That's true for both of us, as it was for my grandfather. And those occasional afternoons or days when you don't have a lot of inbound activity are priceless.

Epilogue

LEAVING

Very few leaders die in harness. When, on average, contemporary college and university presidencies end in their sixth year, it usually is because the president is either pushed out or leaves to take another position. In contrast, after long tenures in office, TR2 and TR3 retired at times of their own choosing, and TR4's twelve-years-and-counting presidency shows no signs of coming to an involuntary end.

Nevertheless, all three Reveley presidents have given considerable thought to the question of how and when a leader should leave.

REVELEY IV, LETTER OF APRIL 30, 2018, TO THE STATE'S COUNCIL OF PRESIDENTS, READ ALOUD AT THE CONCLUDING MEETING OF THE COUNCIL ATTENDED BY REVELEY III AND REVELEY IV TOGETHER: In academic life, spring is the time of transitions. A very personal one of course approaches for the Reveley family. The original "Taylor Reveley" in the family business—W. Taylor Reveley II—retired from the presidency of Hampden-Sydney just over 40 years ago this spring, in 1977. And my dad now is poised to conclude his majestic run at William & Mary with the close of this school year.

Perhaps even more notable about this generational transit is that my dad and I have had the chance to be doing this job at the same time together these past five years—likely a first in American higher education. It's been a chance for me to marvel firsthand at his feats, done with such elegant panache—admiration even more powerful because I know myself now how much of your utmost these jobs demand.[1]

REVELEY III: That fell sweetly on my ears when I heard it, and came as a total surprise. But it's still good to remember that you've got a finite amount of decision-making capital, political capital, as president, and you're spending it all the time. You can renew it to some extent, but after a while it's largely spent. Eventually on most campuses there is an appetite for a new leader, just to see what a new cat would be like and could accomplish. If, on the whole, you're doing a wonderful job, you're probably good for fifteen presidential years or thereabouts. Much more than that, even if you are able to linger, lingering likely isn't in the school's or your best interests.

Reveley IV: Every situation is different, but as a generalization that may be about right. The job is hard. It's almost like playing professional sports. It just takes a lot out of you to work through yet another season.

And my dad also is right that each squeeze of WD-40 that you use to solve a problem depletes your total supply of WD-40 and there comes a time when the can is empty, you've used it all up.

There's a great Bill Bowenism that you want to leave while the band is still playing.[2]

Reveley III: As opposed to one step ahead of the mob.

Reveley IV: Exactly. So that would be a different aspect of the calculus: what's the body politic feeling like?

Reveley III: My situation was somewhat unusual. I didn't become president until I was somewhat long in the tooth, sixty-five.

Reveley III, "Self-Evaluation" section of *Annual Report to the Board of Visitors*, 2013: I'm seventy. That's old, I realize, to be the chief executive of any college or university, especially a public institution in these frisky times for higher education, public schools in particular. A reasonable question is whether I have enough fire in the belly to continue as William & Mary's president. . . .

My conclusion is that plenty of fire remains in the belly. Thus I am game to serve for a few more years *if four circumstances exist:* (1) my body and brain continue to be up to the mission, as they now are; (2) I have the confidence and support of the overwhelming majority of the members of the Board of Visitors, preferably unanimous support, because the sort of progress W&M needs to make won't happen unless the board and president are moving forward together; (3) a critical mass of alumni, faculty, students, and staff continue to want me as their president, which I believe is now the case; and (4) I'm personally confident of my ability to keep doing compelling good for William & Mary.

The board kept renewing TR3's contract, but by his tenth year as president he was ready to retire, months after turning seventy-five, on June 30, 2018. He announced this in early 2017 to provide William & Mary ample time to find his successor and ensure an effective transition. At no point did he become a lame duck, consistent with the axiom that it is better to leave when people want you to stay than to stay when people want you to leave.

REVELEY III: When I got to be seventy, I started looking at newspaper obituary pages even if I didn't know anyone who'd died, just to see when people were kicking off. It turned out the Grim Reaper had a real taste for people in their eighties. I started saying seventy-five and a half would be a good time for me to quit. Then I'd have four and a half years of retirement R&R before entering the dangerous eighties.

This worked well because I was able to leave William & Mary in great shape and moving forward at flank speed. The bands actually were still playing and the flags flying. And unbeknownst, finishing in 2018 was gracefully ahead of Covid.

My father's situation was different. He was beginning to suffer from Parkinson's and later Alzheimer's. He had begun occasionally to forget things he'd told people he would do. He realized it was time to quit. So he left the presidency after fourteen years, with the satisfaction of knowing what an enormous difference for the better he had made. After retiring as president, he and Mother spent a glorious year in England while he was a fellow at Cambridge University. Then he returned to Hampden-Sydney and taught and participated fully in the life of the college for another three or four years before retiring completely. It was a matter of him realizing there were things he could still do well, but being president wasn't among them. He left the job amid warm thanks and gratitude for all he had done and for the person he was.

It was sad because he knew, and the family knew, he was entering cruel diseases that would destroy him, bit by bit, until the marvelous person he had been was wholly gone and only the shell of his body remained to die. Mother, with indomitable commitment, nursed and comforted him at home until the end. Theirs was a love story for the ages.

March 1, 1993, resolution of the Hampden-Sydney Faculty following TR2's death, adopted with a standing minute of silence: Dr. Reveley was elected President of Hampden-Sydney . . . at the beginning of a discouraging period of stress and discomfiture on campuses across the land. Yet, during his fourteen-year tenure the College endured and expanded, reaffirming long-term commitments as it grew in numbers both of students and of faculty.

Dr. Reveley brought to us in maturity the qualities manifested in his youth and early career, qualities that served us both well: a long-suffering tolerance, dignity, concern for his fellows and the community at large, gentle good humor, and a winsome humaneness of spirit. His was the touch of the conciliator, so welcome as so needful in troubled times.

Reveley IV: Something all three of us, starting with my grandad, have agreed on, I think, is that these jobs are monogamous relationships at their best—that when a presidency is really working, when you put your whole heart into it, you just don't think about doing it somewhere else. TR2 was totally committed to Hampden-Sydney, even though he had other opportunities to lead other institutions. For TR3 it was William & Mary, though likewise with a number of other opportunities. And maybe by dint of Longwood rolling along really well, I am contacted frequently by firms in the search-industrial complex about various openings. But even though I can imagine myself doing other things at some point in life, it's difficult to fathom being a college president anywhere else. I feel a great passion for what Longwood can achieve, and I still bounce out of bed in the morning thinking about all the things we can get done.

Reveley III: That's the crucial test.

Reveley IV: And it can weigh on you to think, what will this place be like when there's no person who can do all the things I can do? But the deeper reality is, of course, the Earth will keep turning, the rivers will still run into the sea, and the sea will not become full.

Afterword

I was fortunate to work closely with Taylor Reveley III and Taylor Reveley IV when they assisted the National War Powers Commission that Warren Christopher and I cochaired in 2008.

I was already familiar with the father and son, and their intelligent, thoughtful, and gentlemanly demeanors. TR3 was a noted legal scholar on national war powers who had become president of William & Mary shortly after the commission started its work. TR4 was well-versed in American presidential history as managing director of the University of Virginia's Miller Center and on his way to becoming Longwood University president five years later.

Soon I began to appreciate their shared traits that later helped each serve far longer than the average tenure of a university president, one of the most demanding jobs in the country.

Both men are what I like to call *principled pragmatists.* Each carries firm ideals in both their public and personal lives. Yet they recognize that the art of negotiation is based on all sides coming to agreement. For both TR3 and TR4, compromise is not a dirty word; it is a way to find the common ground needed to develop successful policies.

Their results-oriented focus made them perfect fits to assist the National War Powers Commission and its membership, which included very liberal Democrats and very conservative Republicans. And it also made them ideal candidates to be college presidents.

Few jobs are as hard as university president, and the successful ones have a unique blend of skills. To be atop their game, they must be futurists who accurately foresee the path of higher education. They must be educators who understand that teaching is more than ensuring that students learn; it must inspire them to strive for achievement.

Above all, a university president must adroitly navigate the rising cultural and political polarization that has stricken our nation, and particularly its college campuses. In a country fracturing along racial, ethnic, and other lines, presidents often are stuck between competing interests—students, their parents, faculty members, trustees, local community leaders, and a media looking for any weaknesses. The Reveleys' brand of principled pragmatism is a key ingredient for success.

I understand some of the pressures that confronted the Reveleys in academia—being part of a family lineage that pursues the same profession.

As the scion of a notable legal family in Texas, I wanted for little and got a first-class education. At the same time, from the moment of my birth, my mother and father constantly reminded me of my duty to uphold the family legacy.

After graduating from law school, I suspected that people were quietly saying: "If Jimmy succeeds, what did you expect? His father, grandfather, and great-grandfather were all lawyers."

And had I failed, they would have said: "What did you expect? His father, grandfather, and great-grandfather were all lawyers."

The Reveleys succeeded because of their laser-like determination to get the job done. The two of them can teach a masterclass on that subject and have done so in this book.

JAMES A. BAKER III
Baker Institute for Public Policy
Rice University

APPENDIX
INSIGHTS INTO LEADERSHIP

Leadership is more than a series of aphorism, and studies of leadership are best when embedded in the contexts in which leaders act. Nevertheless, aphorisms have their place, as this appendix, based on earlier pages, indicates.

Motivation

If you don't want to lead, the odds that you're going to do a good job are very small. Don't get seduced by the gold braid if you don't want to do the work, if you've got no idea what's entailed and aren't game for the downsides as well as the upsides of leading.

A leader can do really important things while being a fundamentally good person. Contrary to the mystique that holds among some, you don't have to be a jerk to be a leader of consequence.

Around age thirty-five you're basically old enough to be taken seriously by society at large. You're still young but not prohibitively young.

Whether it's sports or theater or some other collective enterprise, when I have something hard to do as a leader, I tell myself it's not harder than waking up before dawn or staying up late to go practice. There's also the spirit of teamwork that teaches you how to work with and rely on other people and let them rely on you.

Ambition and the desire to serve aren't always easy to neatly sort out, but if you acquire power for purposes other than trying to do good, it can be very dispiriting for the institution and for you.

People

It's vital that a leader create a context in which other people in the organization can relax, hold anxious gossip to a dull roar, and get on with doing their best work. As long as they believe there's a firm hand on the wheel, the ship isn't about to hit the rocks, and it's sailing on a promising course, they're fine.

You cannot lead in isolation. Leadership always occurs in a crowd. And I often have this military phrase in mind when hiring people for consequential positions: Can they hold a command? Do they have the ability to rally the troops to get the job done?

If you care about people and like them, they will respond in kind. It enhances your effectiveness as a leader and makes the job more fun.

People need to be heard, and their leader needs to hear them. You can help, even if it's just by listening and making clear that you understand what they're saying. If you do that, in a friendly and approachable way, you build confidence and legitimacy and amass political capital you can draw on when you've got difficult issues to resolve.

Nonanswers—pablum—from people in charge usually are counterproductive. Sometimes candor creates problems. More often, it is disarming.

A presidency on the one hand is a CEO endeavor of knowing what functional thing needs to happen at what functional moment. But in a deeper way it's also an exercise in having the grace and gravitas, by one's presence, to be a force for harmony and good.

Perspective

Nothing of real significance gets done without leadership. Without leaders, it's very hard for people to do anything but keep repeating what they're used to doing.

A leader needs to comprehend that, "You will do this because I'm telling you to do it" won't work very long or for many things, but

"I think we should do this for these good reasons" has a real chance of succeeding.

Be willing to challenge people when they say, "Can't do that" because of some law or reg or policy. Instead say, "Show me where it says that." As often as not, the law or reg or policy isn't dispositive, if in fact it exists at all.

There's a saying that morale is to the physical as three is to one. You can have all the resources imaginable, but if morale is low, you're in tough shape. And if, by contrast, all the bridges are burned and food is scarce but morale is high, you can carry the day.

Accept the fact that you're constantly choosing among competing goods, and you often have to pick just one. If you let that gnaw at you too much, it will be debilitating.

Success will have persuasive power for the rest of the body politic, even those who would have strongly objected to an initiative on its merits or for fear of failure. If you wait for everyone to be on board before moving out, you may never move out, or you'll do it late, allowing people too much time to tie themselves to the mast of their objections.

People will come to you every day wanting you do to this, that, or the other. Unless you're careful, your agenda for what most needs doing can easily get hijacked. One day you realize it's been replaced by everyone else's agendas.

It is impossible to be right about everything all of the time. Knowing this, paralysis can ensue. But if you try to be right in all of your initial decisions, you will take too few risks. More important than initial omniscience is the willingness to acknowledge error and correct your mistakes.

When you've dealt with the media a great deal, your skin becomes thicker and you know that headlines come and go.

The idea that *Ecclesiastes* was written by King Solomon seems perfectly plausible because it seems to express the experience of someone who knew what it was like to hold a position of consequence and feel the weariness that can come from that.

Adversity

Academia gets very tempted to operate by veto rules, so that if a particular faculty member or trustee or other stakeholder objects, that's enough for everybody else to say you can't do it. The fact is there's always dissent and as long as you steel your souls and go about things in a principled way, dissent is an aspect of the process as opposed to a defect.

There's flak coming in all the time, and if somebody has not had the experience of dealing with flak, it can be easy for them to think that the latest round is the most important thing that's going on, and that's rarely true. If you can't take it, can't stop thinking about it in the middle of the night—it's time to think seriously about laying down your mantle and letting someone else lead.

Not every battle is worth fighting. It's always prudent to keep in mind what the consequences of winning might be for future effectiveness. It's not good if people feel dragged behind your chariot wheels.

It's hard to admit it when you make mistakes. You've got to avoid the impulse to blame malign fate or other people, anything but yourself. Instead you need to say, early on, I whiffed, I goofed, I blew it, I'm sorry, and I won't let it happen again.

Boards

Presidents who lack board experience sometimes view the board as an alien infestation that needs to be fenced in as much as possible, a problem to be managed as opposed to what it really is at its best: a fount of practical wisdom that helps the president navigate the enterprise toward good opportunities and away from trouble.

When the board chair and the president work together, you've got a really powerful engine. The chair needs to encourage the president to spend enough time with the board, and explain enough to the board, and be patient enough with the board to get it to understand and support what he or she thinks needs to be accomplished, as modified and improved by the board's good advice.

By contrast, for the board chair to have an obsessive zeal for every detail being exactly one way won't work. You need somebody who is giving wise counsel but not wanting the paper clips a half inch from the side of the page rather than a quarter inch.

If all board members do is show up for meetings, they aren't going to feel like they're making any difference. You need to find something that each member of the board can do that he or she finds fulfilling and that the school actually needs.

Money

Money isn't everything, but it's everything else.

It's tempting for people to think that the art of raising money is a mystical exercise in which the president somehow performs exotic feats of psychology to persuade donors to do things they don't want to do. In reality, you are helping the donors as much as they are helping the institution. Donors often find that making a major gift is one of the most meaningful things they do in their lives.

The relationship you forge with a prospective donor has to be nurtured and cultivated. It helps if you like each other, but it's still the case that you are leaning on them to part with significant resources. You have to be willing and able to look them in the eye and make "the ask," especially if it's for mega-bucks.

Giving responds much more readily to reports of success than to cries of doom. To plaintively plead that the university barely has one nostril over the waves, so please come to its relief, is not very effective. Far better to trumpet that the juggernaut is rolling, so come get on board and help push alma mater to ever greater glory.

NOTES

Preface

1. "World University Rankings 2023," *Times Higher Education*, https://www.timeshighereducation.com/world-university-rankings/2023/world-ranking; "2022–2023 Best Global Universities Rankings," *US News*, https://www.usnews.com/education/best-global-universities/rankings; "QS World University Rankings," *QS Top Universities*, https://www.topuniversities.com/qs-world-university-rankings.
2. CNBC, "America's Top States for Business," July 11, 2024. The survey ranked Virginia first in education, taking into account both K–12 education and higher education.
3. *US News*, "Top Public Schools, 2024," last corrected October 27, 2023.
4. Nationally, the Gallup Poll found, the share of Americans with either "a great deal" or "quite a lot" of confidence in higher education fell from 57 percent in 2015 to 36 percent in 2023. Megan Brenan, "Americans' Confidence in Higher Education Down Sharply," Gallup, July 11, 2023. Virginia poll results were supplied to the author by the Virginia Business Higher Education Council. Other public opinion surveys within the state show similarly high levels of satisfaction. See, for example, "Kirk Cox, 'It's Time to Invest in Virginia's Talent,'" *Growth4VA*, Fall 2023, and Dennis Treacy and Taylor Reveley, "To Bridge the Workforce Gap, Virginia Must Invest in Higher Ed," *Richmond Times-Dispatch*, September 22, 2023.
5. Andy Tomason, "Is College President 'the Toughest Job in the Nation'?" *Chronicle of Higher Education*, May 1, 2018.
6. Doug Lederman, "College President as the 'Toughest Job'? Military Hero Doubles Down," *Inside Higher Ed*, July 18, 2023
7. Stephen Joel Trachtenberg, Gerald B. Kovar, and E. Grady Bogue, *Presidencies Derailed: Why University Leaders Fail and How to Prevent It* (Baltimore, MD: Johns Hopkins University Press, 2013), 11.
8. John R. Thelin, *A History of American Higher Education* (Baltimore, MD: Johns Hopkins University Press, 2004), 423.
9. Hanna Holborn Gray, *An Academic Life: A Memoir* (Princeton, NJ: Princeton University Press, 2018), 276.

10. Three brothers were mid-twentieth century presidents of American universities: Karl Compton (MIT), Arthur Compton (Washington University in St. Louis), and Wilson Compton (Washington State University). Like TR3 and TR4, all were Princeton alumni whose father was a Presbyterian minister.
11. Jenna Johnson, "Virginia's Academic Dynasty," *Washington Post*, May 19, 2013. The headline appeared in the newspaper's print edition.
12. *The American College President, 2023 Edition* (Washington, DC: American Council of Higher Education, 2023).
13. "The Commonwealth Needs a University of Reveley," editorial, *Richmond Times-Dispatch*, April 10, 2017.
14. Two of the six sections in a Spring 2023 *Chronicle of Higher Education* report called "Trouble at the Top: Meeting the Daunting Challenges of Today's College Presidency" were titled: "Welcome to Hell" and "Is This an Impossible Job?": https://store.chronicle.com/products/trouble-at-the-top. A May 22, 2024, *New York Times* story by Alan Blinder and Stephanie Saul was headlined, "Anyone Want to Be a College President?" with the subhead, "The job is not what it used to be."
15. Rhodes was Southwestern at Memphis before being renamed in 1984.
16. Karen Kapsideles, "For Longwood President, Higher Ed Runs in the Family," *Richmond Times-Dispatch*, September 1, 2013.
17. Michael Nelson, *Celebrating the Humanities: A Half-Century of the Search Course at Rhodes College, 1945–1995* (Nashville, TN: Vanderbilt University Press, 1996).
18. Marie Eason Reveley, "Our Years at Hampden-Sydney College: July 1963–May 1981," typescript, in Hampden-Sydney College Archives and Special Collections, VA .

Prologue

1. Jonathan Mahler, "The Most Dangerous Person in the World Is Randi Weingarten," *New York Times Magazine*, April 30, 2023, 30.
2. Copies of the quoted emails were supplied to the author by Taylor Reveley IV.
3. As noted in the preface, unless otherwise indicated, all quotations from Taylor Reveley III and Taylor Reveley IV are from the long series of oral history interviews conducted with them by the author.
4. Paul Fain, "Facing Ouster, William and Mary's President Makes Dramatic Exit," *Chronicle of Higher Education*, February 13, 2008.
5. Union Presbyterian Seminary was known as Union Theological Seminary until 1997 and from then until 2009 was called Union-Presbyterian School of Christian Education.

6. The Prince Edward County case was *Davis v. County School Board of Prince Edward County* 100 F. Supp 337 (1952). On the student-led walkout and Prince Edward County's response to *Brown*, including Longwood's and Hampden-Sydney's role, see Bob Smith, *They Closed Their Schools: Prince Edward County, Virginia, 1951–1965* (Farmville, VA: Robert Russa Moton Museum, 2008), and Amy E. Murrell, "The 'Impossible' Prince Edward Case: The Endurance of Resistance in a Southside County, 1959–1964," in *The Moderates' Dilemma: Massive Resistance to School Desegregation in Virginia*, ed. Matthew D. Lassiter and Andrew B. Lewis (Charlottesville: University of Virginia Press, 1998), 134–67. On the school integration issue more generally in Virginia, see Frank B. Atkinson, *The Dynamic Dominion: Realignment and the Rise of Two-Party Competition in Virginia, 1945–1980*, 2nd ed. (Lanham, MD: Rowman & Littlefield, 2006), chaps. 8–11. On the school desegregation litigation, see Richard Kluger, *Simple Justice: The History of* Brown v. Board of Education *and Black America's Struggle for Equality* (New York: Vintage, 1975, repr. 2004).
7. Robert F. Kennedy, "Law Day Address at the University of Georgia School of Law," May 6, 1961, https://www.americanrhetoric.com/speeches/rfkgeorgialawschool.htm.
8. *Griffin v. County School Board of Prince Edward County* 377 US 218 (1964).

Part I. Paths to the Presidency

1. John R. Thelin, *A History of American Higher Education* (Baltimore, MD: Johns Hopkins University Press, 2004), 168. As Christopher Jencks and David Riesman note in chapter 8 ("Protestant Denominations and Their Colleges") of their 1969 book, *The Academic Revolution*, "a century ago this would have been Chapter 1 of any book on American colleges." Jencks and Riesman, *The Academic Revolution* (Garden City, NY: Doubleday, 1969), 312.
2. Thelin, *A History of American Higher Education*, 165.
3. Michael D. Cohen and James G. March, *Leadership and Ambiguity: The American College President* (Watertown, MA: Harvard Business Publishing, 1986), 20.
4. The University of Virginia's Darden School of Business dean, Scott C. Beardsley, found in a study of 248 liberal arts college presidents that in 2014, "traditional" presidents—whom he defined as having climbed the academic tenure-track ladder at some point in their career—served an average 3.9 years as president, compared with 6.9 years for "nontraditional" presidents. Beardsley, *Higher Calling: The Rise of Nontraditional Leaders in Higher Education* (Charlottesville: University of Virginia Press, 2019).

5. Louis Guard and Joyce P. Jacobsen, *All the Campus Lawyers: Litigation, Regulation, and the New Era od Higher Education* (Cambridge, MA: Harvard University Press, 2024).
6. Patricia E. Salkin, *May It Please the Campus: Lawyers Leading Higher Education* (New York: Touro University Press, 2022), 11.
7. All three Reveley presidents have been, in Robert Birnbaum and Paul D. Umbach's term, "spanners," who before becoming president had careers outside higher education as well as recent job experience at a college or university, rather than "strangers," brought in as president entirely from outside higher education. The former tend to do better than the latter, they found. Birnbaum and Umbach, "Scholar, Steward, Spanner, Stranger: The Four Career Paths of College Presidents," *Review of Higher Education* 24 (Spring 2001): 203–17.
8. Judith Block McLaughlin and David Riesman, *Choosing a College President: Opportunities and Constraints* (Princeton, NJ: Carnegie Foundation for the Advancement of Teaching, 1990).

1. Taylor Reveley II and Hampden-Sydney College

1. Unless otherwise indicated, all quotations from Marie Eason Reveley are from her unpublished memoir: "Our Years at Hampden-Sydney College: July 1963–May 1981," typescript, Hampden-Sydney College Archives and Special Collections, VA.
2. Alan Taylor, *Thomas Jefferson's Education* (New York: W. W. Norton, 2019), 233.
3. Union Presbyterian Seminary adopted its current name in 2009. Long called Union Theological Seminary, it was often confused with Union Theological Seminary in New York City.
4. D. B. Prentice and B. W. Kunkel, "The Colleges' Contribution to Intellectual Leadership," *School and Society* 32 (November 1, 1930): 595–600.
5. W. Taylor Reveley II, "Optimist Club, Richmond, Wednesday, November 10, 1965," in *Collected Speeches and Sermons of W. Taylor Reveley II* (privately published by W. Taylor Reveley III and W. Taylor Reveley IV, 2003), 22. Hampden-Sydney College Archives and Special Collections, VA.
6. Graves H. Thompson, "Taylor Reveley: A Memoir," *Record of the Hampden-Sydney Alumni Association,* March 1977, 8–11.
7. Joel Sweet, "A Time to Teach, a Time to Fade Away," *Record of the Hampden-Sydney Alumni Association,* Summer 1981, 16–18.
8. Ibid.
9. "Hart Retires as Director of Education," *Richmond Times-Dispatch,* December 23, 1930.

NOTES TO PAGES 15-28   241

10. "Thomas D. Eason," *Richmond Times-Dispatch*, November 3, 1939.
11. The "one other person" was Bill Bowen, TR3's mentor and friend.
12. Dan Caldwell and B. L. Bowman, *They Answered the Call* (Richmond, VA: John Knox Press, 1952), 75.
13. James E. Roper, *Southwestern at Memphis, 1948–1975* (Memphis: Southwestern at Memphis, 1975), 10.
14. All letters in this chapter may be found in the Rhodes College Archive, Memphis, TN.
15. W. Taylor Reveley II, "A Christian Critique of Modern Liberal Democratic Theory as Reflected in the Writings of Jacques Maritain, A. D. Lindsay, and Reinhold Niebuhr," in *Collected Writings of W. Taylor Reveley II* (privately published by W. Taylor Reveley III and W. Taylor Reveley IV, 2003), 251–674, Hampden-Sydney College Archives and Special Collections, VA. On the origins of the Man course and its development during the period TR2 taught at Rhodes, see Michael Nelson, "The Founding Era, 1945–1958," in *Celebrating the Humanities: A Half-Century of the Search Course at Rhodes College*, ed. Michael Nelson (Nashville, TN: Vanderbilt University Press, 1996), 3–32.
16. James M. Vest, "Influences beyond the Walls," in Nelson, *Celebrating the Humanities*, 138–75.
17. Reveley II, "A Christian Critique of Modern Liberal Democratic Theory," 652.
18. Roger L. Geiger, *American Higher Education since World War II: A History* (Princeton, NJ: Princeton University Press, 2019), 168.
19. Sweet, "A Time to Teach, a Time to Fade Away."
20. Ibid.
21. "Faculty Pushes LeMoyne College Financial Drive," *Sou'wester*, May 5, 1949.
22. W. Taylor Reveley II, "The Southern Church, the State and the Negro—An Appraisal," in *Collected Writings of W. Taylor Reveley II*, 701.
23. The Presbyterian Church U.S. was the denomination's southern branch. It was formed in 1861 and endured until 1983, when it joined with the northern-based United Presbyterian Church to form the Presbyterian Church (USA).
24. At considerable risk to their job security, personal safety, and general standing in the white community, two Longwood professors, Marvin Schlegel and Gordon Moss, were especially outspoken on behalf of school integration, as was Mildred Dickinson Davis of Hampden-Sydney. Amy E. Murrell, "The 'Impossible' Prince Edward Case: The Endurance of Resistance in a Southside County, 1959–1964," in *The Moderates' Dilemma: Massive Resistance to School Desegregation in Virginia*, ed. Matthew D. Lassiter

and Andrew B. Lewis (Charlottesville: University of Virginia Press, 1998), 152–57. The social abuse Moss experienced is described (without referring to Moss by name in an effort to protect him from further abuse) in Irv Goodman, "Public Schools Died Here," *Saturday Evening Post,* April 29, 1961, 32–33, 85–89. As president, TR4 renamed one of the newly refurbished high-rise dormitories on campus after Moss.

2. Taylor Reveley III and William & Mary

1. I define "working years" as beginning when one enters the workforce.
2. Hunton & Williams became Hunton Andrews Kurth in 2018.
3. TR3's experience of Memphis in the 1950s is consistent with modern urban planning notions of the "15-Minute-City," in which people live within a short walk of all their basic needs. See, for example, Chris Stanford, "The 15-Minute City," *New York Times,* March 1, 2023.
4. The effort to broaden the economic and geographical talent pool from which Princeton recruited its undergraduate student body was a major priority of Harold W. Dodds, who served as president from 1933 to 1957. Jerome Karabel, *The Chosen: The Hidden History of Admission and Exclusion at Harvard, Yale, and Princeton* (Boston, MA: Houghton-Mifflin, 2005), ch. 8.
5. Solid accounts of Princeton's history are James Axtell, *The Making of Princeton University: From Woodrow Wilson to the Present* (Princeton, NJ: Princeton University Press, 2006), and Don Oberdorfer, *Princeton University: The First 250 Years* (Princeton, NJ: Trustees of Princeton University, 1995).
6. Adroitly, Goheen, persuaded in 1967 by his new provost, Princeton economist Bill Bowen, that the university needed to admit women, appointed Harold Helm, an opponent of coeducation on the board, to study the issue. Persuaded by the evidence, Helm led his fellow trustees to approve the admission of women in 1969. Oberdorfer, *Princeton University,* 176–81. See also Karabel, *The Chosen,* 427–439.
7. Reveley's summer work with Bowen is described in Nancy Weiss Malkiel, *Changing the Game: William G. Bowen and the Challenges of American Higher Education* (Princeton, NJ: Princeton University Press, 2023), 229.
8. William J. Baumol and William G. Bowen, *Performing Arts—The Economic Dilemma: A Study of Problems Common to Opera, Theater, Music, and Dance* (New York: Twentieth Century Fund, 1966). On the book's acknowledgments page, the authors thank "Taylor Reveley, who saw us through the critical final months. And who, in the process, gave up nights and weekends."

9. Bowen died in 2016, by which time TR3 had been president of William & Mary for eight years and had served with Bowen on multiple boards. Speaking at his memorial service, TR3 said, "I've never known anyone whose work ethic, sheer energy, and delight in the chase was as robust as Bill's. Work, for him, was not work as most mortals experience it. This was, in part, I believe, because he was so good at what he did." Quoted in Kevin Guthrie, "Introduction," in William G. Bowen, *Ever the Leader: Selected Writings, 1995–2016* (Princeton, NJ: Princeton University Press, 2018). Among Bowen's other works on higher education are *Lessons Learned: Reflections of a University President* (Princeton, NJ: Princeton University Press, 2011) and *Ever the Teacher: William G. Bowen's Writings as President of Princeton University* (Princeton, NJ: Princeton University Press, 1987).

10. Virginia's constitutional revision process is chronicled in A. E. Dick Howard, "Constitutional Revision: Virginia and the Nation," *University of Richmond Law Review* 9 (Fall 1974): 1–48.

11. Meador's own account of his deanship is Daniel John Meador, *The Transformative Years of the University of Alabama Law School, 1966–1970* (Montgomery, AL: NewSouth Books, 2012).

12. "Presidential War-Making: Constitutional Prerogative or Usurpation?," *Virginia Law Review* 55 (1969): 1243–305.

13. See, for example, "Constitutional Aspects of United States Participation in Foreign Internal Conflicts," in *Law and Civil War in the Modern World*, ed. John Norton Moore (Baltimore, MD: Johns Hopkins University Press, 1976), and "The Power to Make War," in *The Constitution and the Conduct of Foreign Policy*, ed. Francis Orlando Wilcox (New York: Praeger, 1976).

14. For a fuller discussion of TR3's work as clerk, with a particular focus on *Goldberg v. Kelly*, see Michael Nelson, "*Goldberg v. Kelly*: The Case, the Clerk, and the Justice," *Journal of Supreme Court History* 47 (2022): 162–78. See also Martha F. Davis, *Brutal Need: Lawyers and the Welfare Rights Movement, 1960–1973* (New Haven, CT: Yale University Press, 1993). Brennan's life and work on the court are ably chronicled in Seth Stern and Stephen Wermiel, *Justice Brennan: Liberal Champion* (Lawrence: University Press of Kansas, 2010).

15. Stephen G. Breyer, "*Goldberg v. Kelly*: Administrative Law and the New Property," in *Reason and Passion: Justice Brennan's Enduring Influence*, ed. E. Joshua Rosenkranz and Bernard Schwartz (New York: W. W. Norton, 1997), 245. Brennan is quoted in Stern and Wermiel, *Justice Brennan*, 336.

16. Letter from Taylor Reveley to "Aunt Pink and Virginia," January 15, 1970 (supplied to the author).

17. Hunton & Williams' storied history through 1986 is told in Anne Hobson Freeman, *The Style of a Law Firm: Eight Gentlemen from Virginia* (Chapel Hill, NC: Algonquin Books, 1992). "Style" in this context refers to the name of the firm, which was Hunton, Williams, Gay, Powell & Gibson when TR3 joined it in 1970.
18. The political and legal battles spawned by LILCO's effort to build and operate nuclear power plants on Long Island are recounted in Joan Aron, *Licensed to Kill? The Nuclear Regulatory Commission and the Shoreham Power Plant* (Pittsburgh, PA: University of Pittsburgh Press, 1997).
19. At Justice Thomas's invitation, TR3 wrote the foreword to John Charles Thomas, *The Poetic Justice: A Memoir* (Charlottesville: University of Virginia Press, 2022), vii–ix.
20. Freeman, *The Style of a Law Firm*.
21. The roster of boards discussed in this chapter reflects their importance and relevance to TR3's later presidency and makes no pretense to completeness. Even in retirement he serves on the Medical College of Virginia Foundation Board, St. Catherine's School Board, and Rockefeller Trust Committee (his only for-profit board), the latter chaired until 2016 by Bowen in ways that "resembled his leadership of the Princeton board: collegial, gracious, low-key, listening respectfully, making sure that everyone had the chance to participate." Malkiel, *Changing the Game*, 329.
22. Santul Nerkar, Rob Copeland, and Maureen Farrell, "Calls to Divest from Israel Put Students and Donors on Collision Course," *New York Times*, May 3, 2024.
23. At the time, Princeton was one of the few universities whose president chaired the board.
24. See Bowen's nuanced presentation of the issue at a 1985 campus forum, "Divestment and South Africa," in Bowen, *Ever the Teacher*, 29–36.
25. In 1987 the board did vote to divest from the Raytheon and Schlumberger Corporations. Malkiel, *Changing the Game*, 221.
26. For a similar account involving polo at Yale, see Hanna Holborn Gray, *An Academic Life: A Memoir* (Princeton, NJ: Princeton University Press, 2018), 229.
27. See David L. Holmes, *Glimpses of a Public Ivy: 50 Years at William & Mary* (Atglen, PA: Schiffler Publishing, 2022), 77–80.
28. TR3 was fortunate in his timing. Nationally, law school applications, which had suffered a period of steady decline from 1990 to 1997, rose steeply during the decade of his deanship, only to fall sharply again after he became president. Benjamin H. Barton, *Glass Half Full: The Decline and Rebirth of the Legal Profession* (New York: Oxford University Press, 2015), 160.

29. Douglas succeeded TR3 as dean after TR3 left the deanship to become president. Douglas served as dean throughout TR3's entire presidential tenure before returning to the faculty in 2020.
30. These are among the insights TR3 published as "Cultural Musings of a Non-Traditional Dean," *University of Toledo Law Review* 31 (Summer 2000): 725–29.
31. W. Taylor Reveley III, "The Citizen Lawyer," *William & Mary Law Review* 50 (2009): 1309–21. For a thoughtful discussion of the enduring influence of a law school class taught by Reveley on the subject, see "Teaching the Virtues of Civil Discourse," published in the May 8, 2023, edition of the *Richmond Times-Dispatch* by U.S. District Court judge Thomas T. Cullen.
32. For an additional discussion of TR3's becoming president, see the prologue.
33. Gene Nichol, "Statement from Gene Nichol: Feb. 12," WM.edu, https://www.wm.edu/news/announcements/2008/statement-from-gene-nichol-feb.-12.php.
34. "Statement about Nichol's Resignation from the Board of Visitors," *Richmond Times-Dispatch*, February 12, 2008.

3. Taylor Reveley IV and Longwood University

1. Even in the 1990s, recruited athletes and legacies made up a significant part of Princeton's student body. Jerome Karabel, *The Hidden History of Admission and Exclusion at Harvard, Yale, and Princeton* (Boston, MA: Houghton-Mifflin, 2005), 550, 552.
2. Or, as former University of Texas president Peter T. Flawn put it, "You must suffer the fool and the jackass." Flawn, *A Primer for University Presidents: Managing the Modern University* (Austin: University of Texas Press, 1990), 21.
3. William G. Bowen, *The Board Book: An Insider's Guide for Directors and Trustees* (New York: W. W. Norton, 2012), 155.
4. Baliles's interest in higher education leadership was longstanding. For example, he chaired the Association of Governing Boards of Universities and Colleges' Task Force on the State of the Presidency in American Higher Education, which in 2006 released a report titled *The Leadership Imperative*. The report stressed that at a time of uncertainty for American higher education, closer communication and collaboration between presidents and boards was essential.
5. Jim Jordan, "The Longwood Revolution of '76," Longwood.edu, Summer 2017.
6. This position is also effectively defended in Charles T. Clotfelter, *Big-Time Sports in American Universities*, 2nd ed. (New York: Cambridge University Press, 2019.)

Part II. The Reveley Presidencies

1. John Dickerson, *The Hardest Job in the World: The American Presidency* (New York: Random House, 2020), xvi–xiii.
2. Warren G. Bennis, "Searching for the 'Perfect' University President," *Atlantic*, April 1971, 39–53.

4. Fostering Pride and Morale

1. See, for example, "One Tribe, One Day: Selfies with Reveley," and "One Tribe, One Day: The Taylor Reveley Show" at YouTube.com.
2. *Hampden-Sydney Record*, October 1963, 3.
3. Robert Gates '65 was secretary of defense and CIA director; James Comey '82 was FBI director; Jonathan Harvis '75 was National Park Service director; Christina Romer '81 chaired the Council of Economic Advisers; and Eric Cantor '88 was House majority leader.
4. In spring 2015, TR3 was able to claim that William & Mary was the nation's "most efficient university" after *US News* ranked it thirty-third in overall quality but one-hundred-tenth in financial resources. "That 77-point gap between resources and quality," he wrote in the alumni magazine, "is by far the largest among the top 50 universities in the magazine's rankings." W. Taylor Reveley III, "The Efficient University," *W&M Alumni Magazine* (Spring 2015).
5. Shortly before Generals Grant and Lee negotiated the Army of Northern Virginia's surrender at Appomattox courthouse in 1865, they both progressed through Farmville. Union and Confederate forces met in battle near the north end of the Longwood campus. The Black students' walkout from the Moton school in 1951 that led to one of the *Brown* cases occurred near the south end of campus.
6. "The Commonwealth Needs a University of Reveley," editorial, *Richmond Times-Dispatch*, April 10, 2017.
7. Owen Norment, "W. Taylor Reveley—A Personal Remembrance," 2000, unpublished manuscript supplied to the author.
8. "If you give them a good, honest, efficient administration you will have their support," argues former University of Texas at Austin president Peter T. Flawn. Flawn, *A Primer for University Presidents: Managing the Modern University* (Austin: University of Texas Press, 1990), 79. Former University of Chicago president Hanna Holborn Gray adds, "Things on the whole are going pretty well when people are not thinking about what the administration is up to now. It suggests the administration is doing its assigned job to help free everybody else to do theirs." Gray, *An Academic Life: A Memoir* (Princeton, NJ: Princeton University Press, 2018), 295.

9. According to Hank Wolf, W&M's rector, "The president was not willing to have a raise until other people at William & Mary can get raises." Brian Whitson, "W&M BOV Renews Contract for President Reveley," W&M News Archive, May 16, 2010,
10. Letter addressed "To President Reveley" and signed by forty-eight members of the faculty. Hampden-Sydney College Archives and Special Collections, VA.
11. Like William & Mary, "A growing number of research universities have formalized teaching tracks, with security of employment." Beckie Sepiano, "Can a Teaching Track Improve Undergraduate Education?," *Chronicle of Higher Education*, July 19, 2022. David Figlio and Morton Shapiro argue that although it is axiomatic among academics that good teaching requires ongoing research and publication, the evidence does not support that conclusion. Figlio and Shapiro, "Staffing the Higher Education Classroom," *Journal of Economic Perspectives* 35 (Winter 2021).
12. Jordan Weissman has found that what matters most to students is not whether their instructors are tenured or nontenured but whether they are full-time or part-time. Weissman, "Are Tenured Professors Really Worse Teachers: A Lit Review," *Atlantic*, September 25, 2013.
13. Brian Rosenberg, *"Whatever It Is, I'm Against It": Resistance to Change in Higher Education* (Cambridge, MA: Harvard Education Press, 2023), 103.
14. Unless otherwise indicated, all quotations from Marie Eason Reveley are from her unpublished memoir, "Our Years at Hampden-Sydney College: July 1963–May 1981," typescript, Hampden-Sydney College Archives and Special Collections, VA.
15. William E. Thompson, *Her Walls Before Thee Stand: The 235 Year History of the Presbyterian Congregation of Hampden-Sydney, Virginia* (privately published, 2010), 520–37.

5. Forging Constructive Governing Relationships

1. Owen Norment, "W. Taylor Reveley—A Personal Remembrance," 2000, unpublished manuscript supplied to the author.
2. Nancy Weiss Malkiel, *Changing the Game: William G. Bowen and the Challenges of American Higher Education* (Princeton, NJ: Princeton University Press, 2023), 206–11.
3. One relatively brief but instructive board experience for TR4 was joining a team that included former University of Virginia president John Casteen and former state attorney general Tony Troy to try to save Virginia Intermont College, which was experiencing accreditation issues born of low enrollment and financial difficulties. Virginia Intermont was a small

private liberal arts college in Bristol, at the far southwestern corner of Virginia. The start of TR4's presidency abbreviated his role, and the college eventually closed in 2014.

4. See, for example, Nick Anderson, "In Texts, Youngkin Appointee Plots 'Battle Royale for the Soul of UVA,'" *Washington Post*, February 23, 2023.

5. In the years spanning TR3 and TR4's presidencies, the governorship went from Democratic to Republican in 2009, Republican to Democratic in 2013, and Democratic to Republican in 2021. Neither TR3 nor TR4 has had to deal with highly partisan boards, but some Virginians expressed concern at Governor Glenn Youngkin's appointments of conservative activists to various public university boards. See, for example, Bob Lewis, "Thought Policing Va.'s Schools: Youngkin Consolidates His Grip on Education's Ruling Boards," *Virginia Mercury*, December 6, 2023.

6. Youngkin solicited an October 2, 2023, advisory opinion from Republican state attorney general Jason Miyares, who concluded that the primary legal responsibility of the boards of visitors of public universities is to the state rather than to the university. At the November 14, 2023, orientation of new board members, Youngkin decried the "myth that board members are cheerleaders for the university and cheerleaders for the president." Instead, "I appoint you to play that role as a responsible extension of the executive branch." Jessica Blake, "Who's the Boss of Virginia's Public University Boards?," *Inside Higher Ed*, November 30, 2023.

7. William G. Bowen, *The Board Book: An Insider's Guide for Directors and Trustees* (New York: W. W. Norton, 2012), 155. Interestingly, TR3 was one of Bowen's invited commenters on the manuscript, in which he is quoted by name three times. See also Robert A. Scott, *How University Boards Work* (Baltimore, MD: Johns Hopkins University Press, 2018).

8. Jim Collins, *Good to Great: Why Some Companies Make the Leap and Others Don't* (New York: HarperCollins, 2001).

9. Between 2002 and 2022, out-of-state admissions at flagship public universities increased in forty-five states, in some cases dramatically. At the University of Alabama, for example, the share of out-of-state students rose from 23 percent to 65 percent during these two decades. Audrey Williams June, "Flagships Are Enrolling More and More Freshmen from Out of State," *Chronicle of Higher Education*, January 24, 2024.

10. W. Taylor Reveley III, "William & Mary Came First. Why Care?," *University of Toledo Law Review* 35:185–88.

11. North Carolina's public universities are governed by a centralized board of governors whose members are appointed by the state legislature (in effect by its majority party). Along with the legislature, the board of governors

appoints the members of the board of trustees of each campus within the system.
12. William & Mary's board approved a proposal that increased annual undergraduate tuition 20.2 percent in FY2014, 19.2 percent in FY2015, and 12.5 percent in FY2016.
13. The headline in the April 22, 2013, edition of *Inside Higher Ed*, an online publication widely read in higher education circles, was: "William & Mary Adopts New Financing Model, Embraces High Tuition/High Aid."
14. Bowen had "a strong presumption against the university as an institution taking positions on external issues. . . . The university—and its president—should speak out on matters central to its own functioning as an educational institution." William G. Bowen, *Lessons Learned: Reflections of a University President* (Princeton, NJ: Princeton University Press, 2012), 37–38.
15. Some examples: "Reveley: College Affordability Is the Heart of Democracy," *Richmond Times-Dispatch*, August 18, 2014; "College Dorms Are Training Grounds in Political Civility," *USA Today*, August 14, 2018; "America's Civic Duty: Start Teaching Democracy," *Time*, October 3, 2016; "The Conversation: Is Democracy Dying?" *Atlantic*, November 14, 2018; "Fixing College Sports Is Vital to Increasing Public Support for Colleges," Fox News, January 6, 2019; and "Trump, Biden and the Untimely Death of the Handshake," *Wall Street Journal*, September 25, 2020.
16. Mary Grauerholz, "Master Mind," TraditionalBuilding.com, September 21, 2023.
17. The acquisition of Hospitality House alone (renamed One Tribe Place) added 3.7 acres, 318 rooms, and 316 parking spaces to the college's physical plant.

6. Reforming the Curriculum

1. See, for example, Michael Nelson, ed., *Alive at the Core: Exemplary Approaches to General Education in the Humanities* (San Francisco: Jossey-Bass, 2000).
2. Peter T. Flawn, *A Primer for University Presidents: Managing the Modern University* (Austin: University of Texas Press, 1990), 85.
3. President's Commission on Higher Education, *Higher Education for American Democracy* (New York: Harper & Row, 1947). Both the Truman Commission report and, despite their differences, *General Education in a Free Society*, commissioned by Harvard president James B. Conant and released in 1945, conceived of higher education as "the key ingredient for the production of democratic citizens" and general education as "the best way

to prepare citizens for democratic life." Christopher P. Loss, *Between Citizens and the State: The Politics of American Higher Education in the 20th Century* (Princeton, NJ: Princeton University Press, 2012), 138. See also the special issue of the *Peabody Journal of Education* 98 (2023): "Promises Made: The Truman Commission at 75."

4. Michael Nelson, "The Founding Era, 1945–1958," in *Celebrating the Humanities: A Half-Century of the Search Course at Rhodes College*, ed. Michael Nelson (Nashville, TN: Vanderbilt University Press, 1998), 3–31.

5. James M. Vest, "Influences beyond the Walls," in Nelson, *Celebrating the Humanities*, 138–75.

6. By 1968, the faculty had increased from thirty-three to forty-one, even as the number of alumni on the faculty fell from twelve to eleven. By the time TR2 left office in 1977, the faculty had increased to fifty-five, only five of whom were alumni. John Lester Brinkley, *On This Hill: A Narrative History of Hampden-Sydney College, 1774–1994* (Hampden Sydney, VA, 1994), 797.

7. Vest, "Influences beyond the Walls," 160–61.

8. Brinkley, *On This Hill*, 803–4.

9. For a serious critique of AP courses, see Annie Abrams, *Shortchanged: How Advanced Placement Cheats Students* (Baltimore, MD: Johns Hopkins University Press, 2023).

10. Christine Sampson, "W&M Adopts New General Education Curriculum," *Virginia Gazette*, December 14, 2013.

11. The $2.6 million grant funded the W. Taylor Reveley III Interdisciplinary Faculty Fellows program to support faculty who actively contributed to COLL.

12. W. Taylor Reveley III, "The Citizen-Lawyer," *William & Mary Law Review* 50 (2009): 1309–21.

13. TR4's great-grandfather, Thomas Eason, chaired Longwood's Biology Department from 1911 to 1918.

14. Students begin at the Foundation Level with courses such as Inquiry into Citizenship, advance to the Perspectives Level with courses such as Global Inquiry, and conclude with Symposium on the Common Good.

15. For example, in a February 5, 2023, address titled "What Universities Owe Democracy," Johns Hopkins University president Ronald J. Daniels singled out four institutions for their exemplary new curricula: Johns Hopkins, Stanford, Purdue, and Longwood (text supplied to the author by TR4). See also Daniels's book of the same title, coauthored with Grant Shreve and Phillip Spector: *What Universities Owe Democracy* (Baltimore, MD: John Hopkins University Press, 2021). In an article headlined "American Democracy Is Cracking. These Ideas Could Help Repair It,"

renowned political journalist Dan Balz featured Civitas as a curriculum "that encourages active citizenship and perhaps over time a reduction in the country's tensions and divisions." *Washington Post,* December 21, 2023.

7. Enhancing the Student Experience

1. James Shulman and William G. Bowen, *The Game of Life: College Sports and Educational Values* (Princeton, NJ: Princeton University Press, 2002).
2. "Students in my Econ 101 classes were invaluable sources of information as to what was working and what needed fixing at the university, and talking with them was a good corrective to obligatory meetings with many politically engaged student leaders who visited me in my office." William G. Bowen, *Lessons Learned: Reflections of a University President* (Princeton, NJ: Princeton University Press, 2012), 138–39. See also Peter T. Flawn, *A Primer for University Presidents: Managing the Modern University* (Austin: University of Texas Press, 1990), 104.
3. For a contemporary view, see Evan Tucker and Michael Nelson, "Between Division III Athletes and Professors," *Inside Higher Ed,* August 24, 2017.
4. *National Collegiate Athletic Association v. Alston* (2021). One response was that Hampden-Sydney, William & Mary, and Longwood all fostered donor-supported NIL collectives to facilitate the distribution of NIL-related funds to athletes. Hampden-Sydney was the first Division III school to do so.
5. Although the number conceals a massive amount of variation, the average NIL compensation for Division I athletes in the first year was $3,711. Josh Moody, "The Current State of NIL," *Inside Higher Ed,* June 7, 2023. Transfer portals and even unionization by Division I athletes seeking legal status as employees of their universities pose additional challenges for big-time intercollegiate sports. See, for example, Billy Witz, "Are Athletes Truly Employees? NCAA Ideal Faces Big Tests," *New York Times,* March 18, 2024. For an account of how of the NCAA is trying to respond, see Witz, "NCAA Proposes Uncapping Compensation for Athletes," *New York Times,* December 5, 2023.
6. In a March 2024 op-ed, TR4 called on Congress to enact legislation that would "respect the rights and hard work of student-athletes without a turn to pure professionalism." W. Taylor Reveley, "Longwood, JMU Embody the Spirit of March Madness. Congress Must Protect It," *Richmond Times-Dispatch,* March 22, 2024.
7. For an assessment of the effects of adding football, see Welch Suggs, Alex Monday, Jennifer May-Trifiletti, and James C. Hearn, "Institutional

Effects of Adding Football: A Difference-in-Difference Analysis," *Research in Higher Education* (2024).
8. "The Early Decades of the Brafferton Indian School, c. 1700–1740," WM.edu, https://www.wm.edu/about/history/historiccampus/brafferton/indianschool/.
9. In response to the NCAA's 2006 mandate that Native American mascots and nicknames be eliminated, William & Mary abandoned "Indians," its team name since 1916, and adopted "Tribe." As for the new mascot, the four finalists that lost out to the griffin were a phoenix, a wren, a king and queen, and a Napoleonic pug. Dan Troop, "William & Mary's Feathered Future," *Chronicle of Higher Education*, April 11, 2010.
10. "Golfers 'Desperate' to Keep Historic Course Open at Longwood," *Richmond Times-Dispatch*, June 6, 2016.
11. For a full account of Longwood's response to the pandemic, see "Longwood During the COVID Pandemic: An Overview Report by the Administration to the Board of Visitors," June 2021, https://www.longwood.edu/media/presidents-office/public-site/board-of-visitors/BOV-Covid-Report.pdf.
12. The federal government helped offset some of the loss of income that colleges and universities experienced, with half of the $76 billion included in the Higher Education Emergency Relief Fund Act going to students and half going to the institutions,
13. Regional universities like Longwood are important sources of employment and commerce in their communities. See Lydia DePillis, "Colleges Have Been a Small-Town Lifeline. What Happens as They Shrink?," *New York Times*, March 13, 2023.
14. Unusual but not unique in his ambition, Paul Trible '68, one of the first students to matriculate during TR2's presidency, declared while still enrolled at Hampden-Sydney, "I want to be president of the United States." Although he fell short of that goal, Trible was elected to the U.S. Senate from Virginia before serving twenty-six years as president of Christopher Newport University. Located in Newport News, CNU was initially an extension of William & Mary. Brandi Kellam and Louis Hansen, "Paul Trible Transformed the University He Led for 26 Years. Not Everyone Is Pleased," *Chronicle of Higher Education*, December 22, 2023.
15. John Clement, "Reveley Weathered H-SC Change," *Richmond Times-Dispatch*, May 1, 1977; *Collected Speeches and Sermons of Dr. Reveley*, 15, 48; and W. Taylor Reveley II, *President's Report to the Trustees*, April 1969, Hampden-Sydney College Archives and Special Collections, VA.
16. Scott Jaschik, "Reversal on Anti-Gay Bias," *Inside Higher Ed*, March 11, 2010:
17. Reveley III's account is consistent with news reports on the matter. See Katherine Mangan, "After a Speaker Is Shouted Down, William & Mary

Becomes New Flash Point in Free-Speech Fight," *Chronicle of Higher Education*, October 5, 2017.

18. In the interest of free expression, TR3 did allow the Sex Workers Art Show, which had caused so much public controversy during his predecessor's brief presidency, to be held once again on campus in March 2019. But he insisted that the event be accompanied by a forum that involved "serious discussion of issues." Interest in the reformulated event waned. Martin Weil, "Sex Workers' Art Show Back, This Time with Forums," *Washington Post*, March 22, 2009.

19. For a critique of the high cost of college and its negative ripple effects on American life and politics, see Will Bunch, *After the Ivory Tower Falls: How College Broke the American Dream and Blew Up Our Politics—and How to Fix It* (New York: William Morrow, 2022). Among other things, Bunch (56) notes that the Truman Commission called for fourteen years of publicly funded education, adding community college or the first two years of college to high school.

20. See, for example, Mark Rivett, "I Was Trapped in For-Profit Hell: Predatory Schools Trapped Students Like Me into Assuming Huge Debt for Worthless Credits," *Chronicle of Higher Education*, July 11, 2024.

21. "To an architect," writes former University of Texas president Flawn, "the suggestion that he or she should build a structure that resembles one designed by another architect is an insult to his or her creative genius." Giving each new architect free rein may, over time, result in a campus filled with "an offensive conglomeration of closely spaced aesthetically incompatible styles and materials." Flawn, *A Primer for University Presidents*, 61.

8. Engaging Diversity

1. *Regents of the University of California v. Bakke* 436 U.S. 235 (1978).
2. *Students for Fair Admissions v. Harvard* 600 U.S. 181 (2023). See, for example, Liam Knox, "UNC System Board Votes to Eliminate DEI Offices," *Inside Higher Ed*, May 24, 2024.
3. Erin Gretzinger and Maggie Hicks, "Tracking Higher Ed's Dismantling of DEI," *Chronicle of Higher Education*, April 29, 2024. This story continued to be updated in response to ongoing legislative action.
4. Ryan Quinn, "Virginia Officials Scrutinize Two Universities' DEI Course Syllabi," *Inside Higher Ed*, March 18, 2024.; and Quinn, "2 Virginia Universities Won't Require DEI Classes after Governor's Review, Board Pushback," *Inside Higher Ed*, May 13, 2024.
5. Thomas J. Hyatt and Morgan Alexander, "A Primary Loyalty," *Inside Higher Ed*, March 22, 2024.

6. Anne Gardiner Perkins, *Yale Needs Women: How the First Group of Girls Rewrote the Rules of an Ivy League Giant* (Naperville, IL: Sourcebooks, 2019), 16.
7. When it became clear that Princeton was moving toward admitting women in 1969, Brewster quickly persuaded Yale's board to authorize Yale to do the same. For a comprehensive treatment of the history of elite college admissions in the twentieth and early twenty-first centuries, see Jerome Karabel, *The Hidden History of Admission and Exclusion at Harvard, Yale, and Princeton* (Boston, MA: Houghton-Mifflin, 2005).
8. For TR2, coeducation remained an open question whose resolution would depend on the college's ability to attract enough students. During the remainder of his presidency it did, with enrollment increasing to about eight hundred. His successor, Josiah Bunting III, was deeply committed to all-male education, and the Hampden-Sydney board's decision to hire him reflected the depth of its own commitment. John Lester Brinkley, *On This Hill: A Narrative History of Hampden-Sydney College, 1774–1974* (Hampden Sydney, VA: Hampden-Sydney College, 1994), 837–39. In 1995 Bunting became superintendent (president) of Virginia Military Institute and, much to his displeasure, was soon forced by the Supreme Court to admit women as cadets. *United States v. Virginia* 518 U.S. 515 (1996). Peter Finn, "Leading the March into Coeducation—A Smiling General," *Washington Post*, August 15, 1997.
9. See the prologue for an additional discussion of the situation TR2 faced in Prince Edward County.
10. Owen Norment, "W. Taylor Reveley—A Personal Remembrance," unpublished manuscript supplied to the author, 2000.
11. W. Taylor Reveley II, letter to Dr. Wyant Dean, December 28, 1963.
12. The memorial, a large freestanding structure adjacent to the college's original buildings, was completed in 2022. It features all 199 people whom the Lemon Project was able to identify, by name when possible or by gender or occupation when not. The project's research into these and other people enslaved at William & Mary continues. Laurie Lumpkin, "William & Mary Unveils Memorial for Enslaved People," *Washington Post*, May 7, 2022.
13. The 2009 statement acknowledged that William & Mary had "owned and exploited slave labor from its founding to the Civil War" and had "failed to take a stand during the Jim Crow era." The 2018 statement explicitly used the word "apologizes." Brian Whitson, "William & Mary Apologizes for College's History of Slavery, Discrimination," *Williamsburg Yorktown Daily*, April 20, 2018,
14. See also Nick Anderson, "William & Mary Drops a Confederate Emblem and Moves a Plaque," *Washington Post*, August 14, 2015.

15. TR4's maternal grandparents engaged in a creative act of civil disobedience when they married in 1936, defying Virginia's notorious 1924 Racial Integrity Act, which remained law until held unconstitutional by the Supreme Court in the 1967 case of *Loving v. Virginia* 388 U.S. 1.
16. The encounter drew some unwanted media attention, including from the right-wing news site *Daily Caller*. Reporter Rob Shimshock reveled in TR3's "I don't deal in demands" statement, as well as in a Facebook post by an attendee, who said, "This is what white supremacy looks like." Shimshock, "BLM Activists Furious with College President," *Daily Caller*, March 30, 2015.
17. "Black Student Graduation Rates at High-Ranking Colleges and Universities," *Journal of Blacks in Higher Education*, November 4, 2013
18. Nick Anderson, "Longwood U. in Va. Expresses Regret for Actions in Civil Rights Era, Apologizes," *Washington Post*, January 18, 2015.
19. Nick Anderson, "A Civil Rights Museum, a Public University, and a Reconciliation," *Washington Post*, July 22, 2015.
20. Reveley IV had one of Longwood's newly refurbished high-rise dormitories renamed after Barbara Johns, which prompted her surviving sister, Joan Johns Cobbs, who was denied admission to Longwood in 1955, to gratefully acknowledge in 2020 "how much it has helped to heal the deep wounds we suffered all of those years." Cameron Patterson, email to W. Taylor Reveley IV, July 2, 2020. Marking the seventieth anniversary of the *Brown* decision in 2024, Longwood bestowed an honorary doctorate on Cobbs and awarded honorary juris doctorates to more than one hundred members of the Farmville and Prince Edward community involved in the civil rights era campaign.
21. REVELEY IV: Cookie also wrote a powerful and effective letter to the group, which with her permission I then also shared with the broader campus community that fall going into the holiday season. The letter included this passage: "I am a staunch advocate for kindness. If our world is to change positively, it will not be through adversarial relationships. . . . Kindness is not easy and kindness does not mean we do not hold others accountable for their behavior. Showing genuine kindness to unkind people may be the most difficult task we ask of ourselves, but it can reap amazing rewards."

9. ADVANCING FUNDRAISING

1. Daniel de Vise, "Funding Cuts Leave Area Colleges Gasping," *Washington Post*, September 12, 2009.
2. W. Taylor Reveley II, *President's Report to the Board of Trustees*, Hampden-Sydney College, 1970 and 1973, Hampden-Sydney College Archives and Special Collections, VA.

3. Peter T. Flawn, *A Primer for University Presidents: Managing the Modern University* (Austin: University of Texas Press, 1990), 166.
4. *Collected Speeches and Sermons of W. Taylor Reveley II* (privately published by W. Taylor Reveley III and W. Taylor Reveley IV, 2003), 43, Hampden-Sydney College Archives and Special Collections, VA.
5. W Taylor Reveley II, *President's Report to the Board of Trustees*, Hampden-Sydney College, 1974, Hampden-Sydney College Archives and Special Collections, VA.
6. Lambert's ties to William & Mary were strong. He was class of 1999, his wife was class of 1998, his brother was class of 1997, his aunt, Louise Lambert Kale, was director of the Historic Campus, and his grandfather, J. Wilfred Lambert, headed student affairs from 1945 to 1973.
7. Nick Anderson, "William and Mary Launches $1 Billion Drive," *Washington Post*, October 22, 2015.
8. David W. Chen and Michael Corkery, "A New Playbook for College Donors: Power Politics," *New York Times*, December 13, 2023.
9. Princeton's endowment is about $38 billion, which ranks third or fourth among universities. Its endowment per student, however, is $4.6 million, more than a million dollars higher than the next highest-ranking school.

10. Leading

1. Owen Norment, "W. Taylor Reveley—A Personal Remembrance," unpublished manuscript supplied to the author, 2000.
2. In *Fortune*'s rankings of the "World's Most Admired Companies" in 1983 and 2022, none of the top five companies in either survey was on both years' lists; in fact, none of the top five in 2022 (Apple, Amazon, Microsoft, Pfizer, and Disney) was among the top one hundred in the 1983 survey. In contrast, the top five universities in *US News*'s 1983 rankings were the top five in 2022: Harvard, Yale, MIT, Princeton, and Stanford. Brian Rosenberg, *"Whatever It Is, I'm Against It": Resistance to Change in Higher Education* (Cambridge, MA: Harvard Education Press, 2023), 37–38. Nevertheless, a combination of a decline in the college-age population, rising costs, and growing doubts about the value of a liberal arts education hastened the closure of ninety-one small colleges from 2016 to 2023. Stephen G. Adubato, "Why Closing a Very Small Campus Is a Very Big Deal," *New York Times*, May 2, 2024, and John J. Smetanka, "Yes, Colleges Do Close," *Inside Higher Ed*, April 2, 2024.
3. Marie Eason Reveley, "Our Years at Hampden-Sydney College: July 1963–May 1981," typescript, Hampden-Sydney College Archives and Special Collections, VA.

Epilogue

1. Reveley also received an honorary doctorate from William & Mary at his final graduation ceremony in 2018. The lengthy citation that accompanied the honor concluded, "Truly, if you had not existed, William & Mary would have had to invent you." Erin Zagursky, "A Commencement Surprise for W&M's President," W&M News Archive, May 12, 2018: https://www.wm.edu/news/stories/2018/a-marvelous-commencement-surprise-for-wms-president.php.
2. "I am a firm believer in the adage 'Leave when there is at least some semblance of a band playing.'" William G. Bowen, *Lessons Learned: Reflections of a University President* (Princeton, NJ: Princeton University Press, 2011), 142.

INDEX

Italicized page numbers refer to photographs; page numbers preceded by a "g" (e.g., g1, g2) refer to photo gallery pages.

Adams, John, xvii
Adams, John Quincy, xvii
Advanced Placement (AP), 146–47
Afghanistan, 85, 217
Alabama, 29
Aldrich, Griff, 159
Alexa (virtual assistant device), 153
Allianz, 117
American Association of University Professors (AAUP), 108
American Civil Liberties Union of Virginia (ACLU of Virginia), 170–71
American Political Development (APD), 81
American presidency: xvi, 1, 34, 35–36, 79–86, 92, 100, 119, 156, 165, 194, 212, 217, 219–20, 222, 229; and Miller Center, xvii, 79–86; and National War Powers Commission, 1, 36, 73, 79, 81–86, 149, 229; and TR3's war powers scholarship, 1, 34, 35–36, 40, 41, 48, 58, 60, 81–86, 94, 229; vice presidential debate of 2016, 103–5; William & Mary historic presidential ties, 101–2. *See also* Miller Center; National War Powers Commission; vice presidential debate of 2016; war powers
American Revolution, 170
Americans with Disabilities Act (1990), 117
Andrew W. Mellon Foundation, xvi, xxv–xxvii, 44, 48, 55–56, 59, 65, 66, 122, 148, g5

Annapolis (U.S. Naval Academy), 177
architecture, 41, 48–49, 66, 92, 96, 108, 116–18, 172–74. *See also* New Urbanism
Artificial Intelligence (AI), 151, 153
Associated Press, 104
Association of Governing Boards of Universities and Colleges (AGB), 245n4
athletics, x, xv, 96, 154–61, 216, 221, 222; and American higher education, xv, 154, 159; and COVID pandemic, 161, 165–66; and diversity, 186; fees, 220; NCAA, 154–60 passim, 165–66; NCAA Division I, 54, 74, 90, 113, 154, 157–58, 165–66; NIL, 157; and Princeton board service of TR3, 52, 54–55, 166; TR2 as athlete, 11, 12, 13, 14, 15, 154–55, 197; TR2 as coach, 5, 18, 25, 155; TR3 as athlete, 31–32, 154; TR4 as athlete, xvii, 72, 74–75, 154; and William & Mary, 65–67, 130. *See also* baseball; basketball; Bowen, William G.; football; March Madness; NCAA
Atkinson, Frank B., 239n6
Atlanta, GA, 24, 43
Atomic Energy Act (1954), 42

Baker, James A., III, xvi, 1, 51, 73, 80, 82–85, 229–30, g3
Baker Institute for Public Policy (Rice), 230
Baker v. Carr (1962), 39

259

260 INDEX

Baliles, Gerald L., xvi, 33, 73, 77–89 passim, 131, 138, 202, 216, 219, g3, g4; and AGB task force, 245n4; and Hunton & Williams, 44, 73, 77–79; and Miller Center, 80–86
baseball, xvii, 5, 11, 12, 14, 15, 18, 155, 216
basketball: and higher education, 103, 159, 174, 221; Longwood and March Madness, 158–59; and NIL, 157; and TR2, 12, 18, 155; TR3 and William & Mary's Griffin mascot, 160. *See also* Aldrich, Griff; athletics; Joan Perry Brock Center; March Madness; NCAA
Baumol, William, 33
Baumol's Curse, 33
Baylor College of Medicine, 72
Belgium, 43
Bennis, Warren, 94
Bernier, Charles (Yank), 12
Bible, 18, 19, 21, 145; 1 John 4:20, 23; Ecclesiastes, 75
Bicentennial (Hampden-Sydney), 198–99, g2
Big South Conference, xxvii, 154, 157, 165
Birmingham, AL, 35
Black Lives Matter, 186–87, 191–92
Blair, James, 7
Board of Christian Education (Presbyterian Church), 23–26, 91
Bond, Everett, 41, 73
Bond, Lurline, 41, 73
Bowen, David, 33
Bowen, Karen, 33
Bowen, Mary Ellen, 33
Bowen, William G.: and athletics, 90, 155–56; coeducation at Princeton, 242n6; on external events/issues, 138, 249n14; insights regarding boards, 87, 122, 129, 248n7; on leaving leadership, 226, 257n2; on presidents teaching undergraduate courses, 156, 251n2; and TR3, xvi, 33–34, 44, 51–52, 55–56, 59, 78, 243n11, 242n7–8, 243n9, 244n21, 244n24, g5. *See also* Andrew W. Mellon Foundation; JSTOR; Princeton University
Bowman, B. L., 16
Boy Scouts of America, xi, 73
Bradford, Fran, 132
Brafferton (William & Mary president's office), 70, 116, 209
Brauer, Cindy, 218
Brennan, William J., xvi, xxiii, 36–40
Brewster, Kingman, 176, 254n7
Brim, Henry, 17
Brinkley, John, 145
Broaddus, Henry, 218
Brock, Joan, 159, 206
Brock, Macon, 206
Brown v. Board of Education (1954), 5, 22, 27, 30, 103, 129, 139, 189, 246n5, 255n20; Reveley views and commemoration, 22, 30, 255n20. *See also* civil rights; integration; Jim Crow; Johns, Barbara; Griffin, L. Francis; Massive Resistance; Moton High School; Moton Museum; Prince Edward County, VA: civil rights history; race
Bunting, Josiah, III, 254n8
Burger, Warren, 102
Bush, George W., 85

Caldwell, Dan, 16
California, xiii, 200
Cambridge University, xxiv, 94, 227
Camp Dorn, 16
Canton, NC, xxi, 11–12
Cantor, Eric, 246n3
Carnegie, Lake, 32
Carter, Jimmy, 103
Carter, Maybelle, xvii
Cash, June Carter, xvii
Centers for Disease Control, 78
Central High School (Memphis), 30–31
Central Intelligence Agency, xi, 102
Centre College, 103
ChapStick, 41

INDEX 261

Charles III, xvii
Charlottesville, VA, 35, 215
Charter Day (William & Mary), 106–7
Chernobyl incident of 1986, 42
Cherokee Nation, 41, 186, 255n15
Chicago, IL, 85
Chidester, Jeff, 105
China, 162
Christianity: and TR2, 19, 22–23, 110, 114, 122, 145–46; and TR3, 57; and TR4, 75. *See also* Presbyterian Church; Union Presbyterian Seminary
Christopher, Warren, xvi, 1, 73, 82–85, g3
Christopher Newport University, 90, 252n14
Church Hill office (Hunton), 43, 45
Church Schools in the Diocese of Virginia, Inc., 218
Churchville, VA, xxii, 4, 29
citizen lawyer, 61, 148, 245n31
citizen leader, 113, 142. *See also* Civitae Core Curriculum
citizenship, 15, 96, 113, 142–43, 148, 150–51, 249n3. *See also* curriculum; democracy; liberal arts
civil rights, 6, 90, 96, 103, 130, 180–81, 189–91, 209–10. See also *Brown v. Board of Education;* integration; Jim Crow; Johns, Barbara; Massive Resistance; Moton High School; Moton Museum; Prince Edward County, VA: civil rights history; race
Civil Rights Act (1964), 6, 180
Civil War, 27, 103, 142, 143, 185, 246n5
Civitae Core Curriculum (Longwood), 96, 148–51, 153; course pilots during vice presidential debate of 2016, 151; and democracy, 149, 250n14–15; development, 100, 113, 148–50; name, 150; and Teagle Foundation, 151, 190. *See also* curriculum; liberal arts
Clinton, Hillary, 104
Clotfelter, Charles T., 245n6

Cobbs, Joan Johns, 255n20
coeducation, 33, 74, 88–89, 93, 176–79, 242n6, 254n7–8
COLL (William & Mary): 95, 146–48; academic rigor, 147; development, 146–47; and Mellon Foundation, 148; and TR3, 146. *See also* curriculum; liberal arts
College Church, 115
College Curriculum (William & Mary). *See* COLL
college presidency, x, xiii–xiv, 208–9, 222–23; career paths to, 7–9; current challenges in, xv, 238n14; and lawyers, 8, 64, 91; prior challenges in, 209–10; representative day in, 216–17, 221. *See also* leadership; success in college presidency
Colonial Williamsburg, 139, 152
Comey, James, 246n3
Commission on Presidential Debates, 103–5, g5
Compton brothers, 238n10
Conant, James B., 249n3
Confederacy, addressing history of, 22, 50, 184–85, 246n5
Congress, 6, 8, 34–36, 81–86, 88, 158, 180; House Foreign Affairs Committee 36, 85; Senate Foreign Relations Committee, 36, 85
Connelly, Marge, 91
Cooper, Richard, 37–38
Cooper Robertson, 173
Cornell University, 55, 102
Council of Economic Advisors, 102
Council of Presidents of State Colleges and Universities in Virginia (COP), 2–3, 162, 208, 225
Council on Foreign Relations, xxiii, 36, 41
COVID pandemic, xxvii, 1–3, 5, 78, 95, 96, 105, 133, 137, 151, 153, 154, 161–66, 191, 192, 201, 227, g6
crew, 31–32, 154–55
Cuccinelli, Ken, 169–70

INDEX

Cullen, Thomas T., 245n32
Cuomo, Mario, 43
curriculum, ix, xv, 94, 95, 96, 141–53. *See also* Civitae Core Curriculum (Longwood); COLL (William & Mary); liberal arts; Western Man (Hampden-Sydney)
Currier, Tom, 35

Dalton, John, 44
Dana, Charles, 198
Dana Foundation, 198
Daniel, John, 88
Daniels, Ronald J., 250n15
Darden Graduate School of Business (University of Virginia), 72
Davidson College, 11–12, 19, 143, 151, 178
Davis, Mildred Dickinson, 241n24
Davis v. County School Board of Prince Edward County (1952), 239n6
DEI. *See* Diversity, Equity, and Inclusion
democracy: and education, 74, 96, 105, 142–43, 149–51, 153, 250n15; TR2 on, 19; TR4 on, 138, 249n15; Truman Commission, 142–43. *See also* citizenship; curriculum; liberal arts
Denison University, 56
desegregation. *See* integration
Diehl, Charles E., 17
diversity, x, xi, xv, 4, 70, 95, 97, 113, 153, 175–92, 196. *See also* Diversity, Equity, and Inclusion; race
Diversity, Equity, and Inclusion (DEI), 175–76, 186. *See also* diversity; race
Dodds, Harold W., 242n4
Douglas, Dave, 58, 245n29
Driscoll, Terry, 160
Dubill, Andrew, 83, 84
Duke University, xxii, 4, 18, 20, 29, 93
Dupont de Nemours, Inc., 25
Durham, NC, 19–20

Eason, Carrie Rennie (TR2's mother-in-law), 15, 30

Eason, Thomas D., Jr. (TR2's brother-in-law), 15
Eason, Thomas D., Sr. (TR2's father-in-law), 15, 90, 250n13
Eckerd College, 143
Eisenhower, Dwight, 93
Elizabeth II, xvii
Ellis, Tim, 45
Elwood (Longwood mascot), *g4*
ESPN, xviii
Esso, 30
Evans, Mike, 76, 192

FAFSA (Free Application for Federal Student Aid), 171
Fairmont-Hoge Presbyterian Church, 17
faith, 6, 11, 16, 22–23, 57, 75, 106–7, 145–46, 181, 223. *See also* Christianity; Presbyterian Church; Union Presbyterian Seminary
Fan District (Richmond), 48–49, 140
Fan District Association, xxiv, 48–49
Farmville, VA: as America's first two-college town, 5, 14, 139; civil rights history, 5, 28, 96, 103, 129, 139, 149, 163, 181, 190, 191, 246n5, 255n20; Barbara Johns statue, 190; and Medical College of Virginia, 12, 51; and TR2, 5, 14, 28, 88, 90, 120, 181; and TR4, 2, 14, 72, 88, 90, 96, 103, 113, 120, 129, 138–40, 159, 163, 190, 191, 217; and Union Presbyterian Seminary, 12, 51. *See also* Prince Edward County, VA
Farmville Female Seminary Association, 7
Farmville Herald, 28, 137, 138
Farmville State Teachers College, 14
Federal Bureau of Investigation (FBI), 102
financial crisis of 2008. *See* Great Recession of 2008
Finnegan, Patrick, 91
Flawn, Peter, xi, 194, 246n8, 253n21
Florida Southern College, 218
Floyd, George, 191, 215

football: benefits of, 13, 74–75, 159; and COVID, 165; and higher education, 159; and NCAA's origins, 158; and NIL, 157; and TR2 as athlete, 12, 13, 154–55; TR2 as coach, 5, 18, 155; TR3 on, 32, 107, 116, 159; TR4 as athlete, 72, 74–75, 154. *See also* athletics; NCAA
Ford, Gerald, 103
For the Bold, 95, 199–202, 205, *g3*; billion-dollar goal, 199–200. *See also* Gerdelman, Sue; Lambert, Matthew
Fortune 500, 210
Fox, Michael, 218
Franklin & Marshall College, 73
FrederickPolls, xiii
Free Application for Federal Student Aid (FAFSA), 171
Freeman, Anne, 46
Freeman, George, 40
Frick Museum, 55
Fritzius, Cassi, 218
Fulbright & Jaworski, xxvi, 76

Gallup Poll, 237n4
Game of Life, The (Shulman and Bowen), 155–56
Gastanaga, Claire Guthrie, 170
Gates, Robert M., ix–xi, xvi, 102, 246n3, *g6*
Gaza, 215
George Mason University, 78, 90, 176
Gerdelman, Sue, 200. *See also* For the Bold
GI Bill, 17, 18–19
Gilmer, Thomas, 27
Glover, Chon, 4, 70
Goheen, Robert, 33, 242n6
Goldberg v. Kelly (1970), 38–39, 243n14
Golden, Jim, 112
golf, 159, 161
Good to Great (Collins), 129–30
Gray, Hanna Holborn, xiv, 171, 246n8
Great Depression, 11
Great Recession of 2008, 4, 71, 85, 95, 109, 193, 195, 199

Greek, 74, 94, 112, 141–42, 144–45
Greenwood Presbyterian Church, 22–23
Griffey, Ken, Jr., xvii
Griffey, Ken, Sr., xvii
Griffin, L. Francis, 6, 181
Griffin (William & Mary mascot), 159–61, 252n9, *g4*
Griffin v. County School Board of Prince Edward County (1964), 6, 255n20
Grinch Who Stole Christmas, The (Seuss), 107–8
Guthridge, Charlie, 88

Hall, Tim, 158
Halleran, Michael, 108, 146–47
Hamas, 170
Hampden, John, 12
Hampden-Sydney College xiv, 4, 5, *g1–g2*; athletics, 154–56; civil rights and integration, 120–21, 179–81, 188–89, 198; coeducation, 176–79; computers and technology, 151–52; curriculum, 141, 143–46; fundraising, 193–94, 196–99; governance as private institution, 119–20, 125; government relations, 130; history, 4, 5, 7, 12, 51, 88, 139; and Longwood, 14, 88; and Medical College of Virginia, 12, 51; modernization of college administration, 208–9; and Presbyterian Church, 121–22; and Marie Eason Reveley, 113–16; students, 166, 167–69; TR2, climate prior to, 5–6, 27–28, 99, 101; TR2 and board, 119–22, 125; TR2 and faculty, 108–10; TR2 as president, xxiii–xxiv, 4–6, 8, 25–28, 93–94, 111–12, 144, 225–28; TR2's reflections on leadership, 209–10, 212, 221, 223; TR2's student years, xxi, 11–15, 101; and Union Presbyterian Seminary, 12, 51. *See also* college presidency; leadership; Middlecourt; Reveley, W. Taylor, II; success in college presidency

Hampden-Sydney Record, 101
Harbour, Bill, 156
Hardy, Carroll, 184
Harlan, John Marshall, II, 38
Harvard Law Review, 37
Harvard Law School, 62
Harvard University, 74, 111, 145
Harvest Foundation, 77–78
Harvis, Jonathan, 246n3
Hay-Adams Hotel, 84
Helm, Harold, 242n6
Hendrix College, 143
Henry, Patrick, 12
Hettrick, George, 45
Higher Calling (Beardsley), 239n4
Higher Education Act (1965), 8
Higher Education Emergency Relief Fund (2020), 252n12
Hodges, Courtney, 202
Holton, Linwood, 82, 131
Hospitality House, 140, 249n17
Howard, A. E. Dick, 34–35, 76
Howard, Chris, 189
Hungarian uprising of 1956, 31
Hunton Andrews Kurth (formerly Hunton & Williams)
— and TR3, 1, 29; early career of, xxiii, 36, 40; legal education service and board service, 47–57 passim; and LILCO/Shoreham Nuclear Power Plant, 41–43; as managing partner, xxiv–xxv, 43–47, 131; and Fran Minner, 218; and *The Style of a Law Firm*, 46, 243n17; and William & Mary, xxv, 57–59 passim, 66, 247n30; and war powers, 36, 81
— and TR4, 1; and Gerald Baliles, 44, 73, 77–78, 79, 81, 131; early career of, xxvi, 1–2, 72–73, 76–79; and Tim Ellis, 45; and hospital and healthcare practice, 1–2, 78–79, 162; name change of firm, 242n2; and Lewis Powell, 40, 44, 46, 131, 175; and Chuck Robb, 44, 45 131; and John Charles Thomas, 44–45,77; transition to Miller Center, xxvi, 79.
See also Baliles, Gerald L.; Powell, Lewis; Reveley, W. Taylor, III; Reveley, W. Taylor, IV; Thomas, John Charles

in loco parentis, 167–69
integration, 5–6, 23, 110, 120–21, 130, 149, 179–81, 198, 241n24; *g1*. See also *Brown v. Board of Education*; Massive Resistance; Prince Edward County, VA: civil rights history; segregation
International Baccalaureate (IB), 146–47
Irwin, Don, 48
Israel, 52, 170, 215
Ivy League, 155, 163, 165, 176

James Madison University, 78, 90
Jarman, Jospeh L., 15
Jaworski, Leon, 76
Jefferson, Thomas, 12, 61, 66, 101, 148, 160
Jeffries, John, 82, 84, *g3*
Jenkins, Matt, 78
Jim Crow, 35, 182, 184, 187; Longwood apology, 189–90; William & Mary apology, 184. See also *Brown v. Board of Education*; segregation
Joan Perry Brock Center (JPB), 159, 206
Johns, Barbara, 5, 129, 190, 246n5, 255n20; statue in U.S. Capitol, 190. See also *Brown v. Board of Education*; integration; Massive Resistance; Moton High School; Moton Museum; Prince Edward County, VA: civil rights history
Johns Hopkins University, 102, 250n15
Johnson, Lyndon, 34
Johnson, Stanhope, 41
Jones, James A. (Jas A), 25–26
Journal of Blacks in Higher Education, 188
JSTOR, xxv–xxvi, 56

INDEX   265

Kaine, Tim, 82, 85, 104, 131, 151
Kale, Louise, 116, 256n6
Kennedy, David, 81
Kennedy, John F., 32, 95, 120
Kennedy, Robert, 5–6, 120, 180–81, *g1*
kindergarten (integrated under TR2), 115, 180–81
Kindon, Victoria, 104
King, Martin Luther, Jr., xvii
King, Martin Luther, Sr., xvii
Kinney, Lawrence, 17, 18
Kissinger, Henry, 102
Kline, Matt, 84

Lambert, Matthew, 199–201
Lambert, Wilfred J., 256n6
Latin language, 13, 74, 94, 141–42, 144–45, 150, 175
leadership, 208–23; and American presidency, 86, 92, 100, 119, 165, 194, 212, 217, 219–20, 222; and athletics, 13, 32, 74–75, 156; James Baker on, 229–30; and Gerald Baliles, 77, 86–88; and board service, 56–57, 120–30; and William Bowen, 33–34, 59; crisis as a test of, 1–9; and delegation/teamwork, 218; Robert Gates on, ix–xi; and intergenerational learning, xvii, 15, 16, 25, 73, 89, 150, 225; learning to lead, 31, 219; and liberal arts, 165; and mentors, xvi, 33–34; and Reveleys, 96, 231–35; and Peyton Rhodes, 23–26, 144; strategic planning, 111–13. *See also* citizen lawyer; college presidency; success in college presidency
Le Corbusier, 173
Lee, Robert E., 190
legal education, 32, 47–48. *See also* citizen lawyer; University of Alabama School of Law; University of Virginia School of Law; William & Mary School of Law
Lemon (enslaved person), 183, 184

Lemon Project, 183–84, 254n12. *See also* slavery, addressing history of
Lemoyne-Owen College (formerly Lemoyne College), 22
Lexington, VA, 11
liberal arts: and COVID, 165; as descriptor of a college or university, 4, 17, 21, 154, 155, 156, 176, 177; and Hampden-Sydney, 143–46; history of, 141–44; and Longwood, 90, 148–51; and Mellon Foundation, 55, 148; and Reveley presidents, 96, 141–51; and Rhodes College, 143–45; and Teagle Foundation, 151; and TR4, 73–74; and Truman Commission and democracy, 142–43; and William & Mary, 146–48. *See also* citizenship; curriculum; democracy; Civitae (Longwood); COLL (William & Mary); Western Man (Hampden-Sydney)
liberal education. *See* liberal arts
LILCO. *See* Long Island Lighting Company
Lilly Foundation, 22
Lincoln, Abraham, 217
Lindsay, A. D., 19
Loch Willow Presbyterian Church, xxii, 16
Locke, John, 19, 96
Log Cabin (Hampden-Sydney), 115
Long Island Lighting Company (LILCO), 41–43, 47, 58
Longwood House, 117–18, 161, 165
Longwood University xiv, 5, *g4–g6*; architecture and grounds, 172–74; athletics, 154–61; ceremony, 106, 108; computers and technology, 151–52, 153; cost of college, 171–72; and COVID, 1–3, 161–66; curriculum, 141–43, 148–51; diversity, 175–76, 186, 188–92; fundraising, 193–96, 202, 203–6; governance as public institution, 119, 122, 125, 130–31;

Longwood University (*continued*)
government relations, 130–36; and Hampden-Sydney, 14, 88; history, xiv, 5, 7, 87–89, 102, 139, 149; and Marlo Smith Reveley, 113, 117–18; and media, 136–38; students, 166–67, 169–70; and town-gown relations, 138–40; TR4, climate prior to, 89–92, 99; TR4, family ties, 15, 88; TR4 and board, 120–21, 122–29; TR4 and crisis leadership, 1–3; TR4 and faculty, 108–11; TR4 on length of tenure in office, 225–28; TR4 and morale focus, 99–103; TR4 as president, xxvii, 8, 87–92, 95–96; TR4's reflections on leadership, 208–23; TR4 and strategic planning, 111–13; vice presidential debate of 2016, 103–6. *See also* college presidency; leadership; Longwood House; Reveley, W. Taylor, IV; success in college presidency
Loving v. Virginia (1967), 255n15
LSAT, 62
Lynchburg, VA, 41, 162

Madison, James, 12, 74
Malkiel, Nancy Weiss, 122
Man in the Light of History and Religion. *See* Search course (Rhodes)
March Madness, 158–59. *See also* basketball; NCAA
Margiloff, Colleen, 113
Maritain, Jacques, 19
Marrakesh, Morocco, 44
Marshall, John, 61, 62
Marshall, Thurgood, 62
Martin, Almon, 41
Martin, Jeremy, 218
Martinsville, VA, 78
Mary Baldwin College, 178, 197
Mason School of Business (William & Mary), 152
Massive Online Open Course (MOOC), 152–53

Massive Resistance, 5, 120, 189–91; Longwood apology, 189–90. *See also Brown v. Board of Education;* Johns, Barbara; Griffin, L. Francis; Prince Edward County, VA: civil rights history; segregation
Mathews, David, 35
McAuliffe, Terry, 131
McCain, John, 85
McCarthy era, 170
McDonnell, Bob, 170
McGregor, Matt, 158
McGuireWoods, 44
McRaven, William, xiii–xiv
McWilliams, Matt, 105
Meador, Dan, 35
Medical College of Virginia, 12
Meese, Ed, 82, 83
Mellon Foundation. *See* Andrew W. Mellon Foundation
Memphis, TN, xxii–xxiii, 4–5, 13, 17–25 passim, 30–31, 46, 72, 94
Middlecourt, 27, 51, 114, 118, 121, 166, *g1*
Mikva, Abner, 82, 83
Miller, Marlene, 115
Miller Center (University of Virginia): and American Political Development (APD), 81; and James Baker, 82–86, 229; and Gerald Baliles, xxvi, 73, 79–81, 82–86 passim, 86–88, 131, 202; and Jeff Chidester, 105; and Warren Christopher, 82–86, 229; focus on American presidency and national affairs, 1, 79; National War Powers Commission, xxvi, 1, 36, 73, 79, 81–86, 149, 229, *g3*; Presidential Oral History Program, xvii; and TR3, xxvi, 1, 81, 82–86, 229; TR4 as managing director, xxvi–xvii, xxvii, 1, 8, 29, 73, 79, 80–81, 87–92, 95, 131, 173, 202, 229; and vice presidential debate of 2016, 105. *See also* American presidency; Baliles, Gerald L.; National War Powers Commission; Reveley, W. Taylor, III; Reveley, W. Taylor, IV; war powers

INDEX

Millsaps College, 19, 143
Minner, Fran, 218
Mississippi, 16, 22–23, 29
Mississippi River, 41
Miyares, Jason, 248n6
Monroe, James, 102
Monticello, 101
Monument Avenue (Richmond), 48–49, 72, 116
Moore, Thurston, 77
Morehouse College, 177
Moscow, Russia, 44
Moss, Gordon, 241n24
Moton High School, 5, 6, 129, 189, 246n5. See also *Brown v. Board of Education*; integration; Johns, Barbara; Griffin, L. Francis; Massive Resistance; Moton Museum; Prince Edward County, VA: civil rights history
Moton Museum, 96, 129, 139, 189–91, 192; Longwood-Moton partnership, 190. See also Moton High School
Mullins, Eddie, 88

Name, Image, and Likeness (NIL), 157, 251n4–6
National Cathedral, 92
National Collegiate Athletics Association. See NCAA
National Park Service, 102
National Public Radio, 85
National Science Foundation, 152
National War Powers Commission, xxvi, 1, 36, 73, 79, 81–86, 149, 229, g3; and James Baker, 82–86, 229; and Gerald Baliles, 81–86 passim; and Warren Christopher, 82–86, 229; and John Jeffries, 82, 84; and Tim Kaine, 82, 85; and TR3 and TR4, xxvi, 1, 36, 81, 82–86, 229; War Powers Consultation Act, 83–85. See also Miller Center; Reveley, W. Taylor, III; Reveley, W. Taylor, IV; war powers

NCAA, 154–60 passim, 165–66; Division I, xxvii, 54, 74, 90, 113, 154, 157–58, 165–66. See also athletics; basketball; football; March Madness
New College Institute, 78
New Jersey, 31
New Urbanism, 96, 139–40. See also architecture
New York City, 29, 36, 43, 46, 54, 200
New York State Siting Law, 42
New York Times, 13, 41, 80
New York Times v. Sullivan (1964), 39
Nichol, Gene, 3–4, 64, 67–71
Niebuhr, Reinhold, 19
NIL (Name, Image, and Likeness), 157, 251n4–6
Norfolk Southern Corporation, 64
Norment, Owen, 108, 121–22, 180, 208–9
Northam, Ralph, 164
North Carolina, 11, 20, 72, 134, 135, 176, 177, 248n11
Nuclear Regulatory Commission (formerly Atomic Energy Commission), 41–43
Nude Olympics, 53
Nystrom, Scott, 88

Obama, Barack, 85, 105
O'Brion, Cameron, 169
O'Brion, Emily, 132
O'Connor, Sandra Day, xvi, 102
Oklahoma, 41
Oklahoma State University, 67
Olympics, 157
online education, 142, 151, 152–53, 163–64
Osman, John, 17
Othello (Shakespeare), 150
Overbrook Presbyterian Church, 15

Palmer, Benjamin, 22
pandemic. See COVID pandemic
Patrick Henry Memorial Foundation, xxiii

Patterson, Cameron, 191–92, 255n20
Pence, Mike, 104
Performing Arts–The Economic Dilemma (Baumol and Bowen), 33, 242n8
Perkins, Ken, 149
Perkins, Lee, 73–74
Philippines, 16
Pierson, Tim, 192
Pope, Dean, 46
Pope, Justin, 104, 159, 165
Powell, Lewis, xvi, 40, 44, 46, 131, 175
Powell, Michael, 4, 68–69, 126
Presbyterian Church: during civil rights era, 22, 180; and Hampden-Sydney, 121–22, 145–46; and higher education, 7, 11–12, 24, 27, 145–46, 193, 197; history of, 22, 121, 167–68, 241n23; and Nelson Reveley, 51, 57; and Reveley family, 6, 11, 16, 22–23, 57, 75, 106–7, 145–46, 181, 223; and TR2, 4, 7, 13, 16–18, 22–26, 29, 91, 93, 120, 123, 145, 146. *See also* Christianity; Union Presbyterian Seminary
presidential debate of 1976, 103
presidential election of 2016, 104, 105–6. *See also* vice presidential debate of 2016
presidential election of 2020, 162
President's House (William & Mary), 116, 118, 128, *g4*
Prince Edward Academy, 6
Prince Edward County, VA: civil rights history, 5, 6, 22, 27, 28, 120, 163, 179–81, 188–89, 239n6, 255n20; *g1;* Farmville as college town, 5, 14, 139; Barbara Johns statue, 190; and Medical College of Virginia, 12, 51; and TR2, 22, 27, 28, 120, 179–81, 188–89, *g1;* and TR4, 2, 91, 113, 163, 188–89, 255n20; and Union Presbyterian Seminary, 12, 51. *See also* Farmville, VA
Princeton University: and William Bowen, xvi, 33–34, 44, 51–52, 122, 156; coeducation, 33, 177, 242n6, 254n7; and Compton brothers, 238n10; and Harold Dodds, 242n4; endowment, 204; and football, 74-75, 154, 159; and Robert Goheen, 33; history and church ties, 7, 145; motto, 175; as residential campus, 172; and Everett Reveley, 116, 166; and Nelson Reveley, 166; and Helen Lanier Reveley Ramirez, 166–67; and Harold Shapiro, 51, 52, 54; and Samuel Stanhope Smith, 7; TR3 as student, xvii, 1, 7, 24, 25, 31–34, 94, 154, 155; TR3's board service, xxiv, xxv, 48, 51–55, 59, 63, 82, 123, 125, 166; TR4 as student, xvii, 1, 7, 72, 74–75, 95, 116, 154, 166; and William & Mary, 65, 66, 67, 111; and Woodrow Wilson, 148. *See also* Bowen, William G.; Reveley, W. Taylor, III; Reveley, W. Taylor, IV
Public Opinion Strategies, xiii
Purdue University, 250n15

race, x, xv, 15, 16, 22, 26, 53–54, 90, 115, 175–92 passim; 229. *See also Brown v. Board of Education;* civil rights; Confederacy, addressing history of; diversity; integration; Jim Crow; Johns, Barbara; Griffin, L. Francis; Massive Resistance; Moton High School; Moton Museum; Lemon Project; Prince Edward County, VA: civil rights history; slavery, addressing history of
Radcliff, Marianne, 89, 127
Radcliffe, Jeremy, 72
Rainey, Gordon, 77
Randolph Macon Women's College, 178
Regents of California v. Bakke (1978), 175–76
Reveley, Chris (daughter of Hampden-Sydney's Reveley), 5, 17, 18, 25, *g1*
Reveley, David (cousin of Hampden-Sydney's Reveley), 11–12

INDEX

Reveley, Everett (son of TR3), 41, 116, 166
Reveley, Helen Bond (wife of TR3), xviii, 40–41, 48–49, 67–71 passim, 73, 90, 116–18, 166, 173, *g2*
Reveley, Marguerite Grayson (TR2's mother), 11
Reveley, Marie Eason (wife of TR2), xvii–xviii, xxii, 11–28 passim, 30, 73, 90, 91, 94, 114–16, 176, 227, *g1, g2*; memoir observations 121, 168, 177, 180, 194, 197–98, 212
Reveley, Marlo Smith (wife of TR4), xviii, 72, 88–90 passim, 117–18, 153
Reveley, May (daughter of TR4), 88, 117, 153
Reveley, Nelson (son of TR3), 41, 51, 116, 166
Reveley, Quint (son of TR4), 88, 117, 153
Reveley, Robert (TR2's father), 11
Reveley, Walter Taylor (TR2's uncle), xviii, 11
Reveley, William Alexander (distant relative), 51
Reveley, W. Taylor, II, *11*, 11–28, 93–94, 96–97, *g1, g2*; army chaplain service, xxii, 16–17; and civil rights, 5–6, 13, 16, 21–23; 27–28, 110, 115, 120–21, 130, 179–81; early life, xxi, 11; ministry, xxii, 16; and Presbyterian education board, 23–24; modernization of college administration, 208–9; and Marie Eason Reveley, xxii, 15; and Rhodes College, xxii–xxiii, 17–18, 19–21; selection as Hampden-Sydney president, xxiii, 8, 25–28; as student, xxi, xxii, 11–16, 18–20, 101. *See also* college presidency; Hampden-Sydney College; leadership; Reveley, Marie Eason (wife of TR2); Rhodes College; success in college presidency
Reveley, W. Taylor, III, *29*, 29–71, 94–95, 96–97, *g1–g7*; board service, xxiv–xxvii, 48–57; dean of William &

Mary Law School, xxv–xxvi, 57–64; early life, xxii, 29–31; For the Bold, 95, 199–201, 205; and JSTOR, xxv, 56; and Hunton & Williams, xxiii, xxiv, 41–47; Lemon Project, 183–84, 254n12; National War Powers Commission, xxvi, 81–86; and Helen Bond Reveley, xxiii, 40–41; selection as William & Mary president, xxvi, 8, 64–71; as student, xxiii, 31–33, 34–36, 154, 155; Supreme Court clerkship, xxiii, 36–40; Virginia Commission on Constitutional Revision, 35; war powers scholarship, 34, 35–36, 40. *See also* college presidency; Hunton Andrews Kurth; leadership; Reveley, Helen Bond (wife of TR3); success in college presidency; war powers; William & Mary; William & Mary Law School
Reveley, W. Taylor, IV, *72*, 72–92, 95–96, 96–97, *g2–g7*; and Gerald Baliles, xxvi, 76–79, 86–87; Cherokee citizenship, 186; crisis leadership through COVID, 1–3, 161–66; early life, xiii, 73–74; hospital and healthcare law, 78–79; and Hunton & Williams, xxvi, 76–79; Miller Center, xxvi–xxvii, 80–81; National War Powers Commission, 81–86; partnership with Moton Museum, 96, 129, 139, 189–91, 192; and Marlo Smith Reveley, xxvi, 72; and Richmond city government, 76; selection as Longwood president, xxvii, 8, 87–92; as student, xxv–xxvi, 74–76, 154. *See also* college presidency; Hunton Andrews Kurth; leadership; Miller Center; National War Powers Commission; Reveley, Marlo Smith (wife of TR4); success in college presidency
Reveley Ramirez, Helen Lanier (daughter of TR3), 41, 116, 166–67
Rhodes, Dan, 143

Rhodes, Peyton Nalle: Hampden-Sydney address, 144; Rhodes College renaming, xvi, 144; at Southwestern at Memphis, 19–26; and TR2, xvi, 19–26 passim, 33, 144
Rhodes College: coeducation, 93, 177; curriculum, xvii, 94, 143–44, 145, 151; renaming, xvi, 144; as residential campus, 172; and TR2, xvii, xxii–xxiii, 4–6, 8, 13, 17–27, 26, 29, 30, 73, 106, 109, 120, 155; and TR3, 5, 13, 18, 30–31. *See also* Rhodes, Peyton Nalle; Reveley, W. Taylor, II; Search course (Rhodes)
Rice University, 230
Richardson, A. L., 168
"Richmond" (as conventional shorthand for Virginia state administration and legislature), 91, 119, 130–34, 161, 164, 169, 195, 221
Richmond, VA, 1, 4, 12, 136, 175; and TR2, 14–18 passim, 23–27 passim, 91; and TR3, xxiii, 30, 41–51 passim, 59, 70, 116, 117; and TR4, xxiii, 72–76 passim, 95, 140. *See also* Fan District; Monument Avenue
Richmond city government, 76, 192
Richmond Symphony, xxiv–xxv, 49–50
Richmond Times-Dispatch, xiv, xv, 15, 105, 138, 161
Riley, Russell L., xviii
Robb, Chuck, 44, 45, 131
Robert, Joseph, 27, 197
Robert Russa Moton High School. *See* Moton High School
Robert Russa Moton Museum. *See* Moton Museum
Roberts, Caroline Eason, 14
Rockbridge County, VA, xviii, xxi, xxiv, 11, 20
Rockefeller Trust, 244n21
Romer, Christina, 246n3
Roosevelt, Franklin D., 217
Rose, Frank, 35
Rowe, Katherine, 201

rowing. *See* crew
Rumsfeld, Donald, 51, 54

SARS (Severe Acute Respiratory Syndrome), 2, 78, 162
SCHEV (State Council of Higher Education for Virginia), 134–35, 164
Schlegel, Marvin, 241n24
"Scholar, Steward, Spanner, Stranger" (Birnbaum and Umbach), 240n7
Scott, Cookie, 192, 255n21
Scott, Robert, 111
Scott, Winfield, 185
Scowcroft, Brent, 83
Search course (Rhodes), xvii, 19, 21, 143–45, 151
search process for college presidency, 8, 25–26, 58–59, 64–67, 88–91, 112, 148–49, 160, 204
Sears, 30
segregation, xv, 5–6, 21–23, 28, 120–21, 179–81, 187, 189–90; *g1*. *See also* *Brown v. Board of Education;* Massive Resistance; Prince Edward County, VA: civil rights history
Severe Acute Respiratory Syndrome (SARS), 2, 78, 162
Sewanee, 19, 143
Sex Workers Art Show, 67–68, 253n18
Shakespeare, 150
Shapiro, Harold, 51, 52, 54
Shoreham Nuclear Power Plant, 41–43, 48
Shulman, James, 155
Simpson, Aaron, 77
slavery, addressing history of, 22, 95, 106, 182–83, 184, 185, 254n12–13; William & Mary apology, 184. *See also* Lemon Project
Smith, Ashley, 72
Smith, Larissa, 91, 149
Smith, Peggy, 72
Smith, Ron, 73
Smith, Samuel Stanhope, 7
Snowden Elementary School, 30

Sopranos, The, xviii
South Africa divestment, 52, 244n24–25
Southwestern at Memphis. *See* Rhodes College
Sou'wester, 18
Spong, William, xvi, 40, 48, 57–58, 121
Sputnik, 143
Squires, David, 115–16
Squires, Sara, 116
Stanford Law School, 62
Stanford University, 81, 102, 250n15
State Council of Higher Education for Virginia (SCHEV), 134–35, 164
Staunton, VA, 29
St. Catherine's School, 75, 244n21
St. Christopher's School, xxv–xxvii, 48, 72, 73–75, 123
Stokes, Kay, 217
Stottlemyer, Todd, 126
student debt, 172
Style of a Law Firm, The (Freeman), 46, 243n17
success in college presidency, xiii–xv; James Baker on, 229–30; concluding tenure in office, 209, 225–28; crisis leadership, 1–9; curriculum reform, 141–53; diversity, 175–92; fundraising, 193–207; Robert Gates on, ix–xi; institutional and campus honors, 110, 228, 257n1; media, xiv, xv; morale, 99–118; peer recognition, 208; and presidential search process, 25–28, 64–71, 87–92; relationships, 119–40; student experience, 154–74; in Virginia, xiii. *See also* college presidency; leadership
Suez crisis, 31
Sullivan, Timothy, 58–59, 64, 65
Sullivan & Cromwell, 55
Supreme Court of Virginia, 45
Sydney, Algernon, 12

Tachtenberg, Stephen, xiv
Teagle Foundation, 151, 190
Tennessee, xxi–xxiii, 176
tenure, 46–47, 60, 63, 109–11, 135, 247n12
Texas, 29, 72, 230
Texas A&M University, xi
Texas v. Johnson (1989), 39
Thatcher, Margaret, 102
Thelin, John, 7
Thomas, John Charles, xvi, 44–45, 77, 244n19, g6
Thompson, Graves H., 13
Three Mile Island incident of 1979, 42
Time, 138, 145
Times Higher Education, xiii
Title IX, 88, 179
Tocqueville, Alexis de, 158
Tokyo, Japan, 16
Totten, Randy, 46
TR2. *See* Reveley, W. Taylor, II
TR3. *See* Reveley, W. Taylor, III
TR4. *See* Reveley, W. Taylor, IV
Traditional Building (magazine), 140
Trail of Tears, 41
Trammell, Jeff, 126
Trible, Paul, 252n14
Trigiani, Pia, 165
"Trouble at the Top," 238n14
Truman, Harry, 16, 142
Truman Commission, 142–43, 249n3, 253n19
Trump, Donald, 104, 105–6, 162
Tutwiler Avenue (Memphis), 17–18, 30
Tyler, John, 102

Union Presbyterian Church, xxii, 16
Union Presbyterian Seminary: and careers outside ministry, 76; history, 12, 51; and Nelson Reveley, 51, 57; and TR2, xxi–xxii, 4, 15, 17, 25; TR3's board service, xxv–xxvi, 48, 51, 57, 59, 123; and TR4, xxv, 51, 57, 72, 75–76, 95. *See also* Christianity; Presbyterian Church
Union-PSCE. *See* Union Presbyterian Seminary

Union Theological Seminary in Virginia. *See* Union Presbyterian Seminary
University of Alabama, 35, 155, 248n9
University of Alabama School of Law, xxiii, 29, 35, 36, 37, 59, 60, 243n11
University of Chicago, xiv, 55, 102, 171
University of Kansas, 155
University of Michigan, 51
University of North Carolina School of Law, 3, 64
University of Texas at Austin, xi, 194
University of Texas System, xiii, 72
University of the South. *See* Sewanee
University of Virginia, xiii, 12, 80, 102; and Miller Center, xvii, 1, 8, 29, 73, 79, 95, 131, 229; and UVA School of Law, 40, 72, 76, 82, 111
University of Virginia School of Law: and A. E. Dick Howard, 34–35, 76; and John Jeffries, 82, 84, *g3*; and National War Powers Commission, 82, 84, *g3*; and Robert Scott, 111; and TR3, xxiii, 1, 34–35, 36, 40, 46, 94, 194; and TR4, xxv–xvi, 1, 72, 76, 95; and William & Mary, 111
university presidency. *See* college presidency
Upchurch University Center (Longwood), 92
U.S. Army, xxii, 4, 16–17, 29, 30, 91, 93, 115, 185
U.S. Capitol, 190
U.S. Congress. *See* Congress
U.S. Constitution, 15, 22, 34–36, 39, 74, 81–86, 94. *See also* U.S. Supreme Court
U.S. Department of Defense, xi
U.S. Department of Education, 158
U.S. Department of Justice, 6
U.S. Military Academy (West Point), 177
U.S. Naval Academy (Annapolis), 177
US News, xiii, 102
U.S. presidency. *See* American presidency

U.S. Special Forces Command, xiii
U.S. Supreme Court: *Brown v. Board of Education* and civil rights, 5, 6, 22, 27, 103, 139, 189; and college athletics, 157; diversity decisions, 175–76; *Goldberg v. Kelly*, 38–39, 243n14; and Lewis Powell, 40, 44, 46, 131, 175; TR3's clerkship, xxiii, 36–40, 94; and war powers, 36, 82. *See also* athletics; diversity; Brennan, William; *Brown v. Board of Education*; Powell, Lewis; Prince Edward County, VA: civil rights history; war powers
UVA. *See* University of Virginia

Verkuil, Paul, 64
vice presidential debate of 2016, 96, 103–5, 106, 151, *g5*; and COVID, 105, 162; and Moton Museum, 190–91; and philanthropy, 206.
Vietnam War, 34, 40, 115–16, 167, 170, 210
Virginia, Commonwealth of: civil rights history, 5, 27, 120, 190, 239n6; and higher education, x, xiii, 1–3, 12, 15, 47–48, 49, 51, 77–78, 90, 96, 119, 125–27, 130–36, 162–64, 176–77, 193, 208; 237n2, 237n4; Barbara Johns statue, 190; and Reveley presidents, ix, xiv, xv, xvii, 1–9 passim, 93, 96, 208; state government, 119, 125–27, 130–36, 162–64, 169, 176, 186, 190, 193; and TR2, 4, 5, 11–16 passim, 20–27 passim, 120, 177, 194, 197, 208; and TR3, 3, 29, 34, 35, 40–47 passim, 50, 61–62, 95, 119, 125–27, 130–38 passim, 162, 169, 185, 193, 200, 205, 208; and TR4, 1, 2, 72, 73, 77–78, 87, 90, 96, 119, 125–27, 130–38 passim, 157, 162–64, 172, 176, 186, 190, 193, 208, 255n15. *See also* Farmville, VA; Prince Edward County, VA; "Richmond" (as conventional shorthand for Virginia state administration and legislature); Richmond, VA; Virginia

INDEX

General Assembly; Williamsburg, VA
Virginia Bar Association Special Issues Committee, xxvii
Virginia Business Higher Education Council, 237n4
Virginia Commission on Constitutional Revision, 35
Virginia Commonwealth University, 49, 90, 176
Virginia Constitution of 1971, 35
Virginia Constitution on 1902, 35
Virginia Department of Health, 164
Virginia Foundation for Independent Colleges, 208
Virginia Gazette, 136
Virginia General Assembly, 3, 50, 68, 69, 78, 119, 127, 130–35, 139, 169, 174, 176
Virginia Historical Society (now Virginia Museum of History and Culture), xxv, xxvi–xxvii, 50
Virginia Law Review, 34, 35
Virginia Military Institute, 176–77, 254n8
Virginia Museum of Fine Arts, xxv–xxvi, 50, 61, 131
Virginia State Bar Section on the Education of Lawyers, 47–48
Virginia Tech, xiii, 78
Virginia Trust Company, xxiii

Wabash College, 177
Wall Street Journal, 80, 138
Ward, Lacy, 189
war powers: and Tim Kaine, 82, 85; National War Powers Commission, xxvi, 1, 36, 73, 79, 81–86, 149, 229, *g3*; and William Spong, 40; and TR3, xxiii, xxiv, 1, 34, 35–36, 40, 41, 48 , 58, 60, 81–86, 94, 229; War Powers Consultation Act, 83–85; *The War Powers of the President and Congress*, xxiv, 36. *See also* American presidency; Miller Center; National War Powers Commission; Reveley, W. Taylor, III; Reveley, W. Taylor, IV
War Powers Consultation Act (proposed), 83–85
War Powers of the President and Congress, The (Reveley), xxiv, 36, 41
War Powers Resolution (1973), 40, 81
Warren Court, 36–40. *See also Brown v. Board of Education;* U.S. Supreme Court
Washington, DC, 29, 31, 36, 200
Washington, George, 101, 190, 217
Washington & Lee University, 59, 177
Washington Post, xiv, 80, 200
Watergate, 76
Weeks, Louis, 51
Western Man (Hampden-Sydney), 94, 143–46. *See also* curriculum; liberal arts
Westminster Canterbury, 75
West Point (U.S. Military Academy), 177
White, Byron, 38
Whitus, David, 140
Who's Who in America, 12, 198
William & Mary xiii, xiv, *g3–g7*; architecture and grounds, 172–73; athletics, 154–61; and Warren Burger, 102; ceremony, 106–8; computers and technology, 151–53; curriculum, 141, 146–48; diversity, 175–76, 181–88; fundraising, 193–96, 199–202, 202–3, 203–6; and Robert Gates, 102; governance as public institution, 119, 122, 125, 130–31; government relations, 130–36; history, 7, 101–2, 139; and Thomas Jefferson, 101–2; and Henry Kissinger, 102; and media, 136–37; and James Monroe, 102; and Sandra Day O'Connor, 102; and Helen Bond Reveley, 113, 116–17; students, 166–67, 169–71; and Margaret Thatcher, 102; and town-gown relations, 138–40; TR3, climate prior to, 3–4, 67–71, 99; TR3 and board, 119–20, 122–30;

William & Mary (*continued*)
TR3 and crisis leadership, 3–4; TR3 and faculty, 108–11; TR3 and morale focus, 99–103, 105–6; TR3 as president, xxvi, xxvii, 3–4, 8, 64–71, 94–95, 225–28; TR3 and strategic planning, 111–12; TR3's reflections on leadership, 208–23; and John Tyler, 102; and George Washington, 101. *See also* college presidency; leadership; Reveley, W. Taylor, III; success in college presidency

William & Mary Law School: citizen lawyer focus, 61, 148, 245n31; history, 102, 134, 139; and Thomas Jefferson, 61, 148. and John Marshall, 61; and William Spong, 48, 57–58; and Timothy Sullivan, 58, 59, 64, 65; TR3 as dean, xxv–xxvi, 1, 3–4, 8, 29, 57–69, 76, 81, 83, 94, 108, 116, 130, 166, 182, 195, 209, 218, 245n30; TR3 as professor, 48; TR3's transition to university presidency, xxvi, 3–4, 64–71, 100, 109, 112, 166; and George Wythe 61–62, 148. *See also* citizen lawyer; Reveley, W. Taylor, III

Williams, John, 84
Williamsburg, VA, 138–40; and TR3, 48, 58, 59, 105, 116, 136, 152, 170, 184, 200
Wilson, Woodrow, 148
Wilson Center, xxiii, 36, 41
Wire, The, xviii
Witherspoon, John, 53
Wolf, Henry (Hank), 64, 68, 126
Woodrow Wilson International Center for Scholars, xxiii, 36, 41
Woodrow Wilson School of Public and International Affairs (Princeton), 31, 33
World University Rankings, xiii
World War II, xxii, 4, 16, 29–30, 88, 93, 142
Wren Building, 107, 116, 185, *g7*
Wren Chapel, 4, 68
wrestling, 54
Wythe, George, 61, 62, 148

Yale Law School, 62
Yale University, 145, 176–77, 244n26, 254n7
Youngkin, Glenn, 131, 176
Yule Log (William & Mary), 107–8